ADOLESCENCE

The Survival Guide for Parents and Teenagers

Elizabeth Fenwick & Dr Tony Smith

Photographs by Barnabas Kindersley

DORLING KINDERSLEY
London New York Sydney Moscow
www.dk.com

A DORLING KINDERSLEY BOOK
www.dk.com

Project Editor **Christine Murdock**
Designer **Ellen Woodward**
Production **Jayne Simpson**

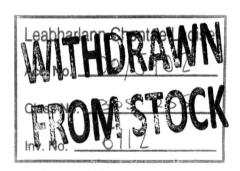

First published in Great Britain in 1993
by Dorling Kindersley Limited,
9 Henrietta Street, London, WC2E 8PS

Revised edition © 1998

A CIP catalogue record for this book is available from the British Library

ISBN 0 7513 0545 6

Reproduced by IGS
Printed and bound in Spain
D.L. TO: 1761 - 1999

Contents

Box Contents

INTRODUCTION

> " *There seems to be only one definite statement one can make about bringing up children — and that is that they should be accepted as individuals in their own right and their differences from their parents and each other tolerated and encouraged. Children develop most satisfactorily if they are loved for what they are, not for what anyone thinks they ought to be.* "
>
> Anthony Storr

THE CHANCES ARE THAT YOU WILL WORRY more about your children in adolescence than at any time apart from early childhood. This is partly because the problems of adolescence seem to be on a bigger scale than those of childhood, more seems to be at stake, and the potential for disaster is much greater. Parents have their eyes very much on the future (will she do well enough at school to get a good job?), while the adolescent's greatest concern is with the here and now (will my spots be gone by Saturday?). Parents also have to learn to play a much more passive role. They can give advice, suggest guidelines, and impose sanctions, but increasingly it is the adolescent who decides whether to accept, follow, or obey.

That adolescence is a time of "storm and stress" for everyone concerned has been said so often that it has become almost an article of faith. Parents are now so primed to expect troubled times and troubled children that they tend to go into the teenage years with their fists already up. But in spite of this, most parents do manage to remain friends with their children, and most families survive the teenage years with only transitory difficulties.

The years between early childhood and the beginning of adolescence are comparatively tranquil: the family is still the centre of the child's world and the main source of emotional support. Most significantly, you think you know your child, and because small children to some extent mirror what you have taught them, you can see your own standards and attitudes reflected in them. It's easy to believe that your children are part of you, that you have "brought them up" to be what they are. Thus lulled into a false sense of security, parents are often unprepared for the sudden metamorphosis of a charming and biddable child into a surly, self-willed stranger whose way of life seems to be entirely at odds with their own, and who monopolizes the phone, the bathroom, and the conversation.

None of this should be surprising if one considers the changes taking place for the adolescent. Physical growth is rapid, and the hormonal changes of puberty are greater than at any other age. The child is developing sexually, a change of immense psychological importance. He or she has to deal with major life events outside the home: the shift from primary to secondary school, the stress of public examinations, the transition to employment, and the fear (and often the reality) of unemployment. Above all, your child faces the need to break away from the family and to establish a sense of his or her own identity. Compared with adolescence, infancy is an island of development entirely surrounded by good advice. Doctors and clinics monitor every phase of development, and books about child-rearing are plentiful; above all, the parents of small children form a pool of shared experience from which they can draw the comforting knowledge that no problem is unique, and that other parents face the same difficulties and deal with them no more or less successfully than they do.

For the parents of adolescents, however, there is no such easy access to professional help, and in any case the adolescent's intense self-consciousness about being different or abnormal may make it difficult for parents to seek it. Moreover, the parents of adolescents tend to isolate themselves, to be much more reluctant to compare notes with each other than the parents of small children. They tend to minimize their problems, probably because they are more likely to feel that confession involves a sense of failure or guilt: it's easier to admit to the foul temper of your toddler than the foul language of your teenager. You may not wonder where you've gone wrong when your four-month-old keeps you up all night; you may well do so when your 14-year-old doesn't come home until morning.

It was for these reasons that we decided to write this book, not as experts, but as parents, backing up our own experience with the knowledge of those who are the acknowledged academic experts in the field. We also gathered our own data by sending a questionnaire to over 100 children in two secondary schools. We asked these children all the questions we wanted to talk about in this book: what they worried about or fought with their parents about; their feelings regarding friends, family, and school; and what anxieties they had about their future lives.

Their answers helped to reassure us, as we hope they will reassure you, that much of the widespread mythology about the awfulness of the teenage years is unfounded. Although there may be difficulties, there need not be disasters. Teenagers can be great company, providing constant stimulation and continual challenge. Growing up is a normal process – all that makes it difficult is the interaction of the child with those around him or her.

HOW TO USE THIS BOOK

Our book is meant to be read by both parents and teenagers. The experiences of growing up generate some straightforward, obvious causes of tension, but some problems may be seen as more important by parents than their children, while others work the opposite way. So we've often written separate sections of a chapter to explain the different outlooks of the parent and the adolescent.

We hope every reader will eventually read the whole book; in fact, we'd recommend it. It is often helpful for teenagers to know what their parents are worrying about (even if they think they are stupid to do so). Our short articles may, we hope, help start some family discussions, possibly about things people find a bit embarrassing.

To make it easier to find your way around the book, we've coloured some of the text for adults grey and the text for teenagers blue (teenagers' text always appears at the back of the chapter). The main text is mostly for parents. We've also organized the text into short, separate articles so that it can be read like a magazine.

The **white pages** are mainly for parents. Topics on these pages are written about more extensively, and text that appears in bold emphasizes important points.

Dialogue boxes are conversations and thoughts familiar to all of us. In most cases, the comments at the bottom suggest ways of reconciling a problem.

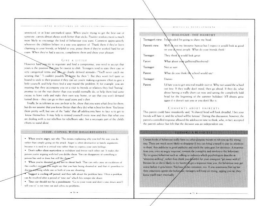

"**Issues**" are those topics parents and teenagers may argue about, such as appearance or curfews, for which it may be hard to find a "middle way".

Grey-tinted boxes are intended to indicate special areas of concern for parents. They include charts, tables, quick-reference boxes, or points to remember.

Quotes from adults are in grey while those from adolescents are in blue. These quotes reflect feelings or situations described in the main text.

Blue boxes are for teenage readers; these pages always appear at the back of a chapter. Quotes from adolescents also appear in blue on the main pages.

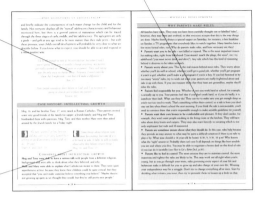

Case histories are about problems – and, in most cases, solutions – from real life. In each instance the parents and teenagers give their side of the story. The comments at the bottom of the box describe what may have been the underlying reasons for the dilemma and how it was resolved (or not, as may happen in life).

Questionnaires are meant to be a private way to help parents and adolescents figure out what their thoughts and feelings are and to decide whether there may be room for a change in their thinking or behaviour. Those that are tinted grey are for parents, while those in blue are mainly for adolescents.

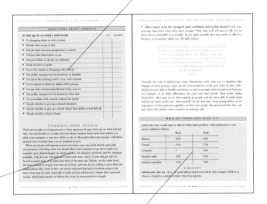

Comments at the bottom of the boxes help to interpret or deal with a situation, such as in a case history, or to evaluate the results of a questionnaire.

Tables are a simple way of representing or summarizing information. Many reflect the findings of our survey, which was undertaken especially for this book.

1

PHYSICAL DEVELOPMENT

Tuesday, September 8th. Lousy stinking school on Thursday. I tried my old uniform on but I have outgrown it so badly that my father is being forced to buy me a new one tomorrow. He is going up the wall but I can't help it if my body is in a growth period, can I?

Sue Townsend, The Secret Diary of Adrian Mole, Aged 13¾

ADOLESCENCE SPANS THE YEARS between puberty, when the secondary sexual characteristics start to appear, and 18, the age of legal adulthood. The term "adolescent" is not one of pinpoint accuracy: it can refer to someone as young as 10 or as old as 18, so it's more useful to think of people as passing through a particular stage of adolescence – early, middle, or late – rather than lumping all adolescents, of all ages, together under the single label "teenagers". Although rates of development differ, the patterns are the same. This first part of the book looks at these patterns and at the impact on the adolescent and the family of each of these milestones.

Perhaps the most obvious sign that a child has become an adolescent is that he or she suddenly shoots up in height. At the peak of this growth spurt, a boy may gain as much as 12–15 cm (5–6 in) in 12 months, so that between his 13th and 14th birthdays he may outgrow all his clothes. It's important to realize, however, that emotional and physical development don't always go hand in hand. A child who is physically well developed won't necessarily be capable of acting in a more "grown-up" way than one who at the same age is still physically less mature. Typically, in developed countries in the 1990s, girls begin their spurt at 10½ years and reach their year of fastest growth at the age of about 12. Boys follow the same pattern two years later, but their peak growth rate is usually slightly faster. Their final height is greater – a genuine sex difference.

Left: Even in a group of adolescents of the same age, variations in physical development are obvious.

During childhood girls and boys are physically alike apart from their genitalia. How much their clothing and hairstyles conform to sexual stereotypes is a matter of choice; many families adopt a unisex appearance of jeans, T-shirts, and sweatshirts for both sexes. There are, nevertheless, a few consistent differences. Girls are more mature than boys at birth (although they are physically slightly smaller, their bones are about five weeks "older"). Throughout infancy they continue to remain slightly ahead: the most noticeable difference is that the permanent teeth appear a few weeks sooner in girls than in boys. Girls reach half their final adult height a month or two before their second birthdays, while boys reach the same target more or less exactly at the age of two. Parents who measure their children's heights at this age will have a good guide to their final height.

Between the ages of three and 10, however, there are no obvious differences in size or in general shape. Girls then begin their growth spurt two years earlier than boys, so that for a while they are both taller and heavier than their male contemporaries. Paradoxically, it is because they mature earlier that girls end up smaller; the end of the growth spurt marks the time that the long bones become fixed in size. Most of the 13-cm (5½-in) difference in height between men and women is due to the extra 8–10 cm (3–4 in) that boys grow between the ages of 10 and 12 years while waiting for their adolescence to begin. Until the growth spurt begins, the limbs grow proportionately more than the trunk; the fact that boys have these two extra years of prepubertal growth makes them proportionately longer-legged than girls as adults.

HEIGHT AND WEIGHT

Your child's final height depends on three main factors: heredity, nutrition, and individual variation. Heredity has an obvious effect: tall parents have tall children.

Nutrition is equally important. In most European countries until very recently, the average height of children of manual workers was about an inch (2 cm) less than that of children of middle-class professionals. As standards of nutrition have improved, these class differences have become less marked and have indeed disappeared in the Scandinavian countries, where overall living standards are high.

The rapidity of their growth often means that adolescents are clumsy and uncoordinated.

The third factor, individual variation, is the most unpredictable. A few generations ago, when large families were more common, six adult brothers might vary in height by six inches even if none was unhealthy. With the smaller families of the late 20th century, this variation is less visible; nevertheless, an individual child may be destined to be substantially shorter or taller than the prediction based on parental average.

Because some studies have shown that taller adults achieve more material success,[1] parents whose children are clearly genetically destined to be short sometimes ask for them to be given growth hormone; this forces the child to grow taller than its genetic potential. However, this is time-consuming and expensive, and no one yet knows what the side-effects of such treatment are likely to be. The main use of growth hormone is to help children who are naturally deficient in the hormone: without treatment such children might grow to be only about four feet tall.

The destiny of the genes is indeed apparent very early on if measurements are interpreted correctly. Parents who wish to monitor their children's health should measure and record their height and weight every six months from babyhood. It will soon become apparent whether the child is on target for the parental average height.

Body weight may double between the ages of 10 and 18. This is due largely to the rapid gain in height, but adolescents also become bulkier. In boys this extra weight is mainly muscle, but in girls it is both muscle and fat, deposited in the breasts, hips, and shoulders to give a rounded, "female" shape. Teenage boys, however, remain slighter than adult men and continue to broaden out until they are about 25.

It it perhaps not surprising that weight-watching is an almost universal pre-occupation among young girls. Teenage girls start to feel fatter because they *are* fatter, and with few exceptions they become, for a while, preoccupied with minuscule gains and losses of weight, tediously concerned about diet, and given to spasmodic bouts of exercise. In moderation none of this does them any harm, although it may cause some family friction.

A few teenagers, however, develop such an overwhelming fear of becoming fat that, left to themselves, they would avoid food to the point of self-starvation. Probably about one teenager in 100 develops a severe eating disorder, anorexia nervosa (see p.240). Nearly all of these are girls, though an increasing number of boys are now being treated.

OTHER BODY CHANGES

Even before the rapid spurt of growth that signals the beginning of puberty, the budding adolescent will have been aware of other body changes. In most young girls, breast development is the first and most obvious of these (although in about a third of girls, pubic hair starts to appear before the breasts start to bud).

The chart (p.19) shows the average age at which each of these changes begins. However, it is important to bear in mind that these are only average ages and that adolescent physical development is immensely and unpredictably variable; a very few children, for example show the first signs of puberty before they are nine years old. Puberty in girls usually begins at 10 or 11. Most girls show some signs of development by the time they are 13 and reach full sexual maturity by the time they are 16. The pattern of sexual development in boys, like the growth spurt begins and ends rather later. Most boys show signs of development by the time they are 14 and are usually sexually mature by 17 or 18.

EARLY AND LATE DEVELOPMENT

Sexual development is influenced by much the same factors as growth: family patterns, general health, and normal variability. This, however, is of little comfort to the anxious 12-year-olds whose development is either ahead of, or lagging far behind, that of their friends. It's often reassuring to point out that all these physical developments come as a package, and that, once the first signs are seen, the rest follow in time.

Some predictions can be made. For example, a girl whose mother started her periods comparatively late is likely to be a later-than-average starter herself, and children who are smaller or thinner than average tend to be late developers. A girl is unlikely to start her periods until she weighs at least 45 kg (99 lb).

CHILDREN WHO MATURE EARLY

There do seem to be some advantages in early development, especially for boys. Children who become physically mature (that is, taller and with other secondary sex characteristics) at an earlier age score slightly higher than average on conventional tests of mental ability; indeed, each extra centimetre (approximately ½ in) of height seems to contribute around two-thirds of a point on standard intelligence tests. That may not seem much, but it may mean that the tallest girls in a typical school class score 10 points higher than the shortest ones. Two other general factors affect performance on IQ tests (the results of which, in all cases, seem to stabilize in the mid-teens): tall children score better than short ones – independently of the early-maturer effect – and children from small families do better than those from larger ones. Some of these effects persist into adult life; about half of the advantage in IQ gained by an early maturer seems to be permanent. These are, however, small differences that are apparent only when large numbers of children are tested.

A child may be physically mature but not
emotionally mature. A 12-year-old may look
15 but act like a 10-year-old.

Early maturing children, particularly boys, also gain in other ways. There is some prestige for a boy in being bigger and stonger than his peers. Such boys may show more athletic prowess – a very important factor in determining a boy's popularity amongst his peers – and may seem to be more outgoing and assured. Adults will tend to treat him as more grown-up and give him more responsibility, even though these expectations may not always be appropriate for the individual boy.

NORMAL ADOLESCENT DEVELOPMENT

GIRLS

Growth spurt (10 to 11)
Consult a doctor if growth spurt starts
before 9 or has not begun by 13.

Breast development (10 to 11)
Breast development is usually the first sign
of puberty. The area around the nipple
swells and the nipple itself starts to stand
out. Consult a doctor if breast buds have
not appeared by 15 (see also *Breasts*, p.23).

Pubic hair (10 to 11); **underarm and body
hair** (12 to 13)
Age of appearance of body hair varies
greatly.

Vaginal discharge (10 to 13)
Decreases once periods begin, but should
not stop altogether.

Production of underarm sweat (12 to 13)
With development of apocrine glands
comes increased underarm sweat and adult
body odour.

Menstruation (11 to 14)
Consult a doctor if periods begin before 10
or have not begun by 16 (see also *Questions
About Periods*, pp.24–5).

BOYS

Growth spurt (12 to 13)
Consult a doctor if growth spurt begins
before 11 or has not started by 15.

Testes and scrotum (11 to 12)
The skin of the scrotum darkens as the
testes grow. Testes should descend in babyhood. Consult a doctor if the testes have not
started to enlarge by 14.

Penis (12 to 13)
The penis starts to lengthen before it
thickens.

Ejaculation (13 to 14)
Ejaculation of a mucus-like fluid begins
about a year after the penis starts to lengthen.
At first the ejaculate contains no sperm.

Pubic hair (11 to 12); **underarm and body
hair** (13 to 15); **facial hair** (13 to 15)
Development of all body hair varies greatly
and depends largely on family patterns. Hair
growth from abdomen up to chest continues
into adulthood.

Development of underarm sweat glands
(13 to 15)
With the development of apocrine glands
comes increased underarm sweating and an
adult body odour.

Deepening of voice (14 to 15)
About a year before the voice starts to
deepen, the larynx (voice box) enlarges
and an "Adam's apple" may develop.

Early maturity does not seem to carry quite the same psychological advantages for girls. A girl who towers above her friends may feel self-conscious and unfeminine, and often such girls develop permanently bad posture because they slouch to look smaller. Early or very noticeable breast development may also be embarrassing. While girls may gain some advantage from being treated as more grown-up by adults, there is also a risk that they may sometimes be regarded as sexually precocious and perhaps put under more sexual pressure by older boys than they can cope with.

LATE STARTERS

For individual teenagers the worrying aspect of the growth spurt is its variability; a school class of 13- and 14-year-olds may include some boys and girls who have virtually completed their growth spurt, and so may be 15 cm (6 in) taller and comparably bigger and stronger than their classmates who have not yet begun to grow.

There seem to be no advantages to either sex in late maturity. Late maturers show a lack of self-confidence and self-esteem and may be tense and anxious. Their social confidence is likely to suffer, and late-maturing boys will be at a particular disadvantage with girls, who are, in any case, usually more physically mature (and often more emotionally mature) than boys of their own age.

What, then, is a parent to do when it becomes apparent that a child's adolescence is delayed? Sometimes the parents of late maturers seek a doctor's advice, convinced that there must be a medical explanation. In practice, however, doctors will rarely show much interest in medical investigation of a short teenager until a girl is 13 or a boy is 15, since they rely on the many studies that have shown that almost all delays are quite normal; the later maturer catches up by the age of 16 (girls) or 18 (boys).

*Children who watch their friends grow while
they remain relatively small may become
worried and miserable.*

It is sensible to consult your doctor for reassurance if your daughter shows no signs of breast development by the time she is 15, or if her periods have not started by 16. Very rarely, delay in starting is due to some underlying hormonal problem; hormone therapy may be prescribed to induce menstruation.

Can the psychological and physical effects of late maturation be minimized? Only by reassurance when the delay is within the range of normal, expected differences. This may be of little comfort when normal variation in height, intelligence, and in psychological characteristics within a family of three or more children is far greater than the average differences between early and late maturers. But children do need to know that the growth spurt will occur in its own good time. Later maturers often end up taller than the average.

EXPECTATIONS

Parents naturally hope that their children will all be beautiful and talented, but of course these are not always reasonable expectations. Children do inherit most of their physical and psychological features from their parents, but the inheritance is rather more complicated than that affecting, say, the colour of the eyes. Height is a good example of this rich and complex genetic inheritance. You can make a reasonable guess about the likely adult height of any one child (add the height of the two parents; for a boy, add 5½ in, for a girl deduct this amount; then divide by two). However, if you look at a family with six or more children who have all grown up, the men and women will be of six different heights, and often they will have six different builds, different hair colours, and so on. This is normal genetic variation. Even if there had been only two children in the family, the parents' predictions would still have had to contend with a great range of possible variation.

In general, tall parents have tall children and short parents have short ones. The tendency is, however, for the children to be closer to the average than their parents, so that very tall parents usually have children who are shorter than they are. This biological principle is known as *regression to the mean*, and what is true of height is also true of other inherited characteristics, both physical and psychological. World-class athletes whose children take up the same sport cannot expect the second generation to be equally outstanding, and parents who are extremely intelligent should expect their children, on average, to be less clever than they are. The importance of understanding this biological inevitability of regression to the mean is that parents should not have unreasonable expectations of their children. It is one thing to wish the best for one's child, but it is equally important to recognize that outstanding abilities are inborn, and most of us do not have them; quite probably they may, in any case, contribute more to problems than to happiness. We should value our children for what they are, not because they might fulfil our expectations or achieve some ambition that we have planned for them from the cradle.

ISSUE: PRIVACY

Adolescents are intensely self-conscious and sensitive about their changing bodies. They are entitled to their privacy: their room is their own territory. Parents should knock if they want to go in, and fix a lock on their teenagers' bedroom door if asked for one.

Free-thinking parents who have always prided themselves on never having a lock on the bathroom door should perhaps modify their behaviour and fix one now. If they have wandered around the house naked, they might wish to consider that this may be embarrassing for their children.

YOUR CHANGING BODY

Your body changes so rapidly and dramatically between the ages of 11 and 16 that it will probably take you a while to feel comfortable with it. The whole shape of your body changes: girls develop a narrow waist and broader hips, and boys broaden in the shoulders. Even the shape of your face changes (more in boys than in girls). Your nose and jaw become more prominent and your forehead becomes higher. You may not feel like an adult, or be ready to have an adult's body. And because people vary so much, you may worry because the changes you notice in yourself aren't quite what you had expected, or what you have noticed in your friends.

All these changes are caused by hormones. These are chemical substances produced by glands (such as, in both boys and girls, the pituitary, and the ovaries in girls and the testes in boys), which affect not only your growth but also your moods. You may notice that one year you may grow three inches and the next year very little, or your skin may be perfect one month and spotty the next. These changes may be unpredictable and may upset you, but they are perfectly normal. As you get a little older, the changes will slow down or won't be quite so drastic.

BODY HAIR GROWTH

The typical pattern of body hair growth in boys and girls varies a lot. It's quite normal for girls to have pubic hair that spreads up their stomach to their navel, for example, or to have occasional hairs around their nipples; some boys will develop hairier chests while some may never even have one hair. Pubic hair won't necessarily be the same colour as the hair on your head.

WHY DO ADULTS SMELL?

During adolescence new sets of sweat glands in the armpits and around the genitals start to work. These are called apocrine glands, and they produce sweat not just when you're hot (to help cool you down) but when you're anxious or excited, too. This adult sweat smells fine when it's fresh, but not so good after a day or so. Young children never really smell "sweaty" in the way that adults do, but as these glands start to work you'll need to wash your armpits and genital area every day, and probably use a deodorant in your armpits. Never use deodorants on or around your genitals because the skin is too sensitive. Washing is enough.

DEVELOPMENT IN BOYS

• **Penis size**   Your penis has special spongy tissue with passageways, and when these fill with blood, your penis becomes stiffer and harder and you have an erection. If you compare penis size with your friends – and most boys do – don't worry if you think yours is small. Although there is a lot of variation in the size of non-erect penises, these differences do not show when the penis is erect because small penises increase in size more than large ones. The average length of an erect adult penis is between 12 and 17 cm (5 and 7 in). Also remember that you probably look at yours from above; that makes it appear smaller than it really is.

• **Embarrassing erections**   Most boys discover that almost anything can give them an erection, however inconvenient or embarrassing the time and place. The easiest way to get it to subside is to think very hard about something else.

• **Morning erections**   You will often find that you have an erection when you wake up in the morning. This is because erections occur automatically during dreaming (whether or not it is a sexual dream) and usually you have a period of dreaming just before you wake up.

• **Wet dreams**   Sometimes when you have an erection during sleep you'll ejaculate. This again is something that happens automatically during dreaming even if the dream hasn't been about sex. Often you'll wake up just after dreaming so it's a good idea to keep a box of tissues by the bed so that you can mop up the semen and don't have to go on lying on a damp patch.

• **Voice change**   Everyone's voice deepens slightly as the voice box (larynx) along with the rest of the body grows larger. In boys, the change is more dramatic than in girls because boys' larynxes enlarge more, and it's the larger larynx that forms the prominent Adam's apple. Your voice will probably deepen gradually although at times you may be embarrassed because you may suddenly produce a squeak when you're talking. Occasionally, though, the voice breaks quite suddenly and rapidly and you may find you have a new, deeper voice all of a sudden.

• **Breast development**   It's disconcerting for a boy to notice that he seems to be developing breasts but this is not at all uncommon during puberty. Any such swelling will usually disappear within about 18 months as your hormones settle down.

DEVELOPMENT IN GIRLS

• **Breasts**   Don't worry if you think your breasts are not developing evenly. It's quite normal for one to "bud" before the other so that you feel a bit lopsided for a while. Even when you're fully developed they may not be exactly the same size; no one's body or face is absolutely symmetrical.

• **Choosing a bra**   You'll probably feel more comfortable if you wear a bra for sports, even if you prefer not to wear one the rest of the time. When you're buying a bra you need to know two measurements: your chest size and your cup size.

To find your chest size, measure around your body just under your breasts. Add 12 cm (5 in) for your final chest measurement. Then measure around the fullest part of your breasts. If this is the same as your final chest measurement you need an A cup. If your cup measurement is 2.5 cm (1 in) more than your chest measurement you need a B cup. If your cup measurement is 5 cm (2 in) more than your chest measurement you need a C cup.

QUESTIONS ABOUT PERIODS

• **Why do girls get periods?** Your monthly cycle of periods – also called menstruation – usually starts between the ages of 11 and 14. Menstruation is the result of your ovaries beginning to release one of about 400,000 tiny eggs you are born with.

• **When will my periods start?** Most people tend to think that periods mark the beginning of puberty, but in fact they are one of the last events to occur. Your periods won't start until at least a year after your growth spurt has begun, after your breasts have started to develop, and after body hair has started to appear in your armpits and in your genital area. A year or two before your periods begin, your vagina will start to produce some clear or white, odourless fluid. You'll probably notice this on your underpants. It can be very worrying if you're not expecting it or don't know what it is, but in fact it's quite normal and nothing to worry about. If there is a lot, wearing panty liners will help to keep you dry. Once your periods start there will be less of this discharge, but there will always be some just as your nose always produces some mucus.

• **Why do some girls start later than others?** Although periods usually begin between the ages of 11 and 14, it's quite normal for them to be delayed well beyond this age. Don't worry if most of your friends seem to have started their periods and you're still waiting. Usually a delay simply means that you're a naturally "late starter". Often this runs in the family, so if your mother's periods started later than average, the chances are that yours will, too. If you're smaller (or thinner) than your friends, you'll probably start your periods later. You are not likely to start your periods until you weigh at least 45 kg (99 lb). Almost all girls will have started by the time they are 16.

• **How long will my period last?** Your first periods may vary in length, but once they settle down, they usually last about five days. This is only an average, however, and periods may last only a day, or as long as eight days, and still be perfectly normal. Bleeding is heaviest on the second and third day, and gets lighter towards the end of the period.

• **How often will I get my period?** At first your periods will be very irregular! There may be gaps of two or three months or more between them at first; this is quite normal. It may take 18 months or longer before they settle down. Usually periods come once a month, so that there is, on average, 28 days between the first day of one period and the first day of the next (this is called the menstrual cycle). But because girls and women are all different from each other, your own cycle may be several days shorter or longer than 28 days.

• **How can I tell when my next period will start?** It's a good idea to mark the first day of a period in your diary or on a personal calendar. At first this won't tell you much because the first few periods are nearly always so irregular. Eventually, though, you'll be able to see that they're settling down to a pattern, with about the same number of days between each period. If you're lucky your periods may become so regular that you'll be able to predict the very day a period is likely to start, but this doesn't happen to everyone. Most girls notice that they have a few more spots than usual during the week before a period starts. You may also notice that your breasts feel a bit heavier, you may gain a few pounds, and sometimes your nipples tingle.

• **Can I use tampons when my periods start?**   Tampons are quite safe for anyone to use but sanitary pads are simpler, so most girls prefer to wear these to begin with. After a few months, when you've grown used to your periods and feel more confident, you may want to try tampons. These are worn inside the vagina. Choose the smallest size to begin with, follow the instructions on the packet carefully, and don't worry if you find them difficult to insert at first. Gradually the opening of the vagina will stretch and insertion will be easier. Tampons are more convenient and comfortable to use if you play a lot of sports. You can wear a tampon when you go swimming, for example. Put on a clean pad or change a tampon at least three times a day.

• **Can I get pregnant once my periods have started?**   Yes, you must assume you can. In practice, though, ovulation (the release of an egg) seldom begins until the periods have become regular. So at first, even though you are menstruating, you may not be fertile. Once your periods have settled down and become regular, an egg will be released from one of your ovaries each month, and if you have sex and the egg is fertilized, you will become pregnant. In a few cases, an egg may even be released before your first period.

• **Will my periods be painful?**   The first periods are usually pain-free, but once a regular cycle is established, many girls have some discomfort just before and during their periods (dysmenorrhoea). You may have a cramp-like pain in the lower part of your abdomen, or an ache in the lower part of your back. The pain lasts only for a few hours, and a pain-killer such as aspirin will usually cure it. If your periods are painful, see your doctor. There are effective drugs available nowadays that can cure bad period pains.

• **Will I outgrow painful periods?**   Many girls eventually do, if not after the first few months, then later in adult life after they've had a baby. Going on the pill can also reduce period pain. But not everyone is the same – some women will always have more pain, or a heavier flow, than others.

• **Can I have a bath or go swimming during a period?**   There's no medical reason why you should not do anything you normally do during a period – it depends only on what you feel like. Some girls avoid sports activities during the first day or two of a period, especially if they have stomach cramps. There is no truth in any of the tales that it's bad for you to have a bath, wash your hair, or go swimming during a period. If you wear tampons, you can swim quite happily at any time. If you wear pads, you may prefer not to swim on the days when the bleeding is heaviest, just in case blood stains your swimsuit. Towards the end of a period there is much less bleeding, and no reason why you should not go swimming without a pad.

2
GROWING UP

"

I would there were no age between ten and three-and-twenty, or that youth would sleep out the rest, for there is nothing in the between but getting wenches with child, wronging the ancientry, stealing, fighting.

"

Shakespeare, The Winter's Tale, *Act III, scene iii.*

ADULT DISENCHANTMENT WITH ADOLESCENCE is clearly no new thing. Some children sail serenely through, passing from childhood to adulthood with the minimum of drama. For other families it's a more turbulent time. Unless parents themselves can adapt to meet the needs of a rapidly changing child, even the best of parent–child relationships is likely to come under occasional strain.

In infancy and early childhood, developmental "milestones" are a useful guide for parents. Each one is seen as a positive achievement, a signal for celebration, and as reassurance that development is proceeding normally.

It's sad that we seldom look upon the changes of adolescence in quite such a positive way. Parents do not often say with pride, "Jon's really starting to think things out for himself now." They are much more likely to complain, "I just can't stand the way Jon contradicts everything I say and starts an argument every time he opens his mouth." It's true that adolescents are sometimes rude, rebellious, egocentric, or surly – but this behaviour is easier to bear if you can see it as part of normal development. You don't have to like it or even tolerate it, but at least you need not worry too much about it, or believe that it will outlast adolescence. The charts below show the main emotional and intellectual "milestones" that have to be passed before a mature human being emerges

Left: The years between childhood and maturity involve more rapid change and more physical, emotional, and intellectual growth than at any other time of life except infancy and early childhood.

and briefly indicate the consequences of each major change for the child and for the family. Not everyone displays all the "typical" adolescent characteristics and behaviour mentioned here, but there is a general pattern of maturation that can be traced through the three stages of early, middle, and late adolescence. The ages given are only a guide – and girls at any age tend to be more mature than their male peers – but with these provisos, your child's overall development will probably be very close to what we describe below. If you know what to expect, you should be able to act and respond in a more positive way.

"I'll be old enough to vote at the next election, but when I said I wasn't going to because it wouldn't change anything, my parents got really worked up. We had quite an argument. They said voting was the only way to change things. Anyway, I won't vote like them, but I might vote – not that it'll make a difference."
Ray, 17

"Most people nowadays don't believe in God, and I see no point in going to church just to please my parents."
Jessica, 14

CASE HISTORY: INTELLECTUAL GROWTH

Meg, 16, and her brother Tony, 17, were raised as Roman Catholics. Their parents invited some very good friends of the family for supper, a Jewish family, and Meg and Tony bombarded them with questions. Meg, Tony, and their mother Mary were then asked around by the Jewish family for a Friday night.

"We were surprised at how keen the children were to go; they haven't been willing to spend an evening with friends of ours for ages."
Mary, 42, and Mark, 43

"Some things about religion seem quite fascinating, but some of it is a bit hard to take. It helps to talk to people about why they believe certain things."
Meg, 16, and Tony, 17

COMMENTS ABOUT INTELLECTUAL GROWTH

Meg and Tony were able to have a serious talk with people from a different religious background and were able to think about what they believed and why.

Mark and Mary were able to explain what Catholicism meant to them. They were quite apprehensive at first, because they knew their children could be quite critical, but they accepted that "you can't make someone believe everything you believe". "Maybe they're not growing up quite as we thought they would, but they're still pretty nice people."

MILESTONES OF EARLY ADOLESCENCE (Age 11 to 14)

MILESTONE	CONSEQUENCE FOR CHILD	EFFECT ON FAMILY
Worries about appearance of developing body	Self-consciousness.	Parents may see this as self-centredness (see p.83).
Hormonal changes	General moodiness. Boys who were previously gentle and easy-going may become much more aggressive. Acne may develop in boys and girls.	Parents may find surliness hard to live with.
Asserts independence and may feel an individual, no longer "just one of the family"	Experiments with dress, speech, manners, etc. in an attempt to find a separate identity of his or her own.	Parents feel rejected and have difficulty accepting the child's wish to be different from them (see p.79).
Rebellious, defiant behaviour	Rudeness.	Parents need to handle children carefully if good relationships are to be maintained (see p.63).
	Demands more freedom.	Parents find that striking a balance between licence and over-protection is not easy (see p.74).
Friends become more important	Wants to identify as closely as possible with friends by having the "right" clothes, hairstyle, etc., listening to the same music.	Parents may be irritated by what they see as conformity and financial demands (see p.86).
Needs to feel a sense of belonging to a peer group: boys form gangs; girls have one or two best friends	Holds friends (and friends' parents) up as a yardstick for their own treatment.	Parents are suddenly criticized by their own children (see p.91)
Has a strong sense of justice, but tends to see issues in black and white and from his or her own point of view	May seem intolerant. Finds it hard to compromise. May be jealous of siblings and fight with them.	Sometimes leads to clashes with school authorities (see p.161). Parents must cope with child's common feeling that "it's not fair".

MILESTONES OF MIDDLE ADOLESCENCE (Age 15 to 16)

MILESTONE	CONSEQUENCE FOR CHILD	EFFECT ON FAMILY
Becomes less self-absorbed and develops greater ability to compromise	More composed, equable, and tolerant. Can accept that others' opinions, even if they are different from their own, may be equally valid.	Parents gradually find that the child is becoming easier to live with.
Learns to think independently and makes his or her own decisions	Reluctant to let parents interfere or control his or her life. Less suggestible and less eager to conform. More discriminating. Friends are less likely to have a strong influence.	Parents have to learn to give up control and to trust the child.
Experiments continually to find self-image he or she feels comfortable with	Clothes, hairstyles, attitudes, and opinions may change frequently.	Parents may take these frequent and often bizarre changes of image too seriously and worry they may be permanent (see p.88).
Needs to collect new experiences, test boundaries, and take risks	Likely to experiment with cigarettes and alcohol and to try soft drugs.	Anxious about risks, parents must decide how and when to set limits (see p.52).
Self-conciousness recedes	More sociable, less shy.	Parents may find a child is prepared to meet their friends.
Starts to build up a set of values, develop a personal sense of morality	Questioning (and possibly setting aside) ideas and values absorbed from the family.	Can lead to problems if the child seems to reject attitudes that the parents value highly (see p.101).
Starts to make lasting and more intimate friendships	Wants to spend less time with the family and more time with friends.	Parents worry about influence of friends and resent being "treated like a hotel".

MILESTONE	CONSEQUENCE FOR CHILD	EFFECT ON FAMILY
Accepts own sexuality, forms sexual relationships that involve feelings he or she may never have had to deal with before	Starts dating. Guards privacy and may seem secretive. Relationships may be short.	Parents' anxiety about child's safety and feelings may make them too intrusive.
Intellectual broadening out, with wider interests and greater awareness of (and curiosity about) the world. Able to think in abstract terms, deal with hypothetical questions	Starts to question things previously taken for granted. Wants to discuss and debate issues.	Parents have a fresh chance to get to know their offspring.
Specific intellectual skills, e.g. ability at maths, science, or languages may emerge	May not be given the chance to develop these skills if "written off" by teachers or parents at an earlier stage.	Parents need to wait until the child's mid-teens before drawing conclusions about intellectual ability.
May develop strong interest in an artistic subject such as music or painting	May neglect schoolwork in favour of the new interest.	Parents need to recognize that their child may have abilities beyond their comprehension or understanding.
Becomes socially and physically adventurous, wanting to travel independently, taking up activities such as rock climbing or surfing	Even mature young adults believe they are immortal; young people may not follow recommended safety precautions.	Parents may want to discourage activities that they know to be dangerous, but risk antagonizing their child.

"Just because I've got a steady boyfriend doesn't mean I'm having sex with him. My parents seem obsessed with my sex life."
June, 15

MILESTONES OF LATE ADOLESCENCE (Age 17 to 18)

MILESTONE	CONSEQUENCE FOR CHILD	EFFECT ON FAMILY
Idealistic	Attempts to find a social or political cause to be committed to. May turn to religious cults or movements (see p.102).	Parents may be distressed at the child's rejection of their own religion or beliefs.
Involvement with life, work, and relationships outside the family	Must learn to cope with the stresses this inevitably brings. Will probably want to go away with friends instead of joining in the family holiday.	Parents' natural wish to protect their child may cause friction. Parents may have the chance to enjoy the kind of holiday they want, without having to take anyone else's wishes into account.
Has to set him- or herself on a course to achieve financial or emotional independence	Anxieties or uncertainty about the future can wreak havoc with temper, confidence, and self-esteem.	Parents may still be financially supporting an adolescent who is not emotionally dependent on them. This can make for an uneasy and unequal relationship (see p.171).
Becomes more able to form stable sexual relationships	Likely to have a serious boyfriend/girlfriend and to spend more time with him or her (see p.99).	Parents tend to worry about a too early or too serious commitment and fear that schoolwork may suffer.
Feels an adult on equal terms with the family	Tends to feel he or she has insights into and experience of the world that parents may lack.	Parents may find themselves being condescended to and resent this role reversal (see p.91).
Is almost ready to become an independent and self-reliant adult	May want to leave the family home and find a place of his or her own.	Parents' own relationship may need some readjustment when their children finally leave home.

PARENTS CHANGE, TOO

You have to adjust to all sorts of changes during your adolescence, but so do your parents. Sharing a home with young adults is quite different from living with small children, and family life can't be organized just on their terms anymore. They probably have less privacy, less time on their own, and a quiet evening by themselves may be a rarity. You are also much more expensive to keep now: the wants and needs of small children tend to be simpler and cheaper than those of teenagers, and so they may be under extra financial strain.

• **Remember they'll need time to adjust.** You're changing so rapidly that it's inevitable that they'll tend to be one step behind. There will be times when you feel they treat you like a child. This is irritating, but it's just as bad to have parents who expect too much of you.

• **Even if you haven't been getting along too well**, try to remember that your parents are basically on your side. If you have a problem, don't assume that they wouldn't understand or be prepared to help you. Other people's parents often seem nicer, kinder, more understanding than your own, but this is often an illusion. Parents put on a good show when there are visitors. They don't (or shouldn't) shout at their children or make them look small in front of their friends. Your parents may seem marvellous to your friends. If you do have difficult parents, your friends will realize it is not your fault (see p.70).

• **Your parents know that you have to grow up and grow away from them**, but they may be hurt (and take it out on you) if they feel you have no time for them any more. If they complain, "You treat this house like a hotel," it doesn't mean they want to stop looking after you. It's a sign that they'd like a little more appreciation, so maybe you could find a little time to talk to them or to do your share of family chores.

Your teenage years may be a difficult time for your parents for other reasons quite unconnected with you. Maybe they are having to take increasing responsibility for their own ageing parents. For many it is a make-or-break time at work; they realize that it is their last chance to change direction if they have not been very happy in their job, or they have to face the fact that they are never going to get that final promotion. And for the many who become unemployed in their middle years, things can look very bleak as the prospects of re-employment are not good. Be tactful about how and when you make demands. If you know that they have their problems, too, choose another moment to complain about the unfair treatment you've been getting. If you know that money is tight, try to wait a bit before asking for an advance or an increased allowance.

> *"Sometimes I feel really depressed and I don't know why. Then just because I don't feel like saying much, or I want to be by myself, my dad says something like, 'Oh, she's just going through a phase.' That makes me really mad. It means they don't understand how I'm feeling."*
>
> Tina, 14

PART TWO

LEARNING TO LIVE TOGETHER

3

FAMILIES AND FEELINGS

All happy families resemble one another, but each
unhappy family is unhappy in its own way.

Leo Tolstoy, Anna Karenina

THERE IS NO SUCH THING AS THE IDEAL PARENT. Every family makes its own rules and draws its own lines, according to the personalities involved. Some styles of parenting, however, seem to make for a less friction-filled life for both parents and child, and this is especially true during adolescence.

A look at "real" families is reassuring. We carried out our own survey in the UK of 120 schoolchildren of all ages. This confirmed that even if they argue a lot with their parents, most teenagers still see the relationship as a good one. In fact, even those with a list of complaints that gave the impression they were living in a top-security prison seldom described their parents as too strict. The overwhelming majority saw their parents as "firm but fair"; it seems that they could accept the ground rules and that, although they would push for every concession they could, they still thought parental lines should be drawn. Our survey also suggested that, on the whole, most adolescents get on very well with their mothers, and that very few had a bad relationship with them. However, boys seemed more likely than girls to maintain a consistently good relationship with their mothers during adolescence: one boy claimed that his mother was perfect!

Relationships with fathers seemed less sunny: fewer adolescents at any age said they got on well with their fathers, and by late adolescence (17 to 18) almost a third of the boys and 14 per cent of the girls said they got on "badly".

Left: The best thing you can learn from family members
is how to make each other feel valued.

QUESTIONS ABOUT PARENTING

Below are some issues that often cause family friction. In each case what would be most likely to happen in your own family? Choose your answer from A, B, or C and jot down the response. Then count up your total of A, B, and C answers to assess your style of parenting.

A You would decide and expect your son or daughter to fall in line with you.

B You would expect to discuss the issue, may try to persuade, but would usually let your child make the final decision.

C You would let your child make his or her own decision without interfering.

How would you approach decisions about the following?	A, B, or C
• Clothes worn outside school	
• A bizarre haircut during the holidays	
• Listening to the radio/watching television while working	
• Going to pop concerts with friends at the age of 15	
• Starting to date	
• Smoking cigarettes	
• Your going away for the night if your 17-year-old is having a party	
• Your child always letting you know where he or she is going	
• Spending pocket money	
• What kind of job to aim for	
• How much help should be given in the house	
• Joining in family outings or holidays	
• Limiting outings during the school week	
• Your youngster seeing a friend you think takes drugs	
• How tidy your child should keep his or her own room	
• A part-time job	
• "Sleeping over" after a party	
• Drinking alcoholic beverages	
• Having a party at home	
• Which examination subjects to study for	
• Learning or continuing a musical instrument	
• What time to be home in the evening	
• Leaving school early	
• How your child should decorate his or her own room	
• What, or how much or little, they eat	
• What TV programmes or videos they watch	
• Giving up a school subject they dislike	
• Whether they should take a part-time or Saturday job	

More than 5 As Authoritarian

On a few issues, it's reasonable to lay down the law, but if you have more than 5 As, your natural inclination may be to want too much control over your children. You tend to be over-protective and perhaps a bit dictatorial: rules are rules and you expect them to be obeyed. In these situations, there may not be much discussion or two-way communication in the family. You probably have high expectations for your children, but may not show them much warmth or approval.

If your child is 17 or over, be wary if you have two or more As: you're probably exercising too much control and must remember that at this age children should be able to take over more responsibility for their lives. Let them make their own decisions, even if you think they're bound to make mistakes.

Remember, too, that a very authoritarian style of parenting can make it difficult for children to grow up and become independent and self-reliant. The youngster who has always been told what to do may find it quite hard to accept responsibility as an adult. If parents are over-protective, never allow their child to take any risks, and never encourage him or her to explore, experiment, or test limits, the youngster may develop into a timid and over-cautious adult. Such children may lack self-esteem and find it hard to break away from the family, staying emotionally dependent on their parents indefinitely.

More than 10 Cs Easy-going

If you score 10 or more Cs, perhaps you're too unconcerned about what is happening to your children. Your attitude tends to be "anything for a quiet life", and you may know very little about what is actually going on in your child's life at any particular time. This casual, *laissez-faire* attitude means that, while you are not a nagger or a disciplinarian, your children don't get very much attention from you. You tend to turn a blind eye to trouble, which, if it comes, may take you by surprise.

Parents who are too permissive can be as disastrous for a teenager as too restrictive ones. It can be quite frightening for youngsters to feel that – no matter what they do, how far they go – no heavy hand is going to come down on their shoulder and say "that's enough". Guidelines are necessary because pressure from friends (as well as the need to experiment and explore) means that children need to know the point at which they can and should draw back. If parents show so little interest in what is happening to their children that they offer no guidelines, it's easy for the children to believe their parents don't care.

Mixture of Bs and Cs Firm but fair

A mixture of Bs and Cs means that you usually strike the right balance between being too easy-going and too strict or over-protective Your policy is not to impose your views on ▷

your youngster, but to avoid confrontation, listen to his or her point of view, and to work out a decision. You set limits, but, at the same time, respond to reasonable demands and recognize that your child has rights too.

Children treated in a fair way have the best chance of becoming self-confident, self-reliant, and responsible. If, when problems arise, you try to cooperate with your teenager in solving them by peaceful means, he or she will feel comfortable about asking for your help if and when real trouble occurs.

If you can manage the mixture of tolerance and firm guidelines that characterizes the firm-but-fair parent, you're off to a good start. However, your child also has to live with you the way you are, just as you have to learn to get along with him or her. If you're naturally happy-go-lucky, you'll probably never make a strict disciplinarian; if you're obsessionally neat and tidy, you may not be able to help nagging the chronically untidy teenager. This doesn't matter, provided that you're consistent and your children know where they stand and what is expected of them.

WHEN PERSONALITIES CLASH

How rough this time is for everyone concerned will depend partly on the personality of the adolescent and partly on your own ability to cope with and adapt to the maturing child. Whatever your parenting style, the chances are that you won't be equally successful in handling every one of your adolescent children. "Of course I always treat them all the same," you say, but of course you don't, however hard you try. Nor should you, because they do not need the same treatment. Each child has his or her own style of temperament, too – and it may or may not mesh easily with yours.

The family is a dynamic system: every relationship is different because every personality is different.

Some children (and some parents) are much better than others at handling problems and coping with stress. This will inevitably affect the way other people react to them: children who have been "prickly" or difficult throughout childhood are not likely to change much during adolescence. What should you do?

- **Don't be critical.**
- **Don't compare one child with another** (see below).
- **Do all you can to boost your child's self-esteem** (see p.83).
- **Remember that one of the most valuable assets** a teenager can have is a family in which people talk to each other, express their feelings, and try to explain why they feel and act as they do.

SIBLING RIVALRY

Only about half the children we questioned said they got on well with their brothers and sisters: on the whole, these relationships seem to be marked more by tolerance than enthusiasm, but real friction seems to be more likely in early adolescence (ages 11–14) when one in five said they got on "badly" with their siblings. By late adolescence (ages 17–18) only one in 20 said they got on badly. Jealousy, a feeling that parents favour a brother or sister, seemed to be more of a problem for girls. Both boys and girls thought that brothers and sisters "interfering" with their lives was one of the main causes of family arguments.

*"When they were smaller they used to play happily all
day long. Now they only have to be in the same room for
10 minutes for one or the other to be screaming and swearing.
I don't understand why it's all gone wrong."*

Alice, 37

When tensions arise there may be times when the adolescent feels (just as the parent does) that he or she can't do a thing right. If there are (temporarily) better-behaved siblings sitting smugly on the sidelines not drawing any of the parental fire, it is easy for the misbehaving child to believe that his or her parents are playing favourites. Dealing with sibling quarrels needs a light and tactful touch:

- **Don't always automatically blame the adolescent** when he or she quarrels with a younger sibling.
- **Don't get over-involved**. You'll simply end up shouting yourself.
- **Don't take sides** or try to find out who started it. Someone will end up feeling hard done by and thinking you're being unfair whatever you do. The origins of most family quarrels are too complex to lay at only one person's door.
- Use **"time out"** (see p.50) to cool everyone down rather than punishing one or both offenders.
- **Act as a mediator** by helping both sides talk about how they feel and what the quarrel was really about – without getting angry yourself.
- **Discover why the same child always seems to be the one you pick on**, the one who causes trouble, the one who is at the centre of every row. You either have an unhappy child or one who is being made the scapegoat for family tensions. Life in a well-balanced family is not like that: everyone causes their share of trouble some of the time.
- **Do not withdraw affection** from even the most troublesome teenager. Make sure he or she realizes that even if you find their behaviour intolerable you still care about them.
- **Value each child as an individual**. Don't compare them with each other and don't seem to value one child's achievements more than those of others.

CHILDREN WHO DON'T FIT IN

Children in the same family are different people. They may have different needs and are probably good at different things. Family life can be particularly difficult for a child who doesn't quite fit the image, hopes, or dreams the parents have always had for their children, perhaps because he or she isn't good at the things the parents value most. If another child in the family does fit the image, then the child who doesn't is doubly likely to feel edged out and rejected. Everyone thrives on success. It's important to help every child find something they can feel they are good at and to show your pride in their achievements.

*"You're always picking on me" is a very
common adolescent complaint.*

CASE HISTORY: NOT FITTING IN

Both Simon and Rebecca's parents were science teachers, so they were especially pleased when Rebecca turned out to be a science "high flier". Simon, on the other hand, showed no interest in any of the sciences. The only subject he really seemed to enjoy was art, which his parents felt wasn't a "real" subject at all, and certainly not a career option. Rebecca's reports each term were always greeted with delight; her examination results were cause for celebration and immediate telephone calls to grandparents and friends. Her parents took a special interest in her projects and were always ready to help or discuss results. Simon's art teacher gave him glowing reports, too, but his parents' response was: "this art stuff is all very well, but you'll have to get down to some real work some time."

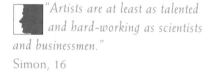

"Science will be the only thing that really matters in the 21st century, so you'd better get your priorities right."
Richard, 52 and Margaret, 49

"Artists are at least as talented and hard-working as scientists and businessmen."
Simon, 16

COMMENTS ABOUT NOT FITTING IN

Simon got good marks in his art examinations and, after a struggle, his parents agreed that he could take up the place he'd been offered at art school. When he came home during vacations, however, he never talked about his work, and his parents didn't ask about it. He now sees his parents very rarely. Simon felt that his parents' running down of art as a serious subject meant that they were running him down. As parents, you may find it difficult to value the subjects that interest one of your children.

Parents shouldn't run a topic down just because they don't understand it or were not good at it themselves.

What Kind of Parents Do Adolescents Need?

As anyone who has lived with adolescents will tell you, there are an infinite number of ways you can put a foot wrong, wittingly or unwittingly. Asking yourselves where you went wrong can be an unprofitable exercise, however. It's much more positive to try to see what you do, or can do, that is right. Modifying your own behaviour is probably the most effective way of altering teenage "stroppiness" and easing the relationship.

Tolerance is essential for living with teenagers, although this does not mean that anything goes. Experts agree that teenagers feel safest when they know how far they can go. They do not expect total freedom to do exactly what they want. However unlikely it may seem, deep down your child actually wants you to impose limits even though he or she may challenge you – sometimes quite loudly – all the way and on every issue. Children do not always expect, and probably do not even want, always to win (see *When to Say No*, p.76). Most of all, children need parents who are warm, loving, and accepting – and those who can continue to be so even when conflict arises

Where to Start

• **Decide what matters**. Although you need to set limits, you should not impose them all over the place. Some types of behaviour matter much more than others, either because they present a danger to the child or because they really do make life intolerable for the rest of the family.
• **Set limits that are realistic as well as reasonable**. For example, even if you don't smoke yourself, you can't realistically forbid smoking; you can, however, forbid it in the house, or limit it to the adolescent's own room. Make sure your teenagers know about the undeniable health hazards of smoking. If you smoke, your arguments will carry more weight if you try to give it up.
• **Back off and leave an argument** over something that, on reflection, you decide isn't really important. This isn't being weak or "letting them get away with it". Your son or daughter will soon realize that when you do disagree with them you usually have a good reason and you must think it important, and they will be much more prepared to listen to you.
• **Be willing to discuss issues** and try to respond to reasonable demands. The whole process of growing up is one of change; unless you are flexible enough to adapt to each new stage, tensions are bound to arise.
• **Don't be afraid to change your mind** if it seems appropriate. This isn't a sign of weakness, but a recognition that your children also have rights and that you acknowledge those rights and will try to meet your child's requests halfway.
• **Don't be nagged or bullied** into accepting behaviour you do not like and do not want. If teenagers get their own way because you have given in to their manipulation, they'll try it again and again.

A UNITED FRONT

Although the politics of family life work best with a strong parental coalition, this is more difficult to achieve during your children's adolescence than at any other time. For one thing, you are dealing with your own past and experience as well as with new issues; also, your long-term aim is to give up control rather than to establish it.

Adolescents are learning to argue and reason their way around problems, and, if they can play their parents off against each other, they will.

● **When challenged by a teenager** who says, "But Dad said last night I could", try not to reply, "And I say you can't." It's better to keep all options open by saying, "Maybe you can, but Dad doesn't realize how I feel because I haven't had a chance to discuss it with him yet. Just give us a chance to talk it over".

● **Accept that there are bound to be times** when you and your fellow parent may disagree about how this is to be done or about the limits you should set, so it's important to keep in touch with each other to work out a common policy.

● **Be careful not to let yourself be drawn into an alliance** with the teenager against the other parent. It's unfair to pass the buck by saying, "You'll have to ask your mother," or "If it was up to me I'd let you, but you know that your father…"

● **If you and your fellow parent are separated or divorced**, it may be more difficult for you to work together and agree a common policy. Your children may be dividing their time between two households in which there are different expectations and in which different limits are set. It may be that you – and they – will just have to learn to live with this. "Well, tough luck, but that is the way things are…" is all one parent can say when their teenagers reproach them with reports of the licence and liberty they are given by the other parent.

FAMILY FEELINGS: ADOLESCENT COMPLAINTS

Our own survey shows how adolescent complaints about their families change with age.

Complaint	Age 11–14		Age 15–16		Age 17–18	
	Boys	Girls	Boys	Girls	Boys	Girls
● Parents fuss too much	70%	76%	59%	55%	45%	54%
● Parents interfere too much	60%	52%	52%	55%	40%	36%
● Parents treat like a child	50%	76%	36%	33%	25%	54%
● Parents expect too much	40%	52%	31%	56%	50%	50%
● Not enough freedom	30%	62%	41%	44%	25%	41%

GETTING ALONG WITH BROTHERS AND SISTERS

In some families brothers and sisters get along well together, but in others they don't. You may find that an older brother or sister ignores you, treats you like a child, shows no interest in your ideas, and won't go out with you. Maybe if you're the older one you may find your younger sibling is a pain, trying to join in the conversation when friends come round, or wanting you to play games that don't interest you when you want to read or listen to music; maybe they always make silly jokes about your clothes or your friends and just like stirring things up.

"My little sister is always hanging around me and my friends and won't clear off when I ask her nicely. Yet if I shout she runs to Mum and makes trouble. What can I do?"
Jack, 14

If you have trouble like this, don't expect your parents to "tell off" your brother or sister. They won't want to take sides. Even if they do help to calm things down for a while, in the end, the two of you will have to sort things out for yourselves.

Have you ever got on well together? If the answer is no, then you may have to accept that this is the way things are, but you both still have to live in the same house. That means you both have to make an effort to avoid fights by being polite, by keeping your distance, and by agreeing on a few things like alternate nights when you choose TV channels or not having crowds of friends around at the same time.

"Karen just doesn't seem to understand that now I'm grown up I've got my own friends and I'm sick of her wanting me to spend all my time with her. She's still just a kid and should stick to other kids her own age."
Mary, 15

But if you have got on well in the past and have been good friends, it's worth trying to patch things up. You could both sit down quietly and write down five things that really annoy you about each other. Then swap the lists, go away to read them, and think about them. Don't even try to talk until the next day. When you both realize what's irritating you, it's easier to talk about it or to persuade someone to be more considerate.

Read the next chapter in this book, *The Tools of the Trade*, because the way to avoid or to resolve fights between parents and children will help you and your brother or sister — especially if you get on each other's nerves.

4

THE TOOLS OF
THE TRADE

"

A family unit is composed not only of children,
but of men, women, an occasional animal,
and the common cold.

"

Ogden Nash

ANY BOOK ON CHILD CARE can tell you how to soothe a crying baby or distract a frustrated toddler; the folklore of babyhood is full of such remedies. Experienced parents know that there are similar management techniques for teenagers. They know, too, that there are fewer battles if you can think of behaviour management in terms of solving problems rather than enforcing rules or punishing their infringement.

You may find it hard to use this problem-solving approach if it's important for you to maintain strong control over your children's lives or if you're naturally an authoritarian parent – but it's worth trying. Most parents find that the basic problem-solving techniques described below work well and help to keep frustration and resentment to a minimum.

Listening to your children makes them feel that what they have to say matters and that you're at least trying to see their point of view and appreciate their difficulties. Teenagers who complain bitterly "they never listen to me" feel both powerless and frustrated and are likely to find far less socially acceptable ways of making their feelings known than simply telling you about them.

Make time to sit down and talk about problems and grievances. This may not be easy if yours is a family in which people don't talk to each other much or express their feelings openly, but it's an essential technique for survival during adolescence (see p.57). It's also a technique you can learn.

Left: Listening is one of the most powerful tools you've got – you will pick up
what your child is feeling and why he or she is feeling that way.

NEGOTIATE

Nearly every disagreement can be more easily resolved by negotiation than by prohibition or a head-on confrontation. Both sides should gain a little, so neither need feel a loser, and, if you're prepared to make concessions, your offspring are much less likely to feel a legitimate sense of grievance. Children who feel they are being wronged feel justified in behaving badly in response: whatever predicament they find themselves in becomes someone else's fault, and their own actions then take on the nature of a crusade.

Negotiating always means that both sides have to give a little and make some concessions. Remember, however, that until they are 16 or 17 most adolescents tend to see things in rigid or absolute terms and may find it hard to compromise. If you do have to join battle, never aim for total victory. You may have to meet them more than halfway – negotiations (and that means continuing the discussion) will probably depend mostly on your capacity for adjustment and on how flexible you are prepared to be.

"I try to listen to my daughter when we disagree.
What I really hate is being shouted at."
Rachel, 41

SHARE DECISION-MAKING

Teenagers are more likely to agree with decisions or respond to rules if they've had a hand in making them, and especially if they can understand why they have been made. When decisions are shared, it also means that the teenager cannot easily play one parent off against the other.

Work out a common policy with your youngster. Rather than simply imposing a total ban on nights out during the week in term-time, for example, discuss what limits would be reasonable in view of their homework commitments and the ease with which they normally struggle out of bed on a school morning.

BARGAIN

Teenagers almost certainly see any quarrels between you both as at least as much your fault as theirs; you may feel the opposite. Conflicts can often be resolved by acknowledging that there is room for improvement on both sides and by making what amounts to a formal agreement that you'll reward each other for a change in behaviour. Make sure the bargain carries a positive, rewarding message rather than a negative one. "If you shout at me once more you'll go straight up to your room" isn't likely to result in any long-lasting improvement in behaviour. The "rewarding" approach goes something like this: "I really do hate being shouted at. If you can be reasonably polite to me until this time tomorrow, I promise I won't nag about your homework." Don't be ashamed of bargaining. It goes on in most relationships and carries the useful message that one way to alter someone else's behaviour is to modify your own.

BE CONSISTENT

Most people, but especially children and adolescents, need to know that their world is in some way predictable in order to feel secure. When it's not, confusion alone may generate behaviour that is ineffective, if not intolerable.

Once a solution to a problem has been negotiated, try to stick by it, bearing in mind that your teenager may forget! He or she needs to know that you're dependable. You may wish to change your mind later, as may your youngster, but, for the time being, stick to your agreements.

"I never really know where I am with my mother. Sometimes she lets me get away with murder, but then she'll turn on me for the least little thing."

Jim, 14

EXPLAIN

During adolescence, children are starting to think for themselves and make their own judgements. They will no longer happily accept "because I say so" as a good reason for altering their own behaviour, but they're open to reason. If you can explain why you're feeling or acting in a certain way, your child will feel that you're treating him or her as an equal, and they'll be much more likely to accept and respect your reasons.

Give the real reason for feeling as you do, even if it's simply a "gut" feeling or something you're slightly ashamed of, rather than a rational objection.

"One of the things I like about my parents is that they can admit it when they're wrong."

Bill, 16

DON'T PUSH

If you state your views very forcibly, your children may feel obliged to take up an opposing and equally outspoken position, thus painting themselves into a corner. If you manage to remain (or appear to remain) dispassionate, they can make a decision freely; the chances are that it may even be the one you would have made yourself.

However strongly you feel, and however powerful your argument, it's sometimes best to play devil's advocate, putting forward the pros and cons of any argument, but letting teenagers draw their own conclusions, rather than trying to force one on them. By making it clear that the decision is theirs and not yours, you're giving them a dignified let-out and making it easier for them to back down.

REWARD GOOD BEHAVIOUR

If behaviour attracts attention, it's more likely to be repeated. Unfortunately what tends to happen is that bad behaviour attracts plenty of attention, while good behaviour goes unnoticed, or at least unremarked upon. When you're trying to get the best out of someone, carrots almost always work better than sticks. Positive reinforcement is much more likely to encourage the kind of behaviour you want. Comment appreciatively whenever the children behave in a way you approve of. Thank them if they've been charming to your friends or helpful to you; praise them if they've worked hard for an exam. When they've had a success, compliment them and show your pleasure.

GIVE A LITTLE

However hard you try to negotiate and find a compromise, you need to accept that yours is the position that may be easier to shift. Teenagers tend to state their case in very categorical terms and take up clearly defined attitudes ("You'll never catch me wearing that." "I couldn't possibly be home by then."). But they won't feel quite so bound to stick to their position if they can see you're making a genuine effort to give a little yourself and help them find a way round the problem. If, for example, you are insisting that they accompany you on a visit to friends or relatives they find "boring", promise to cut the visit shorter than you would normally do, or help them find some excuse to leave early and make their own way home, or say that you won't demand formal dress – they can go in their usual jeans and t-shirt.

Finally, be as tolerant as you can bear to be, show that you want what's best for them, but do not assume that you know (better than they do) what is best for them. You know them pretty well, but one of the "tasks" that all adolescents have to face is to get to know themselves. It may help to remind yourself every now and then that what you are dealing with is not rebellion for rebellion's sake, but a necessary part of the child's efforts to stand alone.

ISSUE: COPING WITH DISAGREEMENTS

• **When you're angry, say why.** This means explaining why you feel the way you do rather than simply going on the attack. Anger is often destructive in family arguments because it is used in a critical way rather than to express your own feelings.

• **Don't suffer silent martyrdom** or withdraw and freeze each other out. It makes the person you're arguing with feel you dislike them. You can disapprove of something a person has said or done but still like them.

• **When you're shouted at, try not to shout back.** That can only cause an escalation of the conflict. Instead, you might say that you hate being shouted at and that it's pointless to discuss anything while one or both of you are shouting.

• **Suggest a cooling-off period** and then talk about the problem later. Often a problem can be resolved after a period of "time out", which lets temper die down.

• **Time out should not be a punishment.** "Go to your room and don't come down until I tell you to," is not time out and solves no problems.

DIALOGUE: THE HAIRCUT

Teenager's view: I've decided I'm going to shave my head.

Parent's view: Well it's not my favourite haircut but I expect it would look as good on you as most people. What do your friends think?

Teenager: They think it would look great.

Parent: What about your girlfriend/boyfriend?

Teenager: Not so sure.

Parent: What do you think the school would say?

Teenager: Dunno.

Parent: I'd hate you to get into real trouble over it. Why not sound the school out first. If they really don't mind, then go ahead. If they do, what about having a really short cut now and saving the completely bald head for the beginning of the summer holidays? It'll always grow again if it doesn't suit you or you don't like it.

COMMENTS ABOUT HAIRCUTS

This parent could have mistakenly said, "A shaved head will look dreadful, I bet your friends will hate it, and the school will be furious." During this discussion, however, the parent's controlled response allowed the adolescent time to think, who, in fact, then accepted the parent's advice, but felt that the decision was an independent one.

TURNING A BLIND EYE

Certain kinds of behaviour really have no other purpose except to rub you up the wrong way. These are much more likely to disappear if you can bring yourself to pay no attention to them. Any publicity is good publicity and much the same goes for attention. A response from you, even an angry response, rewards the youngster and reinforces the behaviour. Try to ignore behaviour such as sulking or rudeness, which psychologists describe as "attention seeking", rather than think you shouldn't let your youngster "get away with it". Because he or she is likely to try harder to get a response from you, the behaviour may get worse before it gets better. You have to be consistent, too. If you sometimes flare up but then sometimes ignore the behaviour, teenagers will keep on trying, egging you on; they know you'll react eventually.

RULES

Family life can be chaotic if everyone does things in a different way at a different time, so almost every family has "convenience" rules that are generally accepted by everyone simply because they make family life more orderly and happen to suit most of the family most of the time. This might mean supper is eaten at 8 p.m., everyone puts their own laundry in the washing machine, and the person who runs the car empty of petrol takes the responsibility for filling it. But apart from these guidelines made for convenience, rules are the least successful tool to use with teenagers, largely because they tend to be, by definition, inflexible. Some issues really do need strict rules because they affect the child's own health and safety – not driving after drinking, for example. But if everything seems to be disapproved of or forbidden, rules will inevitably be broken and cause only resentment for both you and your child. What should you do?

• **Keep rules to a minimum but make them clear**. Be explicit about what you expect from your children. You may, for example, want to make it an absolute rule that you know where they are when they go out in the evening or that they never drink and drive. There will be others that you feel strongly about because the behaviour taxes your own patience beyond endurance. It's reasonable to expect some help with household chores, for example, or to designate smoke-free zones in the house if you don't smoke and your children and their friends do. You may also be unable to tolerate frequent rudeness or foul language. You should try, however, to be as tolerant as you can be about those aspects of adolescent life that, although they may irritate you hugely, do no serious harm – such things as the width of their trousers, the length of their hair, their general untidiness, the amount of time they spend in the bath, on the telephone, or lying in bed in the mornings.

• **Never expect your children to follow rules you never keep yourselves**. Let them know, for example, where you will be if you are going out and what time you expect to be back. Let them see that you take the no-drink-driving laws seriously and keep within the limits yourself.

• **Leave the teenager some room for manoeuvre** so that he or she can learn to act responsibly, not just blindly follow the rules you make. As your children grow older, the rules you impose should be fewer. Too many rules suggest that you are too anxious to keep control; teenagers may then have a hard time persuading you to let them become more independent. Perhaps the more serious consequence of your control is that your son or daughter may be less capable of independent judgement and less confident as an adult.

Teenagers have a strong sense of fairness
and justice. They won't respect or obey rules
if they detect hypocrisy or double standards.

ISSUE: COMPROMISE

When it looks as though a compromise is proving impossible, it can be worth subjecting the problem to analysis. Everyone concerned should write down their side of the argument and what they believe are the other side's objections to it. Once these are written down, it should be possible to see how realistic a view each party has of the situation, and also to reach a consensus on which reasons are the best and should carry most weight. However, this works only if everyone is prepared to put down their real reasons: these may be quite different from the arguments they have been using up to this point. Below is an example that shows how Adam and his mother used this method when he wanted to have an ear pierced and she objected.

Adam's view
- I want to look different.
- I like the look of it.
- It's the fashionable thing.

Adam's mother's view
- Real men don't have pierced ears.
- It's probably against school rules.
- It'll probably give him a punky image, which may prejudice others against him.
- I'll have a hard time explaining it to friends and relatives who disapprove.
- It might give him AIDS.
- It might make people think he's gay.

Why Adam thought his mother disapproved
- She's a snob.
- She thinks it means I'm gay.

Why Adam's mother thought he wanted it done
- He wants to rub me and his father up the wrong way.
- He wants to look as weird as possible.
- He wants to look like all his friends.

Adam's mother's objections arise mostly because she feels protective about him. It's easy to scoff at her for worrying about what "other people" may think, but it's natural for her to want to protect her son from criticism: natural, but perhaps not reasonable, especially if Adam is prepared to put up with it himself.

Adam reassured his mother that plenty of people nowadays had pierced ears, both gays and non-gays. He didn't want to look weird, just fashionable. However, he didn't want to get into trouble at school, and realized that his mother genuinely worried about what her mother, Adam's grandmother, would think, and he didn't want to distress either of them. He agreed that, if no more fuss was made about the ear-piercing, he wouldn't wear his earring at school or when visiting his grandparents.

SANCTIONS

Sanctions are the ultimate deterrent, a point of no return, in a sense: they make it clear to your child that what he or she has done is very serious, reprehensible, and not to be tolerated. Sanctions should be only a last resort if you fail to negotiate a settlement by peaceful means, but if your son or daughter knows that there is an ultimate deterrent, it may be reassuring. It enables a youngster to realize, for example, that he or she has reached the limits allowed and can back down without losing face.

Give prior warning if you are going to use sanctions, and try to use them for specific offences and not arbitrarily, so that the youngster realizes that a particular course of action on his or her part (for example, coming home later than the arranged time without letting you know) is bound to have predictable repercussions.

Sanctions should never be demeaning, and
physical punishment should never be used
against a young adult.

The most appropriate punishments involve withdrawal of privileges rather than loss of dignity. Any sanction that affects their money supply is usually hard to ignore: deprivation of new clothes, no financial help with travel expenses or entertainment – these are punishments that most teenagers will take seriously. "Grounding", or anything else that puts restrictions on their social life, such as having no friends to stay for the weekend or not going to the football match, can also be effective. You might impose a weekend curfew, or withdraw use of the family car, put restrictions on television watching, or choose the weekend family video yourselves instead of letting the teenager do this. Perhaps the best sanctions are those that benefit somebody and aren't simply punitive. Extra domestic commitments, such as help with the shopping, home decorating, or weeding the garden, might be appropriate.

Whatever the sanction, it should have a definite time-limit. If it is imposed indefinitely, or for some arbitrary length of time, it is unfair on the teenager and asking for more rebellious, sanction-busting behaviour. Don't make idle threats or impose sanctions that may be almost impossible to enforce, or which may turn out to be as inconvenient for you as for the youngster. Make sure that when you do impose sanctions, it's because your teenager has done something to deserve it, not just because you happen to be feeling particularly tired, irritable, or at the end of your tether. What has to be avoided is a sort of smouldering warfare with an angry parent adding ever more sanctions for a rebellious teenager who is finding ways of evading them. It may be a good idea to wipe the slate clean once a week – maybe on Sunday – and to try to identify the main problems that are causing the hostility. It will also give you a chance to repeat or re-negotiate the limits of acceptable behaviour, if this is appropriate.

WHY PARENTS MAKE RULES

All families have rules. They may not have been carefully thought out or labelled "rules", however; they may have just evolved, so that everyone accepts that this is the way things are done. Maybe there's always a special supper on Saturday, for instance, a late breakfast on Sunday, a TV programme that everybody likes to watch together. Many families have a few more formal rules too. Why do parents make rules and how necessary are they?

* **Parents want you to be safe** – not killed or injured. This is the most important reason for making rules, right from babyhood ("you mustn't touch the plugs, the stove", etc.) to adulthood ("you must never drink and drive"). Any rule that has this kind of reasoning behind it deserves to be taken seriously.

* **Parents worry about you.** This is the real reason behind most rules. They worry about whether you'll do well at school, whether you'll get a good job, whether you'll get pregnant if you're a girl, whether you'll make a girl pregnant if you're a boy. If you feel hemmed in by too many "worry" rules, try to work out what your parents are really frightened about and take it up with them. If you can reassure them that their fears are groundless, maybe they'll relax the rules.

* **Parents feel responsible for you.** Whether or not you work hard at school, for example, is actually up to you. Your parents feel that if you don't work hard, or if you do badly, it is their fault. What can they do? They can try to make sure you get enough sleep so you're not too tired to work. That's something within their control, so a rule is born: you don't stay out late when there's school the next day. If you think the rule is unreasonable, you'll need to convince them that you're responsible enough to make sensible guidelines for yourself.

* **Parents want their own homes to be comfortable** and pleasant. If they don't smoke, for example, they won't want people smoking in the living room or the kitchen. They will have rules about dirty boots and carpets. They may also react fiercely to swearing, which is not only unpleasant but rude and ill-mannered.

* **Parents are sometimes unsure about what they should do.** In this case, rules help because they provide an easy answer to what may be quite a difficult situation if there is no rule to play it by. What time should a 14-year-old be home? 8.30, 9, 9.30, 10 p.m? Who knows what the "right" answer is? Probably there isn't one! It all depends on things like how sensible you are and where you live. You may be able to negotiate a better deal on this kind of rule if you can do it tactfully (see *How to Get a Better Deal*, p.81).

* **Parents like to feel in control.** The more anxious they are to maintain control, the more numerous and tighter the rules are likely to be. This may work out all right when you're young, but, as you go through your teens, rules governing every aspect of your life and behaviour make it difficult for you to grow up and take charge of your own life. Winning your independence may be a struggle. Don't try to change everything all at once. Start by deciding what irritates you most, then try to persuade them to loosen up a little on that.

5

TALKING TO TEENAGERS

ALTHOUGH YOUNG CHILDREN USUALLY EXCHANGE thoughts and feelings quite easily, adolescents are not often so communicative. It takes a real effort to keep the channels of communication open with someone who is apparently determined to shut you out and to be as monosyllabic as possible. But it's essential to keep talking – and keep *listening* – if you are to survive your children's adolescence intact. If you can manage it and are still on speaking terms with your adolescents by the time they reach their late teens, you'll find they may actually *want* to talk to you and that it's once again rewarding to have conversations with them.

Failure of communication is just as much about one person's failure to listen as another's inability to talk. How many of the battles between parents and children arise because neither side has made the effort to understand?

• **Learn to listen**. This means giving your full attention. Turn off the television. Put down the newspaper. Nothing is more infuriating than trying to talk to someone whose attention is somewhere else.

• **Be ready to respond**. Youngsters don't always choose the most convenient moment, but you may not get a second chance.

• **Ask for their advice or opinion** sometimes, and show that you listen to and respect what they have to say and find their ideas interesting, even if you don't agree.

Left: "They never listen to me," is one of the commonest complaints teenagers have
about their parents – and vice versa.

- **Keep an open mind** when you're discussing something about which you feel strongly. Hear your youngsters out, and don't prejudge what you think they'll say.
- **Don't feel that you must always try to protect them** by not talking about family crises or difficult decisions. Teenagers are not stupid; often they sense that things are not right, and it may lessen family tension if a problem is brought out into the open.
- **Talk about feelings as well as facts** – your own as well as theirs. If you reveal who you really are, they will trust you and let you see who they are.

"Jim comes in from school and I say, 'Had a good day?' and he says, 'All right.' Then I say, 'What did you do?' and he says, 'Nothing.' Then he disappears into his room. Getting conversation out of him is like pulling teeth."

Ruth, 48

CONVERSATIONS ADOLESCENTS WANT TO HAVE

Adolescents like to talk about issues that might affect them or their friends, even if you hope they won't! For example, they might discuss whether a pregnant unmarried teenage girl should have an abortion, and whether the boy should be involved. They have strong views about capital punishment, war, police violence, miscarriages of justice – many have more global worries about the environment or the possibility of nuclear war. If they want to sound off about these topics, listen; and be careful not to give the impression you think you've solved all these problems years ago, or to dismiss them as being insoluble.

Adolescents have a strong spiritual side, which doesn't necessarily mean that they're conventionally religious. They may be forming their own views about the concept of God and what it means to them, about whether human beings have a soul or spirit that persists after death. They're usually fascinated by ideas of reincarnation, out-of-body experiences, or anything to do with the paranormal. If your family already belongs to a particular religion or culture, adolescence is the time when your children will want to explore their own feelings about it.

Sometimes it's nice for teenagers to talk to you about something about which they clearly have superior knowledge. Give them a chance to talk about the music they're interested in for example. You'd probably like to know how easy it is to buy drugs in your area, or how many of their friends take them: why not ask? If it's a conversation and not a high-handed inquisition, they may actually tell you.

Finally, like the rest of us, teenagers like to gossip. "How was school?" is a boring question and will probably get a short and pretty boring answer. You're more likely to get a picture of what their school life is like by asking about the people involved: their friends, or even their teachers.

TALKING TO YOUR CHILD ABOUT PROBLEMS

There may be times when you feel fairly sure that something is troubling your child. It can be difficult to tread the fine line between respecting privacy (which is vital) and making sure your child knows you're available to talk. Searching a child's room to find and read letters or diaries is never permissible and is a violation of trust.

If you feel sure your youngster is in trouble but has shown no sign of wanting to talk to you about it, take the initiative. Sometimes youngsters leave clues: a letter or postcard left lying around on the table, for example.

Say you're concerned and ask if anything's wrong. This may provide the opening your child needs and has been waiting for. But if the child clearly does not want to talk about it, don't put pressure on or feel rejected. All you can do is say that you'll be around if they do want to talk or if they need help.

"Jane's having problems with bullying at school. She won't let me talk to the school about it, so I'm trying to persuade her to tell one of the teachers herself. It's hard to know whether to step in or not. It was easier when they were little…"
Evelyn, 41

ISSUE: HOW TO BE ANGRY

Anger is such a powerful emotion that many people are frightened of it. Some families bottle up their feelings and never show their anger: this usually results in resentment, and the real problems never get solved. In other families, showing anger is all too easy, and any trivial argument is likely to develop into a stand-up row. Anger can be destructive if it is used to hurt another person rather than to express your own feelings.

- **If you start to feel frustrated or angry, explain why**. Try to do this in a way that helps the other person step into your shoes and to see exactly how you're feeling.
- **When you ask questions, keep them neutral** so as to invite discussion, not confrontation. Don't ask the kind of closed questions that are bound to produce an aggressive response and force an argument, such as, "Do you call that room tidy?" If you're a teenager, don't say, "You're not going to wear that to my school sports day, are you?"
- **Keep your arguments focused on the subject in hand**. "And another thing…" is a sure way of escalating an argument into a pitched battle.
- **Don't use sarcasm or resort to teasing**. You may think it's good-natured, but it's often hurtful. Some families use this approach to cover up their real feelings or to deal with embarrassment, and they never get around to communicating seriously.

CASE HISTORY: LYING

On holiday in Greece with her parents, Lisa met a young, unemployed American man, Martin, who was 24. Her father thought Martin was too scruffy and too old for Lisa.

"Martin and I got on really well together. We've been writing, and next summer he's going to try to get a job in England so we can see each other again. I can't tell my parents; it was obvious they didn't like him. If they knew, they'd probably try to stop us from seeing each other. Anyway, it's none of their business."
Lisa, 16

"In Greece Lisa was always sneaking off to see this man. We thought it would all come to an end when we came home, but the way she dashes down for the post every morning she's obviously in touch with him. She swears she's not, but I know she's lying. She was always such a truthful child, but now she's being so deceitful we feel we can't trust her at all."
George, 41

COMMENTS ABOUT LYING

Martin was Lisa's first love, and to Lisa the relationship was far too personal and fragile to be exposed to her parents' comments or ridicule. At 16, she is old enough to choose her own friends.

If Lisa's parents had tried to get to know Martin, they would have discovered that he was a pleasant and thoughtful young man; they would have felt easier about the friendship and Lisa would have had no reason to deceive them.

If parents probe too deeply into their youngsters' activities, or demand to know every detail, it is more likely that children will lie to stop parents worrying, to avoid a row if they think parents will disapprove or make a fuss, or just to get parents off their back.

Adolescents will tell the truth if they know from experience that their parents trust them, are willing to help with a problem, and are genuinely interested in what they're doing.

"We were delighted that Chris suddenly seemed to want to talk to us again. We would have long conversations about his friends, his problems, the state of the world, the existence of God. The only thing was he wanted to wake us up and have these talks sitting on the end of our bed at one in the morning when he'd just got home from an evening out with his friends."
Janet, 50

WHY TALKING HELPS

When you're miserable or have a problem, it usually helps to tell someone else how you feel. The other person doesn't need to give you advice; in fact, it's often better if they don't. They may not know all the facts, and if you don't know what you want to do, how can they? They can, however, help you see the problem more clearly so that you understand what your choices are. Then you can work out for yourself what you want to do.

If you want to have a serious talk with your parents, make sure you choose a time when there *is* time: not when they're rushing off to work or are involved with something else. You may have to insist that they pay attention by saying something like, "Listen, I really want to talk to you about something."

Not everyone finds it easy to talk to their parents at the best of times. If you're in serious trouble, it's even harder to pluck up your courage or to find the right words. If you've been getting on badly with them anyway, you're probably going to be even more frightened to tell them something difficult, for example, that you've crashed the car, or have been suspended from school, or about an unwanted pregnancy. Nothing can make it easy, but if it has to be done, get it over with as soon as you can. Waiting and thinking about it is usually worse.

If you're very worried about how they will react, it may help to tell the parent you get on best with. Sometimes it helps to confide in another close relative or family friend (a grandparent, for example) and ask them to help you tell your parents.

Your parents' first reaction may be anger, but this probably won't last – especially if they can see that you're unhappy and worried about what's happened. Basically, they are on your side and will want to help you.

"I was taking cello lessons but hated doing it, and I knew my mother wanted me to keep on, so I only pretended to go for almost two months. I'd go to the library or something instead. When my cello teacher didn't send the bill, my mother found out, of course. She wasn't as angry as I thought she'd be about my not wanting to take lessons. In fact, she was more upset that I felt so afraid to talk to her about it. She agreed that I could stop the lessons right away and told me it was much more important that I should talk to her about anything that was really making me unhappy."

Laura, 13

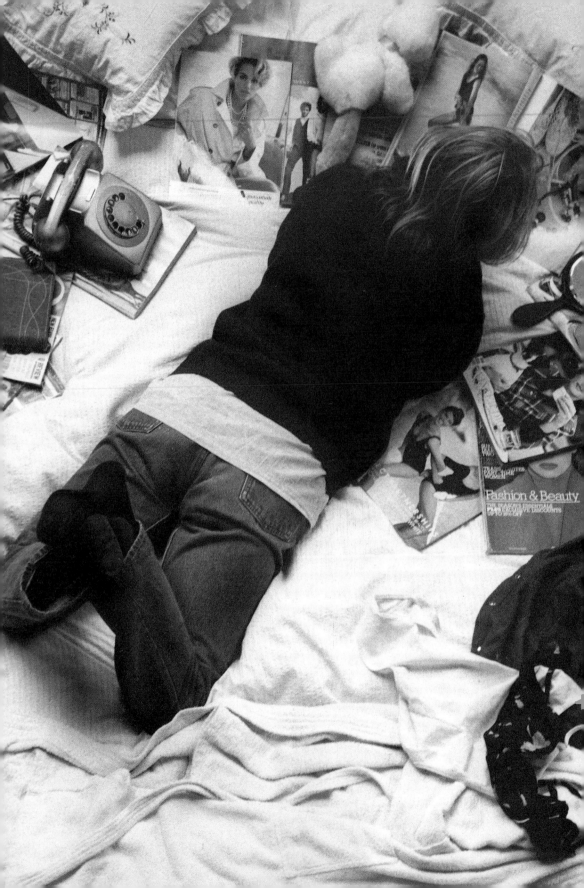

6

Rows, Rudeness, and Rebellion

66 ————————————————————————————

Children aren't happy with nothing to ignore,
And that's what parents were created for.

———————————————————————————— 99

Ogden Nash

THIS IS HOW ONE SET OF PARENTS described the outbreak of adolescence in their family: "It was as though Amy had undergone a total personality change, almost overnight. She seemed to disagree with everything we said and did on principle. She was rude, surly, uncooperative. She overreacted to everything, especially criticism. There were endless tears and tantrums, and she didn't seem to know the reason for them any more than we did. We were totally unprepared for it and found ourselves looking back on the happy, cooperative child we'd known in total disbelief."

Until your child is 10 or 11 years old, you think you know them. Young children do, to some extent, mirror what you have taught them, reflecting your own attitudes, even sometimes copying your mannerisms or bringing out your own turns of phrase. During adolescence, however, you suddenly have to adapt to sharing your lives – and your home – with someone who seems to have discarded your own ideals and attitudes, whose way of life seems to be entirely at odds with your own, but who still expects you to be available whenever you're asked.

You may not always be able to avoid the issues that cause most friction between parents and children, but you can prevent them getting out of hand and putting more strain on family relationships. Parents and teenage children often have different priorities, viewpoints, lifestyles, even a different perception of time. Parents often feel

Left: Messiness infuriates most parents, who see it as inconsiderate and irresponsible. To a teenager, however, a room is a private space.

rejected. Adolescents often feel misunderstood: indeed, they often *are* misunderstood. Much adolescent behaviour is incomprehensible (and often insupportable) to adults because they don't understand the reasons for it; they may mistakenly believe there is *no* reason for some behaviour, and then react in a way that puts an even greater distance between them and their children. The adolescent cries of "you don't understand me" are usually all too true.

Parents, asked what maddened them most about living with adolescent children, replied:
– Rebelliousness.
– Rudeness.
– Lack of consideration.
– Quarrels with siblings.

Adolescents, asked what maddened them most about living with their parents, replied:
– Being treated like a child.
– Lack of privacy.
– Being picked on unfairly.
– Parents always interfering.

REBELLIOUSNESS

Age range: usually peaks around 15 to 16 but should improve thereafter unless mismanaged

The early years of adolescence have been called the time of "normal insanity". Hang on to that word "normal" – it will help you to see things in perspective. Remember that these first stirrings of emotional discord can be tough for the adolescents themselves and sometimes impossible to bear for those near and dear to them.

Rebellion signals the first stirrings of the
child's drive for independence.

Much of the natural rebelliousness of adolescents stems from their need to be different from their parents and to establish a separate identity. At first a young teenager may need to go overboard in his or her efforts to do this and may become quite exaggeratedly different. However, this rebelliousness may not be particularly comfortable even for adolescents: they may make decisions or act in a particular way, not so much because this is what they want to do as because they know for sure that it's what their parents won't want them to do. Indeed, adolescents who show no signs of rebellion, no determination to be separate from the family, may be giving their parents an easy ride, but may also be missing a necessary stage of development before a mature human being emerges.

How easily you cope, and how easily you pass through this stage, will depend on your reactions as much as on your children's actions.

- **Overlook what you can.**
- **Avoid confrontation.**
- **Be as tolerant as you can bear to be.**
- **Remember that even if your child rejects your attitudes** (and prejudices) in favour of his or her own, they are not rejecting you. However hard this is to believe, they still need to know they have your approval and support.

"We'd always prided ourselves on being liberal and tolerant, and we thought our children would respect it. Instead we seem to be living with someone who takes every opportunity to parade his bigoted, reactionary views. I know he only does it to rub us up the wrong way."
Richard, 51

RUDENESS

Age range: worst around 11 to 14 but should improve by 15 or 16

For a good many parents, rudeness comes near the top of the list of complaints about teenagers. It may be more helpful to discover what provokes it rather than automatically to play the "don't-you-speak-to-me-like-that" card. Rudeness usually occurs for the following reasons:
- **Thoughtlessness** Youngsters trade insults more easily than compliments, and what seems normal banter to them is often very offensive to adult ears. This is largely a problem of early adolescence (when youngsters are testing limits) and is greatly influenced by friends. Set limits if rudeness or foul language become a habit that spills over into family life and offends you.

Part of growing up is learning that what is acceptable in some company is inappropriate elsewhere.

- **Shyness or self-consciousness** Very often rudeness is the result of social gaucherie. People who are feeling shy or embarrassed (as teenagers often are in social situations) can be abrupt or rude without meaning to be. Teenagers may need some help to overcome shyness (see *Coping with Shyness*, p.92). Point out how the other person might have felt, but be gentle.
- **Tension or unhappiness** Sometimes a surly reply to a perfectly friendly question or comment is a sign that the teenager is anxious or unhappy about something. They may find it hard to tell you what they're really feeling or simply not want to talk about it; hitting out verbally is a way of expressing their feelings. This kind of rudeness is best overlooked; it doesn't need a heavy-handed response (see *Turning a Blind Eye*, p.51). Try kindness or sympathy instead.

• **Frustration** Often the kind of rudeness that adults call "answering back" arises out of frustration, maybe because adolescents feel they're not getting their point across in an argument, or are not being listened to, or are being unfairly treated. Listen to what they're trying to say and why, rather than take them to task for the way they're saying it.

• **Anger** Some parents are regularly faced with extreme, unprovoked, and often quite aggressive rudeness. This usually stems from anger, and may be a deliberate attempt to hurt or to provoke a pitched battle (it usually does both). Unless the issue that causes it is resolved, aggressive insolence may become the teenager's habitual response to almost anything parents say. Sometimes the youngster does not even realize how unattractive it looks to other people, even to their peers.

This is the most difficult kind of rudeness to deal with, especially if it becomes a pattern. Discussing the way you all feel about it is the only course you can take. Be sure to explain exactly how it makes you feel. Teenagers may genuinely not realize how hurtful they're being. Stay calm and try not to shout back.

"I get really embarrassed at Annie's house; she's so rude to her mother."
Sophie, 12

KNOW YOUR OWN STRENGTH

Remember that, although you will have fights with your teenager, all the evidence suggests that most adolescents get on well with their parents most of the time, and that parental approval is important to them. It may not always seem like that. Certainly as you watch them becoming more and more involved with their friends, looking like them, sounding like them, you may feel that your own influence as a parent is being eroded.

Don't believe it! Studies have shown that, however large a part friends play in their lives, teenagers still see their parents as their main source of affection, support, and help in solving problems. Your children won't confide in you or disclose their feelings to you as much as they may have done when they were younger, and they certainly won't want to spend as much time with you, but they still need to know that you love them and that you're there for them when they're in trouble. They may, quite reasonably, reject your views on politics or religion and your advice about what to wear or how to spend their free time. About important issues, however – issues that affect their future, such as education or the choice of a university course or career – your opinion will count for much more than that of their friends, and they will nearly always be swayed by what you say and think. It may not be until they are fully adult that you will realize how strongly they have, in fact, been influenced by you. Watch and wait; you may be surprised.

THOUGHTS: PRESENT AND FUTURE	
Parent's view:	If only he'd work harder, I'm sure he'd do well in his exams next year.
Teenager's view:	What's the point of slaving away now? There'll be plenty of time.
Parent:	If she does well in her exams, she'll have a better chance of a good job.
Teenager:	If I spent as much time working as they want me to, I wouldn't be able to do anything with my friends. Why worry about what might happen in five years' time if it's going to make my life miserable now?
Parent:	I don't see why I should give him an advance. If he really saved up, he'd have enough for an electric guitar next year.
Teenager:	A group is forming *now*. I'll be the only one left out. I have to have money now. I want it more than anything – I can't think of anything else.
Parent:	Honestly, I can hardly see that spot. Anyway, it's just your age. Your skin will be much better in a year or two.
Teenager:	I can't go out like this. What'll I do if it's not gone by Saturday?
Parent:	You promised you'd wash up and the dishes are still in the sink.
Teenager:	What difference does it make *when* I do it? I'm *going* to do it.

I Need It Now

Age range: ongoing, but gradually decreasing as the adolescent matures

Teenagers live largely in the present and can't easily accept short-term misery for long-term gain. To a 15-year-old, a year is an eternity. This different perception of time is another familiar source of family friction for which there may be no real solution; it may help if you can each understand exactly why the other thinks as he or she does.

The Need for Personal Space

Age range: ongoing, rising to a peak around 17 to 18

However close your relationship with your children, from puberty onwards they start to need more and more physical and emotional privacy. To gain this, they may have to start pushing you away, and this can be hurtful. There will be times when the most innocent foray into their "space" will be resented. You might feel that the situation is hopeless, but try to remember these points:

• **Make sure they have their own territory** – a room of their own, if possible, which they can decorate as they like and where they can entertain their friends. You may hate its messiness, but it's important that adolescents have privacy. Because they're in the family home, it's unlikely they'll do anything too outrageous with their friends.

- **Remember how self-conscious teenagers are** about their developing bodies and sexuality. If yours is a family where nudity has always been regarded as natural and taken for granted, you may find this newly emergent modesty irritating, but try to be sympathetic towards it all the same.
- **Don't expect to know all about their emotional life.** It is none of your business, unless they choose to tell you.
- **Offer help** if you think it is needed, and give it if you are asked, but be prepared to stand back if they reject it and want to solve their problems in their own way.
- **Keep talking to them,** despite requests to "leave me alone", which will ring in your ears during these years, reaching their peak in mid-adolescence (around 15 to 16).

DEALING WITH DISHONESTY

Age range: early and mid-adolescence

Among teenagers, shoplifting sweets or small items is often seen as fair game, regarded in much the same light as an adult might see a mild laundering of tax returns or driving after a few drinks. This cavalier attitude towards law-breaking among teenagers still appals most adults, and most parents feel they've failed if they don't instil a sense of values and a conscience that will, at the very least, keep their youngsters out of trouble and perhaps influence them to become what we would consider "good" human beings.

At some time or another, most adolescents, particularly boys, do break the law. They do it for several reasons: mainly to show off to each other, to see what they can get away with or how far they can go, to prove they're not "chicken", or simply to find out how it feels. Trying to get into adult movies, having a drink while under age, avoiding fare-paying on public transport, or sneaking into a sporting event without paying are, unfortunately, activities so widespread that they shouldn't really be regarded as abnormal. How should you react?

- **Don't condone dishonesty.** Repayment and an apology to anyone personally involved are appropriate. If your child suddenly appears with some expensive new item you know they can't afford, ask how they came by it.
- **Don't overreact.** If you make the child feel like a criminal, he or she may be reluctant to come to you for help when they're in real trouble.
- **Stick rigidly to your own standards of honesty.** In the long term, these are the ones your child is most likely to adopt.
- **Make sure that the teenager has a reasonable amount of pocket money** (see *Money Matters*, p.171) so that penury is not used as an excuse to steal.
- **Stress the very real dangers** and disadvantages of tangling with the law. A record, even for a very trivial offence, lasts a long time. Let youngsters know that, when they start to apply for jobs, they will be asked about any criminal offence.

ISSUE: MEALTIMES

Meals are social events for adults, one of the few opportunities for the whole family to be together and talk to each other. It's a shame, then, that even when the family is gathered together around the table, the meal sometimes turns out to be less than a pleasure.

Food and mealtimes are just not that important to most teenagers. They aren't usually interested in what they eat, and they're not, most of the time, particularly interested in talking to their parents. For them, eating isn't a social event but something they do because they're hungry. On the whole, they like to do it as quickly as possible so that they can get on with something more interesting, so it's perhaps not surprising – when parents have so much emotional energy invested in meals, and teenagers have so little – that mealtimes often become a source of irritation to both. They are one of the few occasions when everyone has everyone else's almost undivided attention and thus can become the focus for tensions within the family. Parents should avoid using the time to resolve sibling conflicts (which their children could probably do on their own), or only to insist on better table manners. For their part, children shouldn't use mealtimes as an opportunity to air grievances. They should also appreciate that someone has gone to a lot of trouble to prepare a meal for them.

• **The dripfeed system** of frequent snacks does seem to suit the adolescent constitution better than three square meals a day. It may cause less family aggravation if parents can make allowances for this when planning meals, at least during the school week. If parents prefer to eat quite late, they should have something available for their children to make themselves healthy snacks when they come in ravenous from school (see p.256).

• **Even if they're not popular**, communal meals do provide one of the few chances a busy family has to spend time together. It's fair enough to expect everybody to turn up and at least to start a meal together most of the time; if this is difficult to arrange, try to have at least one special meal at the weekend.

• **It is probably a mistake** to make every meal into a ritual and to force restless 14- or 15-year-olds to stay on acting sociable until the bitter end. There will be times when they'll actually want to do this, but if they don't, there is not a lot to be gained by making them stay and suffer.

• **If mealtimes are to be sociable** and enjoyable, keep carping and criticism for another time and another place.

"All I did was to go down to breakfast and ask John how he was today, and he turned on me and snarled, 'Why are you always going on at me? Can't you leave me alone for a minute?' "
Edward, 49

DEALING WITH PROBLEM PARENTS

What can you do if you have a real problem with a parent who is always nagging or shouting at you?

Your natural reaction to someone criticizing you unfairly may be to fight back. But if you take an extreme stand, you'll never sort out the problem.

You might try it differently:

- **Make a list of the things you argue about most**. Then work out what changes you need to make to get your parents off your back. Often you don't need to do very much. Helping around the house just a little more, shouting at your sister or brother just a little less, keeping your room just a little tidier may well be enough for a quieter life.
- **When you want them to make changes**, work out what the problem is first. If you feel your parents are not letting you be as independent as you'd like to be, or that they're treating you as if you're much younger than you are, try to find specific examples. Don't tackle it all at once; work on it bit by bit.
- **Telling your parents how you feel** gets better results than criticizing the way they behave. They can't deny how you feel. If you say "Why can't you let me come home at a reasonable time like everyone else's parents do?", they'll probably reply, "Because no one else's parents care about what their children are doing." Instead, try saying this: "When I have to come home earlier than everyone else, it makes me feel stupid/as though you're treating me like a kid/that you don't trust me."
- **Tell them what you'd like**. Don't aim too high, and decide what's most important. For example, would you rather have an extra hour added to a curfew on Fridays or Saturdays, or to have an occasional late night during the week for a special concert?
- **Offer something in exchange**. Maybe you could stay in and babysit one weekend a month or do special chores. Remember that your late nights may affect them, too.
- **Stick to a particular issue and resolve it**. Don't use a disagreement as an excuse to rake up old grievances about other times your parents may have been unfair or treated you as a child. Problems are best tackled one by one as they happen.
- **Your parents don't have a right to know every detail of your private life**, but they do need to know you're safe. You should realize how precious it is to have someone who cares about you.
- **If you're very angry**, count to 10 or take a few deep breaths until you've calmed down. Otherwise you're likely to lash out and say things you don't really mean, but which really hurt and will be remembered.

When things are really bad, and you and your parents just can't seem to get on at all, life can feel very bleak. It won't last for ever, but while it does, there are a few things you can do to make life more tolerable.

- **Tell a friend**. Talking about a problem almost always helps a lot. Your friend may have similar problems. Even if they don't, they'll be able to imagine how you feel, and may be able to help you work out ways of dealing with it.
- **Give yourself space**. Keep out of the way as much as possible, especially at times when you know that tempers may be short.
- **If you're feeling miserable**, don't be afraid to cry. It relieves your feelings and will almost certainly make you feel better. It shows other people how you feel, too. Sometimes your parents may not realize how unhappy you are, and they may think you're just being angry or defiant. They're much more likely to be sympathetic rather than angry about real unhappiness – but won't respond to fake tears.
- **Think about which parts of your life** you do enjoy and which activities you're best at, and concentrate on them. Taking part in extra-curricular school activities such as sports or drama may help, and you will spend less time at home.

WHEN YOUR PARENTS HAVE PROBLEMS

If your parents are having a hard time – because of unemployment or money worries, for example, or because their own relationship is going through a bad patch – you may have a hard time, too. People who are worried or unhappy are often difficult to live with. They may be irritable and get angry more easily and more often. If a parent suddenly starts to behave in a way that seems quite out of character for him or her – maybe shouting or even hitting you when they've never done this before – the chances are that this is nothing to do with you or anything that you have done. It is much more likely that they have some problem of their own. If this is so, they may not talk to you about it, perhaps because they are so concerned with their own feelings that they simply want to protect you or feel that this is their problem and has nothing to do with you.

You may just want to keep your head down, keep out of the way, and let them sort things out themselves. But sometimes, if you're really worried, it helps to remind them that you exist and that whatever happens to the family happens to you, too. If your parents are divorcing, for example, what will happen to you? You should be able to say which parent you would like to live with and how often you will be able to see the other. If illness or financial disaster hits the family, you might want to know whether you will have to move house or change schools. Even if what they have to tell you is bad news, it has to be faced some time, and it may be no worse than what you've been imagining. It's important to try to talk; if you really can't discuss things with your parents at least talk to a friend.

7

THE QUEST FOR FREEDOM

"

Most parents interfere in (they would call it guiding)
the choices of their children

"

Martin Herbert, Living With Teenagers

Most OF THE PROBLEMS CHILDREN HAVE in growing up and growing away arise simply because of the parent's natural desire to protect his or her child. How much independence a teenager should be given, and how soon, causes more friction between parents and adolescents than almost anything else.

Part of a parent's job is to give teenagers the freedom to experience life outside the family, but to ensure that they come to no real harm doing so. "Why do you treat me like a child?" "Why must you always interfere?" "Why can't you leave me alone?" These are heartfelt cries every parent is likely to hear during some well-meant attempt to strike a balance.

One difficulty for parents is that emotional and social maturity do not necessarily go hand in hand with physical development. Some parents are tempted to hand over too much responsibility too soon because they expect the child who may tower above them, looking more or less like an adult, to behave like one. Others cannot believe that someone who is less physically mature than his or her contemporaries is capable of assuming some responsibility for his or her own life. With the best will in the world, it is hard for parents to judge the right level of concern.

Families vary greatly in the ages at which they feel it is appropriate to allow their child to do various things. One survey of Australian families found that middle-class

Left: Parents often disagree with teenagers who insist they can do their homework
while listening to music — but it's the teenager's responsibility, not the parent's.

QUESTIONS ABOUT FREEDOM

At what age do you think a child should:

	SON	DAUGHTER
• Go shopping alone or with a friend		
• Decide when to go to bed		
• Decide what television programmes to watch		
• Choose what films/videos to see		
• Choose clothes or decide on a hairstyle		
• Drink alcohol or smoke		
• Go to the cinema with a friend		
• Use public transport for local journeys in daylight		
• Go out in the evenings until 11 p.m. with a friend		
• Go to a party at which no adults will be present		
• Go out with a boyfriend/girlfriend if they want to		
• Use public transport for local journeys after dark		
• Go on holiday with a friend, without the family		
• Decide whether to give up a musical instrument		
• Decide whether to give up a school subject they dislike or find difficult		
• Decide whether to leave school		

COMMENTS ABOUT FREEDOM

There are no right or wrong answers to these questions because there are no hard and fast rules, but you should try to make decisions about freedom based upon how mature you think your youngster is (not how old he or she is). Remember that your teenager will always demand more freedom than you are prepared to give.

What you decide will depend on how you assess your own child and the particular circumstances. Deciding when you should allow your youngster to go out at night, for example, must depend largely on where you live, the distances involved, and the transport available. Girls become self-sufficient sooner than boys, and a 15-year-old girl will see herself as much more of an adult than boys of the same age. Parents, on the other hand, are more protective of girls than they are of boys, and may be less willing to give them the independence they need. In fact, our survey indicated that lack of freedom seems to be more of an issue for girls, especially in early and late adolescence. Maybe this is parental sexism, which leads parents to believe they must be more protective of girls.

parents and children expected responsibility to be handed over to the teenager at a slightly earlier age than did working-class parents and their children. It also found that older parents, and fathers in general, were more likely to hold back from allowing their children to be more independent. Michelle Elliott, author of *Keeping Safe*[1], surveyed 4,000 parents, and found that the only factor that they all agreed should determine the degree of independence children should be given was their maturity, not their age. However, she did find some consensus in a few areas. Most parents thought that, on average, children should be able to go to the cinema or shopping with a friend at about the age of 12; use public transport for local journeys in daylight at about 11 or 12; and go out in the evenings with a friend, provided that they were home by 11 p.m., at about 15 or 16. No parents find these decisions easy to make. Few, whatever the ages of their children, ever reach the stage when they can sleep easily unless they know that their offspring are safely gathered in for the night.

CASE HISTORY: RESPONSIBILITY

Fourteen-year-old Andrew wanted to go on a weekend camping trip with his friends. His parents, Irene and John, weren't quite sure how they should react to this. Initially they were quite reluctant because, although Andrew's friends seemed fairly sensible, Andrew had never been away on his own before. He also might have got quite a different response if they hadn't had a fairly unsatisfactory meeting at a parents' evening with Andrew's teacher the day before.

"If you can't even manage to spend enough time doing your homework, then you're certainly not responsible enough to go off camping on your own for the weekend."
Irene, 37, and John, 45

"That's not fair. My homework's got nothing to do with it. I've often been camping with the Scouts and you know I can look after myself okay."
Andrew, 14

COMMENTS ABOUT RESPONSIBILITY

Judge each request for freedom on its own merits. Parents often latch on to some particular area where the child has shown him- or herself to be immature or irresponsible, and use it to justify or strengthen a position they have taken about something quite different.

Don't expect the adolescent to be all of a piece. The growth towards maturity isn't a smooth process. A 14-year-old, for example, may be capable and responsible in some ways, but still quite childish in others.

Listen to your youngster. If most of your arguments start with him or her complaining, "Why do you always treat me like a child?", then independence is probably a big issue between you. Maybe you're being too slow to let go of the reins.

When to Say No

It is in the nature of adolescents to demand more freedom than they think they will get – and sometimes even rather more than they really want. Don't worry about giving an unequivocal, non-negotiable "no" occasionally. There are times when a course of action proposed is so off-limits that there's little point in even pretending that there's room for discussion. Often in such cases the child has only been testing you anyway; the last thing they expect is to be taken seriously.

Enouraging Self-sufficiency

Adolescents are extremely sensitive to any suggestion that they are not completely capable of organizing their own lives. Parents are accused of interfering if they offer guidance or advice, if they enquire about their youngster's whereabouts or activities, if they comment on the state of their room, or their preparedness (or lack of it) for an exam.

Of the younger adolescents (11–14-year-olds) we questioned in our own survey, half of the boys and three-quarters of the girls complained that they were "treated like a child". Other complaints were about over-protectiveness, lack of freedom, and, very commonly, about parents who "fuss too much". Even in the oldest age group (17–18-year-olds), one-quarter of the boys and over half the girls felt they were treated like children. In fact, this is a feeling which persists into adulthood – how many adults still feel that they have never attained full adult status in the eyes of their own ageing parents? It's worth remembering that a parent's job is to encourage their children to become adults, not to keep them as children. There are helpful ways to do this:

• **Make them financially responsible**. How much pocket money they get will obviously depend on what you can afford, but however much or little this is, give it regularly so that the teenager can plan and budget. This is much better financial training than forking out, however generously, for each demand as it arises.

• **Encourage their relationships** with friends and their involvement in activities outside the family. If you are reluctant to let them meet other people, they may hide their friends from you or feel they have to break away completely.

• **Encourage them to take school trips** and exchange visits abroad if the opportunity for these should arise.

• **Give them some domestic responsiblities**. It needn't be much, but it should be something they're expected to do regularly, whenever it needs doing. An older teenager might also be given responsibility for planning, shopping for, and cooking one family meal a week, with a given budget.

• **Negotiate the areas in which you intend to "interfere"** (progress at school, for example, or their whereabouts when they go out) and those you will leave up to him or her (room-tidying or deciding what to spend money on, for example).

ISSUE: CURFEWS

Disagreements about when a teenager should be home are among the commonest causes of friction during the teenage years. To the teenager, staying out late (or at least staying out later than parents would like) is a hallmark of adulthood and independence. To the parents, this is one fairly clear-cut area where they have a chance – in fact, a duty – to stay in control, and lay down ground rules for the child's own health and safety.

To say with any assurance what time 16-year-olds "ought" to come home is almost an impossibility: there is no magic about any particular hour, and to insist that a youngster always be home by a certain specified time, no matter what, is an open invitation to battle. Obviously during the week, when there may be homework to do and school the next day, it is reasonable to set much stricter limits about going out than at weekends and during holidays (also, some people need more sleep than others). Sometimes the availability of public transport, or a parent's unwillingness to turn out to collect a child after a certain hour, will impose a natural curfew.

What really does matter is that parents know where their youngsters are, and how and at what time they intend to get home. This is much more important than setting an inflexible deadline, and it's not too much to ask of any young adult.

Whatever the house rules about curfews, they should be open to some negotiation. The real value of setting a curfew is not simply to impose discipline, but, as teenagers grow older, to help them discipline themselves. Rather than say, "You've got to be back by 11 p.m.", parents might say, "Be back by 11 if you can, but let me know if you're going to be later". The more say young adults have in setting their own curfews, the more likely it is that they will observe them.

- **Accept your limitations**. You cannot force teenagers to work harder than they want to, or to do homework they have no intention of completing. All you can do is make sure your child is aware of the consequences. Sometimes a "carrot" works: a promise of a contribution to something they're saving for, for example.
- **Let them make their own decisions**, even if you think they're making a mistake.
- **Let them take the consequences for decisions** you have agreed between you are to be their responsibility. If your son cannot find his football kit under the debris in his room, do not backtrack and tidy it for him – even if he howls.
- **Be available to give advice** when you are asked. Remember that even if you're not allowed to interfere, you are still expected to give unequivocal support and be around to act as a backstop in case of emergency.
- **The accusation that "you're always interfering"** peaks in mid-adolescence. If you continue to interfere much beyond this time, then almost certainly you're interfering too much.

WHAT IS AN ADULT?

"You treat me like a child" is a cry heard mostly in early and mid-adolescence. Parents and teenagers often bring out the worst in each other as the teenager tries to grab power, and the parents fight to stay in control. But what does being an adult mean?

For parents, it means being responsible, living up to certain standards which the parent thinks desirable. For teenagers, it means being independent, being allowed to run their lives the way they want to, and choosing their own friends, clothes, and leisure activities. It also means being able to question adult injunctions rather than simply accept them. If each believes the other shares their view, both are bound to be disillusioned.

"Sam's always going on at us to treat him like an adult, but there are times when he seems even more irresponsible than our 10-year-old."

Jane, 41

THOUGHTS: INDEPENDENCE

Parent's view:	He's not a child any more.
Teenager's view:	I'm not a child any more.
Parent:	She should be more responsible.
Teenager:	I want to be more independent.
Parent:	He should choose his friends a bit more carefully.
Teenager:	I'm old enough to choose my own friends.
Parent:	She ought to spend more time working, less time fooling around.
Teenager:	What I do in my own time is up to me.
Parent:	He should be responsible enough to get home at the time we arranged.
Teenager:	Why should I have to get home at the time they said?
Parent:	She's old enough to help around the house a bit more.
Teenager:	I'm tired of them always telling me what to do.
Parent:	He's old enough to keep his room tidy without me nagging him.
Teenager:	It's my room. Why can't I keep it the way I want?
Parent:	She should realize that smoking is bad for her health.
Teenager:	I know smoking's bad for me, but if I want to risk it, that's my business.
Parent:	He's old enough to behave how I think an adult ought to behave.
Teenager:	I'm old enough to decide how to run my own life.

CASE HISTORY: PAINFUL BREAK

When Anna asked if she could go back to a friend's house after school, and to spend the evening there, her parents reacted as if she was proposing something shocking or immoral.

"Why on earth do you want to go to Jane's? Don't you see enough of her at school all day? You need to come home to do your schoolwork without interruption and to have a proper meal. People like Jane's family don't eat as well as we do, you know."
Margaret, 34, and George, 40

"It's so boring eating here every night, watching the same TV, listening to you both saying the same old things about money and politicians. I want time with friends of my own, talking about things that interest us."
Anna, 15

COMMENTS ABOUT PAINFUL BREAKS

Anna's parents had cut themselves off from the rest of the world. Both her parents were very shy; they had never been very sociable or made friends easily themselves, and rarely had people (other than family members) come to visit. They found the idea of Anna developing a life outside the family very threatening.

Anna needed to be quite strong to insist on her right to make her own friends and to spend time with them. She even brought some of her friends home. Although her parents found this hard to accept at first, they gradually managed to relax their grip on Anna. Once she had managed to negotiate the right to spend more time with her friends, Anna was less resentful about the evenings she had to spend at home with her parents. This gradual separation made it possible for her to develop a genuinely close relationship with her parents as she grew into adulthood.

PARENTS WHO CAN'T LET GO

Giving your child more responsibility for his or her own life means that you also have to change as well. For some parents this is hard to do.

If being a parent is something that has always been very important to you, and that you've taken pride in, it's hard to accept that, to some extent, you're becoming redundant. Teenage children do still need their parents, but they no longer need the constant care that you may have provided in the past. A few parents find it particularly hard to let go because of their own needs: maybe the marriage is unhappy, and one or both parents have found much of their emotional fulfilment in the child, or a single parent may have made the child the focus of his or her whole existence. Such parents often continue to expect to come first in their child's life even after that child has grown up, left home, or even married and had a family of his or her own. For some parents, letting go means losing control, and this is something they find very hard to do. It's an illusion to believe that you can shape your children's lives, and you risk losing them altogether if you try too hard to do so. "Mother's always complaining that I won't do what she wants. But why should I?" Why indeed? Any child who has a sense of self-preservation and a sense of his or her own identity will dig their heels in if they feel they're under pressure to fulfil parental expectations that don't broadly correspond with their own. However, because children *do* want to please their parents, there is a real danger that some may go along with the parents' wishes against their own better judgement. You should try to remember these points:

- **Your child is an individual**, not just an extension of you. Don't expect them to share your dreams and ambitions, let alone to fulfil them.
- **Don't burden your child** (especially an only child) with the feeling that they are everything to you; this puts too heavy a responsibility on anyone.
- **Don't try to limit contacts and friendships outside the family**. It is in the very nature of growing up that friends should start to provide the emotional support that used to be derived solely from the family. By trying to hold on too long and too hard, there's a risk that you'll force your teenager to make the break in a way that is painful to everyone, and which may damage the relationship permanently.

> *"My parents are always telling me who I should be friends with,*
> *who to ask over, but sometimes I just want to be left alone. Besides*
> *some of their friends are pretty horrible."*
> Kevin, 15

- **Show an interest in what your teenagers do**, but don't expect them to tell you everything or to share everything with you as they may have done when they were younger. Secrets are a natural part of teenage life.
- **Show that you are not dependent on them**. As your children grow older and need you less, take the opportunity to expand your own life and interests, so that your children and their achievements are not the only source of satisfaction in your life (although they may always remain one of the most important things).
- **Don't play the "hurt parent"** by saying, for example, "You're not going out *again* are you? We never see anything of you nowadays." It is easy to take advantage of most children's natural reluctance to hurt their parents, but it's not playing fair.

> *The family that has always prided itself on being*
> *very close can be difficult for youngsters to break*
> *away from; it may be harder for them to make friends.*

HOW TO GET A BETTER DEAL

Do you feel that your parents give you less freedom than you are entitled to – much less than your friends, for example? Usually this is because they genuinely worry about you, about how you'll keep up with your schoolwork if you stay out too late and too often; about their fear (if you're a girl) that you may be attacked or raped if you travel home alone at night, or end up pregnant if you stay all night at a party; about their terror that you may have had an accident or be in trouble if you don't come home at a pre-arranged time. All these are to some extent realistic fears; they could happen. But these fears are relatively easy to deal with, so long as they're brought into the open and talked about.

It's more difficult if your freedom is restricted just because your parents have fixed ideas about what "ought" or "ought not" to be allowed at a particular age, or if strict rules are laid down which don't seem to make real sense to you. It's quite reasonable to tell your parents that you're the only one of your friends not allowed to do something special – but it has to be done really tactfully. It's easy to rub parents up the wrong way by pointing out how much more freedom your friends are given by their parents. "But Tom's parents always let him…" is likely to be met with only one response: "Well, your parents don't".

POINTS TO REMEMBER

● **They see themselves as** *good parents*. You have to make it easy for them to let go of the reins a little, but still feel that they're doing their job properly. One way to do this is to bring home the friends who are allowed extra freedom, so that your parents can see that they're not wild tearaways who will lead you into deep trouble.

● **Aim for small concessions at first**. There's no point in demanding something you know they're bound to refuse, such as being allowed to come home whenever you like every night of the week. Instead, you may be able to negotiate an extra hour or two out when there's no school next day.

● **Once you've won some concession**, try as hard as you can always to keep your side of whatever bargain was struck. By not coming home at an agreed time, for example, you give them more excuses to restrict your freedom. If you do stick to the agreed limits, it's more likely they'll agree to your next request.

● **Try to get them to say exactly what is worrying them**, rather than merely saying, "You're too young". There's nothing you can do suddenly to age yourself, but you may be able to reassure them about specific worries.

8

BOOSTING MORALE

*If a child tells a lie, tell him that he has told a lie, but
don't call him a liar. If you define him as a liar, you
break down his confidence in his own character.*

Jean Paul Richter

ADOLESCENTS DO SOMETIMES APPEAR BIG-HEADED, but this is more than likely to be bravado, an effort to convince the world that they're more confident than they feel. In fact, they're among the least self-confident of people – they need to be built up, but too often the adults around them see it almost as a duty to cut them down to size, saying things like, "He's big-headed", "She's too clever by half", "He's far too cocky", "She's too big for her boots".

The truth is that people need to feel good about themselves. The way you see yourself colours most of your actions and behaviour. Children with high self-esteem think positively about themselves. As a result, they do better in school, may be more competitive, and they tend to have more friends. They also seem to have a sense of competence about their own lives, a feeling that they are, to some extent, in control of what happens to them.

Parents who are very critical or very punitive will give the impression, rightly or wrongly, that they don't greatly value their child. Inevitably, the child will absorb this negative view of him- or herself, and life can be difficult for people who don't feel good about themselves.

Young people with very low self-esteem are often maladjusted in some way. Teenagers who are bullies, or disruptive in school, or delinquent, tend to have low

*Left: To teenagers, appearances matter very much, and make-up is a way of
building confidence. Be careful how you comment on experiments!*

self-esteem; so do children who become dependent on drugs. Depression seems to be linked with a sense of low self-esteem and a feeling of helplessness in the face of events, and that very little can be done to influence one's destiny. What is it that builds up (or knocks down) a child's self-esteem – a belief that he or she is valuable and worth loving?

BEING VALUED

You learn to value yourself because others value you. Children with high self-esteem know that they are loved. They tend to come from families in which their achievements are valued and praised, and where they have been encouraged to make decisions and have been given some responsibility for their own actions.

How teenagers see themselves depends not only on how others see them, but on how they think others see them. They'll absorb your view of them (or what they think to be your view of them) more readily than you may realize: it is therefore all the more important to make sure the messages they're picking up are positive ones, those that make them feel confident.

Most parents have no idea how much their children need their good opinion. The world is full of adults still striving to gain their parents' approval, and often feeling that nothing they do can ever be good enough. That is an unforgivable burden to impose upon anyone, especially a child.

Self-esteem usually grows throughout adolescence. At first it depends very much on being liked and accepted by friends but, with maturity, it comes more and more from personal achievement – so it matters very much that teenagers should have their share of successes. It doesn't help them at all to find themselves in situations where they are almost bound to fail (see *Life in School*, p.149).

THE GOOD OPINION OF FRIENDS

In early adolescence especially, self-esteem depends very much on friends. People of this age are not yet secure enough to believe that their friends will like them for themselves, and they know that appearances play a large part in the way their contemporaries judge each other. You should realize that it's useless to try to convince any adolescent that appearances do not matter. To teenagers, they matter very much. There is no escaping the fact that very attractive teenagers are usually popular, and that very unattractive ones tend to be unpopular. So, even if it's hard for you to accept that spots, greasy hair, or other problems with his or her appearance are ruining your child's life, these are big issues. Take them seriously and do what you can to help (see *Short Sight*, p.269 and *Teeth*, p.266).

When they're older, adolescents may be able to rely on wit or intelligence or charm or sheer self-assurance to impress other people, but these are skills they're only beginning to develop. In any case, these qualities are not always the ones most appreciated by other adolescents. It takes more self-confidence than most teenagers possess to rely on what you are rather than what you look like to make an impression on other people. What should you do?

- **Try not to be critical.** Even if many of the things you criticize (their hair, their choice of music, their clothes) seem pretty trivial to you, they matter to them. Although it may be hard for you to believe, so does your approval.
- **Praise their achievements**, and give credit where credit's due.
- **If you dislike their behaviour**, make it clear that you don't dislike *them*.
- **Don't feel you should knock them down**, or fail to pass on compliments because you're afraid of making them conceited or big-headed. Few adolescents are so self-confident that they have that sort of conceit. Because they're vulnerable and sensitive, they need to be built up, not knocked down.
- **Don't "label" children.** It may take years for people to stop thinking of themselves as "fat" or "thick" or "clumsy" if this is the identity they've been given in the family and the way they have heard themselves described for most of their lives.
- **Show that you're interested in what they do.**
- **Make them feel that you accept and value them as they are.** They may be very unlike you were at their age, still less like you are now, but you can still respect their interests and opinions, even if you don't share them.
- **Remember how sensitive teenagers can be.** A verbal weapon like teasing can be hurtful even when it's meant to be good-natured, especially when it's directed at the teenagers most private feelings and insecurities. Sarcasm can also be very belittling.
- **Encourage them to find their own area of expertise**, and to do things you know they can do well. Everyone needs to succeed at something.
- **Trust them to make the right choices** for themselves, and reinforce their choices if you can. If cold water is regularly poured on their decisions, they may eventually lose faith in their own judgement.
- **Encourage them to have opinions and values of their own**, and to express them. Then, if they find themselves in a situation where these values are challenged (being offered drugs at a party or being pressured to have sex before they really feel ready for it), they'll have the confidence to defend them.
- **If you criticize, try to be positive rather than hurtful** or destructive, even if the best you can manage is "I think your orange hair last weekend suited you better than this week's green". Like everybody else, youngsters like to be appreciated by the people close to them, and they will be hurt (because, in spite of themselves, they do tend to believe what you say) if you let them know that you genuinely think they look awful.
- **Let them follow current teenage fads and fashions.** Within obvious limits (imposed by money and school rules, for example), teenagers should have the right to look the way they want. Out of school, as far as you can, be tolerant (see *The Age of the Designer Label*, next page), and remember how important appearances are to teenagers.

THE AGE OF THE DESIGNER LABEL

Teenage fashion is no longer just a matter of the width of your jeans or the length of your hair. One quite new problem that most parents now have to face is the demands of children under the ever-increasing influence of designer fashion. It can never be anything but lunacy, for example, for a child whose feet have not yet stopped growing to be bought a £90 pair of trainers, and yet many parents are blackmailed into this kind of expenditure by children desperate to have the "right" label on their feet.

The real tragedy is that there are indeed children whose lives have been made a misery, even to the point of having to leave the school, simply because they have had the "wrong" trainers. When things have reached this pitch, it's clearly time for parents and schools to make a concerted stand. Don't be persuaded to buy anything you can't afford. A school uniform is one way around this problem, and some schools, realizing the extent of the problem, are now reintroducing the uniform they had previously abolished.

"I had this tiny butterfly in a circle of roses tattooed on my left shoulder. No one else knew it was there, but I did, and whenever I thought about it I felt happy, like a different person. My mother was furious when she found out I'd had it done, but I think it's really pretty."
Barbara, 19

- **Try to avoid arguments about any passing fashion** – however much you dislike it.
- **Take your child's genuine worries about appearance seriously** and offer whatever practical help you can. When we asked our sample of teenagers whether, on the whole, they were happy with they way they looked, most said that they were. However, when it came down to specifics, almost all of them had some worries. Hair and spots were by far the most common sources of concern at all ages. For girls, feeling that they were too fat was the next major worry. Having the right kind of clothes also mattered to our teenagers, although again, this was more important to the girls than to the boys.

Although spots are a universal teenage worry, acne can be treated. Suggest a visit to the doctor if over-the-counter preparations don't work (see *Skin*, p.262). If your teenager is genuinely overweight, try to adapt the family's diet so that it's easier for him or her to lose weight sensibly.

Most short-sighted adolescents hate having to wear glasses. A change to contact lenses may do more than anything else to boost their self-confidence and self-esteem (see *Short Sight*, p.269).

If your child's teeth are uneven or crowded, orthodontic treatment can improve appearance. Early adolescence is a good time to start treatment, but a teenager has to make up his or her mind about whether they want it. If a younger child has uneven teeth, do something about it now, and try to help your child feel confident during the time he or she needs to wear braces.

Birthmarks or moles, even if no one else thinks them particularly disfiguring, can cause a self-conscious teenager a lot of distress. Ask your doctor whether plastic surgery or laser treatment would be appropriate.

> *"She stood there in a sweatshirt about 10 sizes too big, and torn jeans about*
> *10 sizes too small, wearing trainers that made her feet look like Minnie Mouse.*
> *I don't suppose her hair's seen a comb in weeks and her make-up*
> *makes her look like something out of a Hammer horror film. She was*
> *pointing to a practically invisible spot and screaming, 'How can I go out*
> *like this? Everyone's going to be looking at this great zit on my chin.'"*
>
> Gillian, 43

CASE HISTORY: MISTAKES

Fifteen-year-old Mark went for a haircut one Friday afternoon in an adventurous and experimental mood, but came home distraught. His mother eventually persuaded him to remove his anorak hood, which had been covering a virtually shaven scalp.

"I just want to look different. I didn't realize how it was going to look. How long does hair take to grow back?"
Mark, 14

"Well, it does look different... I'm afraid it won't grow back by Monday, though."
Helen, 39

COMMENTS ABOUT MISTAKES

Realize that some mistakes are genuine, not done deliberately to provoke parents or school authorities. It may take years for people – even adults – to know what styles are suitable and flattering for them.

Don't make things worse by being overly critical. Parents might not be thrilled with their child's appearance, but shouldn't respond by teasing or humiliating him or her.

Try a cool-headed, practical approach. Both Mark and his mother realized that Mark's shaven head was likely to prove more than his school would happily tolerate, so Helen decided it would be wise to pre-empt trouble. She wrote a note to Mark's head teacher, explaining that her son's new hairstyle had been a misjudgement rather than an act of rebellion, and that he felt as bad about it as the school undoubtedly would. To everyone's relief, the school agreed not to make the haircut a discipline matter, but they couldn't stop Mark from being teased about it. All he could do was to keep a low profile until his hair had grown back a bit.

ISSUE: APPEARANCE

"You're not going out looking like that, are you?"

This may be the only comment about their appearance many youngsters get from their parents. It would put a damper on anyone's evening out, let alone someone who is intensely self-critical of his or her own appearance and who has probably spent hours achieving the effect you have just rubbished. Young people don't look the way they do just to irritate their parents. So why is it that arguments about appearances occur and recur so often within so many families? And what points need to be considered to avoid the same old arguments?

● **An adolescent's appearance ought** to be his or her own affair. Fights about appearance are nearly always started by parents, and occur because the parents worry that other people will judge them by the way their child looks ("How could they let him go around like that?"). Parents should remember, however, that this cuts both ways (see *Feet of Clay*, p.91).

● **Parents should accept,** however difficult it is, that their child's body is their own, and what it looks like is not their business but their child's.

● **Experimenting with dress,** hair, speech, or manners are some of the few ways that 12- or 13-year-olds have of asserting their independence and proclaiming their individuality.

● **Adolescents want to impress** and win the approval of their friends. They are quite unmoved by the thought that their parents' friends or neighbours might dislike the way they look: if anything, this will probably reassure them that they've struck the right note.

● **If parents try to choose clothes** for their teenagers, they're almost certainly going to get it wrong. The nuances of teenage fashion are interesting, but often far too subtle for most adults to grasp. Teenagers learn to get it right with their friends, however peculiar the styles may look.

● **When they're with their own friends,** adolescents should be allowed to dress as they like. At first, most teenagers simply want to fit in, to look like everyone else in their own circle. But by the time they're 15 or 16, they want to develop their own individuality, and the easiest way to do this is by making a strong visual impact.

OTHER REASONS FOR ARGUMENTS

● **Special occasions** On special occasions, especially family ones, it's reasonable for parents to ask their children to compromise a bit, provided that they don't expect drastic changes. Until their late teens, few adolescents find it easy to compromise on their appearance or to adapt it to different circumstances. The way they dress shows what they like to think they are: glamorous, outrageous, unconventional, punk, or whatever. If parents expect their teenagers to present an utterly different image when they go out together (visiting their older relatives, for example), adolescents may feel uncomfortable and resentful, as though they're being forced to pretend to be something they're not. But it's part of growing up to learn that it is not hypocritical but merely good sense and good manners to look and behave differently on different occasions.

- **Worries about sexuality** Quite often battles about appearance really reflect parental fears about adolescent sexuality:

Maria's parents were horrified at the black leather miniskirt and tight black tank top she was wearing to go out to a party. They accused her of looking "tarty", and told her the costume was an invitation to rape.

Jill's parents worried just as much because Jill refused to be as feminine as they would have liked, or to make any real effort to look attractive.

People – even adults – usually have good reasons for choosing the particular image they project. Jill probably deliberately played down her sexuality because she did not yet feel ready to cope with sexual attention, and had found the best defence she could manage. Maria may have wanted simply to prove that she *could* attract sexual attention; she was looking for reassurance that she was attractive, something she'd always found hard to believe. Perhaps if her parents had been able to boost her self-confidence more, she might not have felt the need to go over the top to attract attention.

- **Fathers and sons** Men's fashions have changed faster than many parents have adapted to them, and fathers especially often regard a son's awakening interest in fashion as a form of sexual deviance. It is by no means unusual for men to wear earrings, for example, but a man whose son wants to have an ear pierced is still quite likely to worry that his son might be homosexual or accuse him of being effeminate, so an argument might follow (see *Issue: Compromise*, p.53).

- **School restrictions** Most schools impose some dress restrictions. Adolescents may well try to sail as close to the wind as possible where these are concerned, but it is up to parents to see that they do not flout regulations over dress, jewellery, or hairstyles too flagrantly. Problems are most likely to arise over permanent or semi-permanent looks such as a change of hairstyle which cannot simply be left at home when the youngster goes to school. If teenagers inadvertently go too far in their quest for individuality, they may need to be helped out (see *Case History: Mistakes*, p.87).

- **Tattooing** What should you do when a youngster wants to try something that is permanent and that he or she might live to regret, like a tattoo? Parents often see this as a mutilation of a perfectly good body, and it's true that a few youngsters may use tattooing as a form of self-injury. Among some groups of teenagers, tattooing has become a fashionable or cult thing to do. More often a tattoo is seen simply as adornment or, particularly if the teenager's self-esteem is low, as a way of making themselves feel special. Parents can only stress that a tattoo is not like a haircut, that it is always painful to have done, equally painful to have removed, and will leave a scar (in fact, having a tattoo taken off is likely to prove much more difficult and expensive than having it put on). There is also the genuine risk of contracting hepatitis and even AIDS through the needles if they are not sterilized. If, after all these warnings the teenager is still determined to go ahead and have a tattoo, ask them at least to wait for, say, three months. People do change and it's important for them to be absolutely sure of their decision.

SHYNESS AND UNSOCIABILITY

Shyness can make it hard for youngsters to form friendships even with people of their own age. It can make them seem very unsociable and ungracious if you try to persuade them to put in a social appearance and meet your friends. They may be even less happy if they're forced into the company of children of family friends whom they do not know. These guidelines might help:

• **Don't force painfully shy youngsters into the limelight** or draw too much attention to them. There is a direct conflict of interests here: you want to show them off, they hate to be on show.

"We had some very old friends we hadn't seen for years coming to see us. They brought their 13- and 14-year-old children with them, too – just about the same ages as Matt and Tina, we thought it would be nice for them. But all ours did was skulk in their rooms all day. We had to force them to come down and they were barely polite. We felt thoroughly ashamed – I don't know what our friends must have thought of them."

Robert, 49

• **Don't let them off the hook altogether.** They will learn how to deal with people and how to make friends largely by watching the way their parents behave. If adolescents are brought up in a household where friends seldom call and visitors seem unwelcome, they may not develop the social skills they need to make friends of their own.

• **Remember that teenagers like to choose their own friends** and do not particularly want to be identified with yours. It also takes time and a good deal of self-confidence for them to be at ease with people of their own age they don't know. If you put them into this situation, it's up to you to help them break the ice. Eating together straightaway usually helps. Arranging some sort of expedition or project in which everybody can join is a good idea, too. With luck the youngsters will eventually discover common ground and take off together.

• **Take real phobias seriously.** Mild social fear (such as stage fright or anxiety about dating) is quite common in adolescents, as it is in the general population. However, a few people develop social anxieties in adolescence that are so intense that they amount to phobias (see p.236). Some teenagers who are determined to overcome their fear are able to do this with the support of their family. If you have a child who is suffering from such a socially crippling phobia and seems unable to do anything about it, it is sensible to ask your doctor to refer you to a professional therapist (see also *School-refusers* p.236). Although shyness is not a phobia, it can make life very difficult for the young adolescent who has to change schools, especially if they are entering the new school late (perhaps because the family has just moved house) at a time when other children have settled in and friendships have already been formed. In these circumstances, a shy child may become isolated and an easy target for bullying (see p.164). One of the worst aspects of bullying is that it tends to make people, who may already be lacking in self-confidence and self-worth, feel that there must be something wrong with them. It may deepen a sense of inadequacy so that long after schooldays they are vulnerable to the bullies who exist in all walks of life.

• **Children tend to pick on anyone who's different**, so help your child to blend in with his or her contemporaries as much as you can (see *Coping With Shyness*, next page).

• **Encourage self-confidence in any area**. Whatever talent they have, help them to cultivate it. It can be an advantage for the teenager to join a drama, music, or gymnastic group outside the school so that they can make a new beginning with people who don't have preconceived ideas about them and don't expect them to be shy.

• **Teach them the basic social skills** that will help them not to look as shy as they feel. Shy people tend to scowl, look anywhere but at the person speaking to them, shuffle their feet restlessly as though they can't wait to get away. Learning to look and act friendly and well-disposed towards other people, and not like a hostile alien, is half the battle for shy people.

FEET OF CLAY

Teenagers are usually just as self-conscious about their families as about themselves. Ideally, the parents of an 11- or 12-year-old should be quite invisible to anyone but the child. Certainly they should be as unnoticeable as possible. A 16- or 17-year-old may be proud of his or her parents' achievements and tolerant of their eccentricities, but in early adolescence these serve only to draw other people's attention to the parents, and by association to the adolescent him- or herself.

It may be a blow for parents to discover that they're suddenly being viewed without the rose-tinted spectacles of childhood, and expected to live up to a new set of impossibly high standards. Criticisms may be levelled at defects which have passed unnoticed in your home for years, and agonies of embarrassment suffered about your minor eccentricities – even though children may have lived with these quite happily all their lives. For the time being, keep a profile so low as to be virtually invisible. In a few years' time your child may find you quite acceptable once again.

"If you collect me from Michelle's, please don't wear your jeans because they're too tight or your blue skirt because it's too long or your cloak because it looks funny. In fact, you'd better just stay in the car and I'll come out to you. Then they won't see you at all."
Natalie, 12

COPING WITH SHYNESS

One of the worst things about shyness is the feeling that no one else suffers from it – that everyone around you is having a great time. But it really isn't like that. Almost everyone knows what it's like to feel shy – even people who always seem outgoing and self-confident. Everyone knows the symptoms: feeling anxious, sometimes even sick, at the thought of having to go to a party where you don't know anyone; realizing that your heart's pounding, or your forehead's breaking into a sweat, when you meet someone new (especially if it's someone you want to impress); believing that everyone is looking at you, even laughing at you, watching you blush.

Shyness is uncomfortable. Extreme shyness can be a real handicap. It forms a barrier between you and other people, so that it's hard for you to join in a group and make friends. It can make it almost impossible for you to speak two coherent words to anyone of the opposite sex. What should you do?

• **When you feel shy you are looking inwards**; you want to shrivel up inside yourself. You're far more conscious of the way you feel, or the way you look, or the impression you're making, than of anything else around you. So the first, most important (and, it has to he said, most difficult) step is to forget about yourself. Turn all your attention to what's going on around you. The more attention you pay to any feeling, whether it's pain, tiredness, or shyness, the more intensely you'll feel it. Just by distracting your attention means that you'll feel it less.

• **When you meet someone**, and realize that the feelings of shyness are welling up, focus all your attention on the other person. If they're happy to talk, listen to them. If they're as tongue-tied as you are, it's often easier to acknowledge this. Say something like, "I can never think of anything to say when I meet someone new."

• **Act friendly.** The best way of doing this is simple. It just means looking at other people when you talk to them. Shy people tend to look down at their feet or over their shoulder, or indeed anywhere but at the face of the person they're talking to. But to the other person, this looks as though you're being unfriendly, not just shy. They'll feel you have no real interest in them, and they'll probably feel rejected and back off quite quickly.

• **Think of the other person as the one who's shy.** You know how they're feeling because you've felt that way yourself. Try as hard as you can to put them at their ease. You'll be much more able to forget your own shyness and self-consciousness if you do this.

• **Think of your shyness as an unattractive bad habit** – like biting your nails – and resolve to give it up. When you meet someone new, act out a new, non-shy personality. You don't have to stop *being* shy. The world is full of shy people; they've just learned to act as though they are not. You can do this, too.

COPING WITH BLUSHING

Everyone blushes, and the more self-conscious you are, the more readily you will blush. Most teenagers are very self-conscious indeed, which is why blushing, and the fear of blushing, can be such a real problem during these years. Blushing will become less of a problem as you grow more self-confident, and less concerned about what other people think of you. But meanwhile, it's hard to live with.

Almost any emotion, but particularly embarrassment, shame, or self-consciousness, can cause blushing: that sudden reddening of the face caused by the opening of small blood vessels in the surface of the skin. But you don't necessarily blush because you're embarrassed. More often you're embarrassed because you blush. And this, of course, makes you blush even more. It's a vicious circle.

"Even if I was just asked a question in class, I'd feel myself going redder and redder. Then someone would say, 'Why are you blushing?' and that would make it even worse. It was the feeling that it was all entirely beyond my control that I hated."

Jill, 15

There are various strategies you can try to help stop your blushes. Some people find that learning relaxation exercises, and using these when they feel tense or anxious, helps them to stay calm and to blush less. But this doesn't work for everyone. Probably a better way of tackling the problem is to try to change the way you think about your blushing. This means convincing yourself that it actually doesn't much matter if you blush, that no one else notices it as much as you do, and that anyway, it isn't the end of the world. It doesn't stop you doing anything you want to do or affect the way other people feel about you.

One 17- year-old chronic blusher described her attempts to deal with her blushes like this: "I found it helped to feel I was in control of the situation, even if I couldn't control the blushing. I'd say to myself, 'if I blush I'm going to go on talking and no one else is going to notice'. I'd even make myself take the initiative more, force myself to take part in the conversation and ask questions. Putting myself deliberately in the limelight instead of trying to be invisible seemed to help, although I don't quite know why."

Try to "act" unembarrassed. Even if you don't feel it! Looking at your feet and hoping the floor may swallow you up will only make things worse. You need to use much the same strategies as those suggested for coping with shyness. Turn your attention towards anything or anyone outside yourself; this may not actually stop the blushing, but it will help you not to think and worry so much about it.

PART THREE

THE ADOLESCENT
AND THE
OUTSIDE WORLD

9

FRIENDS AND
FRIENDSHIP

"

*Our mother... had grown up on a farm where families
did everything together. How could I explain to her
how much things had changed, that we kids scarcely
admitted we had parents?*

"

Edmund White, A Boy's Own Story

THROUGHOUT ADOLESCENCE CHILDREN BECOME less "family-centred"
and more "friend-centred". Friends start to play a new and much larger part in their
lives, and friendships teach valuable lessons. Through them the teenager learns to get
along with other people and to adapt as part of a group. For this reason, try not to move
your child to a different area, or at least not to move more than once, during your
children's adolescence. Frequent disruptions of friendships can make teenagers feel
insecure and less able to commit themselves to future friendships.

Friendship in childhood and early adolescence can be a pretty transitory thing,
usually confined to the same sex or based upon shared activities in small groups. As
adolescents mature, these friendships become closer and more durable, and by the late
teens, most youngsters are able to make stable and lasting friendships.

Girls tend to form one or two special friendships, which may be intense, exclusive,
and turbulent. They are also very important: life without a "best friend" to share your
thoughts and feelings with is, at this age, almost insupportable. For boys of this age,
friendships are not usually quite so intimate. Having a special friend is not as important
as being accepted by a particular group or gang.

Around the age of 15, larger mixed-sex groups start to form, and there is usually some
pairing off as the first relationships with the opposite sex are formed (see p.124). By the
late teens these sexual relationships will play an increasingly important part in their

Left: One of the joys of adolescence is the capacity to develop deeper friendships.

lives, and however anxious you feel about this, your children's lives and their need for privacy must nonetheless always be respected.

SOURCES OF FRICTION

Friendships are a vital source of support for adolescents; they can also be a real cause of friction within the family. Below are some of the areas that particularly worry (or irritate) parents.

SLAVISH CONFORMITY

Although adolescents may be trying their hardest not to belong exclusively to the family, they still have a very strong need to belong somewhere. Acceptance by a group or gang makes youngsters feel they belong, and gives them a comfortable feeling of security. As if to emphasize the fact that they do indeed belong, teenagers tend to take on a group identity, especially through clothes, and may conform slavishly to the image their particular group likes to project.

• **Don't dismiss this desire to be like everyone else as trivial**, or put too many stumbling blocks in its way. In early adolescence especially, children do judge each other on what most adults see as very superficial things. Appearances count a lot. It

ARGUMENTS ABOUT FRIENDS

Teenagers often feel torn between family and friends, and our survey of adolescents showed that this conflict lies at the heart of a good many family rows. The table below indicates the main flashpoints.

Reason for argument	Age 11–14 Boys	Girls	Age 15–16 Boys	Girls	Age 17–18 Boys	Girls
• Spending too much time with friends	30%	24%	14%	22%	30%	35%
• Parents disapprove of friends	30%	24%	23%	39%	20%	18%
• Parents dislike a girlfriend/boyfriend	15%	24%	18%	22%	5%	18%
• Parents think youngster is too young to have a girlfriend/boyfriend	10%	33%	9%	11%	5%	9%
• Parents dislike friends being brought home	20%	38%	9%	11%	10%	14%

really does matter to them to wear the right clothes, or have the right hairstyle. Listening to the "right" music is equally important.

• **Whatever they may look like**, don't imagine that adolescents are deliberately drawing attention to themselves. Outlandish clothes and weird hairstyles may look outrageously exhibitionist to adults, but may be a cloak of invisibility to a teenager because "everybody else" – or everybody whose opinion matters to them – has them, too.

• **Don't feel that it will last for ever.** In two years' time or so, the teenager's desire to conform to the group image will have given way to the desire to create an individual look of his or her own. This is not to say that they won't look equally bizarre. They just won't necessarily look like everybody else.

"The grumbles that go on because they have to wear a school uniform you wouldn't believe. And yet when you see them out of school they're as uniform as a regiment – the same hair, the same torn jeans, the same shapeless jackets, the same shoes, the same Walkmans plugged into their ears listening to the same music. Where's all this individuality they keep going on about?"

Anita, 46

SPENDING TOO MUCH TIME WITH FRIENDS

As they grow older most teenagers become increasingly reluctant to take part in joint family activities or to go on family holidays, and want to spend more time with their friends and correspondingly less with the family. Parents, quite rightly, see this as the beginning of the end of childhood. They may also see it as the breakup of the family, and even find it hurtful. It isn't a personal rejection, just a natural and psychologically healthy step in the loosening of family ties.

• **If you feel hurt, don't show it.** The time to worry is when your children don't seem to have close friends, and prefer to spend their spare time with you and other adults rather than frittering it away in the pursuit of idleness with people their own age (see *Issue: No Friends*, p.104).

• **Remember that most teenagers still see their parents as their main source of affection**, support, and help in solving problems, however large a part their friends might seem to play in their lives. Your children won't confide in you or disclose their feelings to you as much as they may have when they were younger, and they certainly won't want to spend as much time with you. But they still need to know that you love them, and that you're there for them to turn to when they're in trouble.

• **Encourage them to use home as a base for their social life**, but understand what this may mean: nine people drinking Cokes around the kitchen table when you're trying to prepare a meal, or occupying all the chairs watching a video when you'd planned a quiet evening with a good book. It means an inevitably increased level of household pollution by loud music, cigarette smoke, dirty mugs, and empty beer cans. Make them welcome, by all means, but lay down simple ground rules. Whatever applies to your own son or daughter (no smoking except in his or her own room, for example) should also apply to their friends.

• **Don't make them lose face in front of their friends by criticizing them**, or embarrassing them, for example, by issuing a torrent of last-minute instructions ("Don't be late" or "Don't drink too much") just as they're going out.

DIALOGUE: HOLIDAY PLANS

Maureen: What are we going to do about a holiday this year? Majorca again? Or Greece for a change?

Mike: Don't mind. Either would suit me, just so long as it's hot and I don't have to do anything for a couple of weeks.

Peter: Well, you can count me out. I'm not coming with you this year.

Vicki: Neither am I. Michelle's having a party and I don't want to miss it. Anyway, I'd rather stay home. There's lots I want to do here.

Mike: What do you mean? Of course you're coming. It's our family holiday. No point in it unless we all go.

Peter: But there's nothing to do, Dad. It's really boring. I hate just lying around on a beach doing nothing. Tina and I want to go climbing instead.

Maureen: You can't just go off on your own. Where would you stay? How would you get there? Suppose you have an accident?

Peter: We could take buses or we might hitch. We'd be staying in a youth hostel and we'll be with the school climbing club. It'll be quite safe.

Maureen: I think you should come on the family holiday just as you always have.

Mike: I agree. You're both coming with us.

COMMENTS ABOUT HOLIDAY PLANS

Mike and Maureen forced two reluctant teenagers to go on the family holiday because they were not yet ready to abandon the family tradition. It was not a happy experience. **Peter sulked and Vicki complained the whole time.** Their parents couldn't believe that they had spent a great deal of money for a family holiday in Greece and it wasn't appreciated.

THE COMPANY THEY KEEP

As your children get more involved with their friends, it's easy to feel that your own influence as parents is being eroded. In some areas, of course, it is. Your children will certainly not want your advice about what to wear or how to spend their free time, and they're more than likely to reject your views on politics or religion. But most are very discriminating about whose opinion finally carries most weight with them. On the issues that are really most important because they affect the youngster's future – education or the choice of a university course or career, for example – your opinion will count for much more than that of their friends, and they will nearly always be swayed by what you say and think.

Your best safeguard is to get to know your children's friends, especially if there are a few friends you're not sure about (see *Case History: Bad Company*, p.103).

CULTURE CLASHES

Teenagers who live in one society, but who belong to a minority creed or culture within it, often find themselves pulled in one direction by their families and in another by the outside world. They may feel they have "two selves", both of which are important to them but which seem to be irreconcilable.

> *"My parents are far more strict than my friends' parents. My*
> *friends are all allowed to go out on dates and wear make-up, but*
> *I'm not. I'd like to go to college and have a career, but they want*
> *me to stay at home and help in the house. My father even threatens*
> *to send me back to Pakistan to get married."*
> Shireen, 16

There is no easy solution. Some families feel able to acknowledge how torn their children feel and try to help them find some sort of balance between their two lives. Cultural, religious, and family roots go very deep; most teenagers value them and do not want to abandon them. The fact that they made friends outside their particular faith or culture, for example, does not necessarily mean they will want to marry outside it, but parents who refuse to compromise at all do run the risk of losing their children altogether. Eventually the youngster may find the only solution seems to be a total break with the family, although this is seldom what they want.

YOUNGER OR OLDER FRIENDS

If your child usually seems to prefer the company of younger children, it may be because he or she feels inadequate with people of the same age. Very shy teenagers can often cope better if they are with others who are younger, or even rather older, than they are, with whom they do not feel in direct competition. Don't worry about these friendships, or try to stop them. They are useful "practice" relationships, and will help to give youngsters the confidence they need to make them feel more secure and at ease with people of their own age.

"Simon always goes about with boys at least two years younger than he is. He seems happy enough, but surely he ought to be making friends more his own age?"
Martha, 36

IDEALISM, CAUSES, AND CULTS

One of the nicest characteristics of adolescents, especially in their late teens, is their idealism, their tendency to question everything, to try to find a social or political cause they can commit themselves to, and to try to find solutions for what ails the world. This makes them interesting and stimulating company, but it can also be threatening to parents who discover that their own ideals and beliefs are being called into question – especially if, for example, a strong religious faith has provided parents with strength and comfort or a sense of cultural identity or "roots".

In this situation it's helpful to remember that there is nothing to be gained by trying to force a reluctant teenager to go to church, temple, or synagogue. Adolescents are not good at paying lip-service to anything, and usually dislike hypocrisy. Also, even if an adolescent does seem to be rejecting the religion he or she was brought up in, such rejection is often only temporary. Many people turn away from a particular faith in adolescence, but rediscover it later in life.

Some adolescents, however – perhaps those who find conventional church services boring – may be attracted to more evangelical or other religious movements that are often livelier, involve a greater demonstration of emotion and feeling, and demand more involvement. Some may be attracted to even more unconventional religious cults. Often such groups have a particular appeal because they are welcoming, and are a boost to the self-esteem of the youngster who is made to feel that he or she has a vital part to play in the movement. Young people who feel depressed, isolated, and in need of friends – often when they're travelling abroad alone for the first time – are especially vulnerable to overtures from cults such as the Moonies.

People who have studied cults of this kind[1] advise that youngsters should be careful of:

• **New acquaintances who invite them to a group dinner** where they will be sure to meet "many interesting and loving people".

• **People who express scepticism** about the goodness of the youngster's family and/or friends, or who try to separate the youngster from their family.

• **Invitations to isolated weekend workshops** with nebulous goals. These may involve sleep and food deprivation, hyperactivity, constant peer pressure, and bombardment by the group's doctrine.

CASE HISTORY: BAD COMPANY

Tess's family had recently moved house, and Tess started in a new school. She missed some of her own friends, and was quickly taken up by an older girl, Laura, who was a poor student with a history of truancy. Tess and her mother Rachel fought about this, and Rachel decided she could do a "damage limitation" exercise if Tess brought Laura home.

"I feel Laura is really a bad influence on Tess. I'm sure they drink when they go out together, and I know Tess has started smoking. They spend so much time together that it worries me. Tess has had her hair cut short to look like Laura's, she dresses like Laura, her opinions are Laura's opinions. I really don't like the girl and I feel she influences Tess more than we do."
Rachel, 37

"My mother won't let me try anything new, she thinks I should be playing with dolls. Laura's older than me, she's doing things I want to try. I'm not a baby any more."
Tess, 14

COMMENTS ABOUT BAD COMPANY

Encourage your child to bring friends home and make sure that when he or she does, they feel welcome.

Don't forbid friends you dislike or disapprove of. You have more control over, or at least more knowledge of, what goes on under your own roof.

Make an effort to get to know the friends, especially the ones you're wary of (which means talking to them). You may discover what it is your child sees in them, and maybe even come to quite like them yourself.

If you have no worries about your child's behaviour, then you probably have no need to worry about his or her friends. A study of delinquents found that 98 per cent had friends who were also delinquents, while only seven per cent of non-delinquent children had delinquent friends.

Explain why you are anxious about the friendship if you really have good reason to believe that a friend is potential bad news.

Trust your child's own sense of discrimination. Remember that as children grow older, increased confidence and social skill makes them more discriminating. While the 14-year-old may drink or smoke just because friends do, the 16-year-old is much less likely to be influenced in this way.

ISSUE: NO FRIENDS

All through her teenage years Helen's parents worried because she didn't seem to have any close friends. The preoccupations of her classmates – pop music, partying – did not interest her; her looks (tall, thin, and gangling) did not appeal to them. What's more, she was a "swot", and did not try to hide it. Even at university Helen was not really at home with her contemporaries. Later, however, she found an interesting and demanding job that brought her into contact with older people who appreciated her talents, and with whom she found she could easily get along.

Not all teenagers find it easy to make friends; indeed, one study has shown that about one young person in five is friendless[2]. A very few people are natural "loners", people who are so self-contained that they don't seem to want or to need friends, but are truly happier on their own, doing their own thing. For most people, however, friendlessness is a miserable state.

Some children fail to make friends because of extreme shyness. For some, like Helen, it's because the youngster just does not fit easily into an adolescent group. Adolescent standards can be very harsh: the child who is too quiet, plain, intellectual, or unathletic may fail to meet these standards, and may also realize that at the moment there is nothing much he or she can do to become more socially successful. It may seem easier simply to opt out of the competition.

Perhaps the most comforting thing for youngsters to realize is that success and popularity at school really have very little to do with what happens in the adult world. There are people who are just not cut out to be adolescents. They come into their own as adults, and it is, after all, as adults that they are going to spend the greater part of their lives.

Some youngsters seem not to know how to set about making friends. Occasionally this is because they come from a family that is so self-contained it has always had few contacts in the outside world, few other interests, and few other friendships. Children learn how to deal with people and how to make friends at least partly by watching the way their parents behave. However, if they're brought up in a household where friends seldom call and visitors seem unwelcome, they may not develop the social skills needed to make friends of their own.

Sometimes it's a matter of personality. Shy children, for example, may give the impression of being unfriendly so that others hesitate to make the first move towards them (see *Coping with Shyness*, p.92).

People can never be forced to make friends, but friendless youngsters may be able to work out just why friends are so hard to come by and improve their chances of making friends (see *What Sort of Friend Would You Make?*, p.106).

IF YOU CAN'T MAKE FRIENDS...

It's nice to be popular, but popularity isn't that important. Popular people whom everybody likes aren't necessarily good at making close friendships. They may have lots of friends, but no special friends.

Even if you feel you've never quite fitted in at school, you may discover that you have qualities that develop and come into their own as you (and your contemporaries) grow more mature. School misfits often find that they can make an impact on a more adult world through being witty or funny, or by having an unusual talent or skill, or even by being eccentric. The same is true about the way you look. As you get older, your own distinct looks should depend more on a personal style rather than on just ordinary "prettiness" or "handsomeness". Ugly ducklings do, quite often, turn into swans.

An American cookery writer, Lora Brody, describes in her book *Growing Up on the Chocolate Diet*[3] how she went back to a school reunion:

"In my high school popularity was unfortunately not based on one's ability to bake a wicked brownie.... Cheerleaders with big breasts, nice teeth, and naturally curly hair got dates.... Being short and skinny with braces and glasses, I was basically ignored by all my heart-throbs. [Skipper Kaufman] made it clear he had no wish to waste his time and energy on anyone sporting less than a 36C. He was so nasty. I hated him. I loved him."

Fifteen years later Lora went back, poised, better-looking, happy – and famous: "Literally nothing about [Skipper] had changed, including his height.... When he got to me it was obvious that he didn't know who I was. I stood up (towering over him I was able to see his bald spot) and shook his hand. This incredulous look came over his face. He began to sputter my name. 'Skipper, why didn't you tell me you knew her,' gushed his wife."

Studies that have looked at the reasons why some children are popular, while others are rejected, have suggested several other factors which influence the way teenagers feel about each other.

Characteristics that contribute to popularity:
- Cheerfulness
- Friendliness
- Likes jokes
- Suggests games and activities
- Attractiveness
- Athletic ability (especially for boys)

Characteristics that contribute to rejection:
- Restlessness
- Over-talkativeness
- Too quiet
- Too shy
- Unattractiveness, especially too fat
- Being "different"

To find out what kind of friend you are, turn the page.

WHAT SORT OF FRIEND WOULD YOU MAKE?

If you want friends but seem unable to make them, you have to start by assuming that somehow what you do or how you behave stops other people wanting you as a friend. There's not much you can do to change other people. But you can try to change yourself, if you want to, and this can make other people behave quite differently towards you. Try looking at yourself from other people's points of view.

		YES	NO
1	**Do you feel you're not really worth having as a friend?** If you feel inferior or play yourself down, this may put other people off. On the whole, people feel more comfortable if they're with someone who feels confident and comfortable being who they are.		
2	**Are you very demanding?** When someone acts friendly towards you, do you immediately want them to be your friend only, want them to spend all their time and give all their attention to you, or feel resentful or jealous if they have other friends or are pleasant to other people? This may frighten people away.		
3	**Are you ever disloyal?** People value loyalty in a friend. They want to know they can trust you, that you'll keep their secrets, and that you'll stick up for them if they're having trouble.		
4	**Are you critical of other people?** On the whole, people like those who seem to like them. When you have a chance to say something nice or complimentary to someone, take it.		
5	**Do you always wait for someone else to make the first friendly move?** Well, you may have to wait a long time. If you're very shy you may give the impression that you're unfriendly, and make other people think that you're being stand-offish. If you need friends, it's up to you to go out and make them.		
6	**Do you offer help when people need it – even if they don't ask?** People appreciate helpfulness, especially if they don't have to ask for it.		

	YES	NO
7 **Do you volunteer to take part in class or school activities, rather than wait to be asked?** Even if people don't always think of including you, it doesn't mean they don't want you. If you never put yourself forward, others may assume you're not interested.		
8 **Do you ever bother to talk to other people who seem shy or short of friends?** Maybe you feel only the most popular people are worth knowing, but they don't actually need more friends. Why not concentrate your efforts on people who do?		
9 **In an argument, do you try and see things from the other person's point of view as well as your own?** If you're having an argument and you only see things from your side, then the other person may think you're being unfair.		
10 **Do you listen when people talk to you?** Giving someone your attention, showing that you understand what they're trying to say, makes them enjoy your company and feel well disposed towards you. If you talk too much yourself, it can give the impression that the only person you're really interested in is you.		
11 **If someone looks miserable, would it occur to you to ask them if anything is wrong, or try to cheer them up?** This is simply being kind – and most people like people who are kind to them.		
TOTAL		

Score one point for each *NO* answer to questions 1–5. Score one point for each *YES* answer to questions 6–11. The higher your friendship score, the easier it probably is for you to make friends. If making friends is difficult, answering these questions honestly may help to show you why. They all concentrate on aspects of your personality you can do something about if you try.

10

SOCIAL LIFE AND
SPARE TIME

WHAT DO TEENAGERS DO? A lot of the time, not a lot. "Hanging out" is a normal teenage activity (along with lying in bed until midday). Few teenagers share the adult belief that a day is incomplete unless filled with action, and this can be very irritating to the frenetic adults who share their lives. On the other hand, a great many of what adolescents think are perfectly normal activities seem to be automatic triggers for either parental wrath or parental concern.

The amount of time teenagers spend on the telephone triggers almost as many arguments between parents and teenagers as clothes do. Some parents impose a total ban, or at least very fierce restrictions, on telephone calls, although this does seem hard on the youngster: telephones play much the same part in the teenager's social life as dinner parties might do for their elders, and provide an opportunity to relax and catch up on the day's events. "Telephone tension" can usually be reduced by less draconian measures.

• **If you need the phone to be free over a certain period**, it is perfectly reasonable to insist that no lengthy calls are taken or made during that time.

• **Consider giving your youngster his or her own phone**. Installation and quarterly charges have become cheaper in recent years and local calls cost very little. Don't buy a mobile phone unless you are prepared to pay the bills, which are much higher than for a standard phone.

Left: Many adolescent friendships (especially those of girls in their teens) seem to be conducted almost entirely on the telephone.

- **Suggest that they take turns telephoning friends,** perhaps on alternate days, so that you don't have to pay the entire bill.

> *"Jane sees Mary all the time at school, and then they spend half the evening talking on the phone. My husband can never even get through to tell me what time to pick him up at the station, and our telephone bills are astronomical. I can't imagine what they find to say to each other."*
>
> Alison, 44

POP GROUPS, CONCERTS, AND MUSIC

Music is a central part of adolescent life, and a constant source of friction in many households. This is usually because it's played at maximum volume, and often because adults dislike the music anyway. It's also because parents tend to distrust the whole pop scene, seeing it as commercial exploitation of their children and imagining that the groups their children go to are only a front for drug-pushers, an excuse for drinking, and a target for police activity.

Why is the teenage music scene so important? Pop music is the common currency of adolescence, and it's really not a bad one. It forms a common bond, a topic of conversation, even a substitute for conversation. Listening to tapes or CDs without saying a word is a perfectly acceptable way for a couple of shy or socially inept teenagers to spend an evening together. Most of all, it provides the sense of identity that is so important in the early years of adolescence. Following a particular group can give the youngster as solid a feeling of being someone as belonging to an exclusive club.

- **Concerts and shows your youngster may want to attend are not wild** or depraved, although the pop-and-rock scene may indeed be commercialized. Soft drugs may be available for those who want them. This is unfortunately inevitable where large groups of teenagers gather, but it's something that every teenager has to learn to deal with anyway. Most of the large rock concerts are well run: the organizers don't want trouble, and in fact seldom get it. The truth is that these occasions are about music.
- **Try not to shout "Turn that rubbish off!"** Don't forget how closely teenagers identify with the music; an attack on their choice of music is an attack on them.
- **Negotiate the volume so that life is tolerable for everyone.** Sometimes you'll have to negotiate between two siblings with separate stereos.
- **Try to introduce them to a broad** spectrum of all types of music. Good music — whether it's opera, jazz, folk, or rock — is always preferable to bad music.
- **Ask your youngster to wear earplugs at rock concerts** (see *Music Can Damage Your Ears*, p.117).

DIALOGUE: DISTURBING THE PEACE

Sally's parents' view: Turn that dreadful racket down. Are you deaf? I'm trying to work.

Sally's view: It's not a dreadful racket. That's what it's supposed to sound like.

Parents: You can't possibly enjoy it when it's as loud as that.

Sally: You don't know anything about it. It's meant to be played loud. There's no point in it if you have to play it quietly.

Parents: Well, you'll just have to turn it off, then. You can hear it halfway down the street. Any moment now the neighbours will start complaining.

Sally: I have to listen to your stupid *Four Seasons* every night, why should I turn my music down?

COMMENTS ABOUT DISTURBING THE PEACE

Sally's parents realized that these regular evening arguments weren't actually changing anything, but simply making everyone angrier. They asked Sally if they could call a "musical truce" and try to work out some sort of compromise that would suit them all.

Sally's parents admitted that at least part of the problem was that they didn't share her taste in music, let alone the level at which it was played, and their nerves might not have been quite so frayed by Mozart or even Manilow. They also realized that they'd been critical of music they didn't know much about; they shouldn't have implied that they thought Sally's music was "bad" or that the music they happened to like was "good".

Sally admitted that perhaps her music was a bit loud for anyone who didn't want to listen to it. She agreed to keep as many doors as possible closed, which cut down noise considerably. Then she agreed that there should be times which should be noise-free (or at least decibel-reduced) when other people in the house were working or when her parents had some of their friends in.

Sally's parents agreed not to complain about the music at other times, and bought Sally a set of headphones.

"Last year we had to move because my dad got a new job. I hated having to leave all my friends and change schools. One of the things that helped me find new friends was the group that I followed. Other people liked their music, too, and it gave me something to talk about."

Sandie, 15

DIALOGUE: DRUGS AND CLUBS

Tim's view: We're going to Angels on Saturday. I'll probably be back pretty late.

Mother's view: Angels? I hear that's a terrible place.
(Her first response is so inflexible that she's left herself little room to manoeuvre.)

Tim: What do you mean? It's brilliant, everybody goes there.

Mother: Well, you're not going. It's full of drugs. Everyone knows that. You'd be crazy to go there and I'd be crazy to let you. I don't want you to end up a junkie.
(What evidence does she have that he will? This leap into the future shows no trust in Tim's judgement.)

Tim: You're stupid. Everyone knows drugs don't do you any harm if you're careful.

Mother: Of course they do. It's wrong to take them and it's dangerous, too.

Tim: Well, I'm going and you can't stop me.

Mother: You're not and I can. You're grounded on Saturday, so you're not going anywhere.
(What might have been a reasonable discussion has generated into a slanging match.)

ALTERNATIVE DIALOGUE

Tim: We're all going to Angels on Saturday. I'll probably be back pretty late.

Mother: Angels, that's that club in Market Street, isn't it? What's it like?

Tim: It's brilliant, the music's fantastic, everybody goes there.

Mother: But it's got a bad reputation at the moment, hasn't it? Everything I've heard about it makes it sound like one of the drug centres of the western world.

Tim: Honestly, it's not really like that. There are drugs about, but you don't have to take them. We just go for the music.   ▷

Mother:	But isn't it difficult not to take them if everyone else is doing it? That's what really worries me. *(This is a real problem for youngsters — better to acknowledge peer-group pressure so that you may be able to help your son or daughter deal with it.)*
Tim:	None of my friends are really into drugs. I mean, there's the odd joint and some of them take Ecstasy, but I wouldn't take anything dangerous. I'm not stupid, you know.
Mother:	I'm not suggesting that you'd mainline heroin or get hooked on crack. But I do worry you might try something that's harmless for most people, and have a bad reaction. That can happen with Ecstasy. People have died. And whatever you take, you never know if it's been mixed with something much more dangerous. *(This is an acknowledgement that, although Tim's mother has strong views and real anxieties about drugs, she cannot actually stop Tim taking them if he is determined to.)* The other thing that worries me is that once a club has a bad reputation, the police are probably keeping an eye on it. So be sensible; you have to remember that even if you don't think taking a drug would do any harm, it's illegal. I don't want to have to bail you out in the middle of the night because there's a police raid. *(Rather than treating it as a moral issue, it's better if you can make teenagers realize you don't want them to get into a situation they can't handle. Tim's mother has given him two practical reasons for not taking drugs which he can use with his friends.)*
Tim:	All right, I get the message. Don't worry. I won't have you dragged out of bed on Saturday.
Mother:	Good.

COMMENT ABOUT DRUGS AND CLUBS

Tim may or may not experiment with whatever the fashionable drug of the moment is, but at least he's aware of the possible risks and consequences. He might think a little harder before doing it.

TV AND VIDEOS

In general teenagers impose a surprising amount of self-censorship on their television watching. While some do spend the whole evening glued to the box, most do not. A 12- or 13-year-old may have to be reminded about homework, but a 15- or 16-year-old should be able to plan an evening and take responsibility for what he or she does (or fails to do). Watching TV may be an excuse for missed homework or social gatherings, when the real problem is that the youngster isn't motivated to work.

Teenagers genuinely believe that a background of music or television helps them to work. Parents genuinely believe that it does not. It isn't really possible to reconcile these views, but it's worth remembering that it is the youngster who is actually doing the homework. You could force teenagers to work in silence, but if they're convinced that it's more difficult this way, neither you nor they will gain very much (see *Case History: Responsibility*, p.75).

VIOLENCE AND VIDEO NASTIES

You have some control over what teenagers watch at home, but if they choose to sit and watch video nasties at a friend's house, you are unlikely to know about it, and in any case, there is not a lot you can do about it. How much does it matter?

Some studies show that when violent films or videos are shown to adolescents, they become more aggressive for at least a few days afterwards. The effects, though, seem to depend to some extent on the "setting" in which the viewing occurs. Disturbed or aggressive children are likely to be most influenced. Whatever the evidence, most parents do have a gut feeling that they care about the mental "food" as well as the physical nourishment their children get, and that a constant diet of violence or horror must have some malign influence.

• **Make sure** that yours is a home in which aggression is neither used nor tolerated. If this is your child's background, viewing an occasional violent film or video is unlikely to cause anything worse than a nightmare.

• **Watch with them** if they want to watch anything you're unhappy about. Discussing it with you may sharpen their critical faculties.

DRINKING IN PUBLIC

Most countries seem to have some type of protective legislation to prevent under-age drinking. In the United Kingdom, for example, currently the law excludes children under 14 from pubs and bars. From the ages of 14 to 16 they are allowed into the bar, but not allowed to buy or drink alcohol there. People between 16 and 18 may drink beer, cider, or perry with a meal in a bar, but cannot buy it themselves. Over the age of 18 they may buy alcohol freely as adults. By comparison, in the United States 21 is now the minimum age for legal drinking in most states. The evidence is that there is no less under-age drinking in the United States than in the United Kingdom. Age restrictions are usually a challenge to adolescents, especially boys, who try to get around them (some may go as far as illegally obtaining false identification). The most parents can do is be familiar with the laws in their country and teach them to their children. Perhaps it's more important to teach them not to drive if they plan to drink no matter where they get the alcohol.

PARTIES

Every parent has some horror story about teenage parties; if they're lucky, the story happened to someone else. There are good parties, which everyone enjoys, and which don't leave the house wrecked and the host (and parents) wretched. But there are others that quickly go wrong and are a disaster for everyone. Usually it's because there has been too little supervision, too little preparation, and too many people.

• **If you can avoid it, don't give parties at all** until your teenagers are about 16. Let someone else cope with the early adolescents, who are at the age when the boys in particular are likely to behave worst. They may be rowdy, are not old enough to drink sensibly, and yet, if you offer them only Cokes, will try to smuggle their own alcohol in and drink too much out of bravado. By the time they are 16 or 17 many of them have discovered that they can still enjoy themselves while reasonably quiet and sober.

• **Stay around** – not necessarily on the spot all the time, but certainly not out of town or away for the night. This is not just for your own peace of mind, but for your son's or daughter's. Nearly always, whether adolescents acknowledge it or not, a party in their own home is quite a responsibility for them. They worry about it getting out of hand, about gatecrashers, about damage being done. However, on principle they will probably try to persuade you to go away as far as possible and for as long as possible and leave them to manage the whole affair. Don't do it, however vehemently they protest that you will ruin the evening if you're within a 100-mile radius.

• **Don't be too much in evidence**, or join in unless you are invited. If the party is for younger teenagers, it's best to stay in the house all the time, but once they are 16 or 17 a good arrangement is to go out and let the party establish itself, then come back later.

A V O I D I N G   M A Y H E M   A T   H O M E

One disadvantage of having a party in a public hall (from the teenager's point of view) is that it usually has to end much earlier than the participants would like. For younger teenagers this may be an advantage, but once they are 16 or 17 they will very much prefer their party to be allowed to draw to a natural end rather than send their friends away at a pre-arranged time. There are a few things you can do to prepare your home for a party which might limit the damage:

- **Make the youngsters and their friends clear away everything breakable** before it begins. Your children cannot be responsible for the behaviour of all their friends; most teenagers are fairly careless about other people's property and, unfortunately, a very few are wantonly destructive.
- **Put out plenty of ashtrays** because the greatest risk is of cigarette burns on furniture and floors.
- **Take up or protect carpets in some way.**
- **Check the volume of the music before the party.** Put the music on full blast, go outside the house and work out how far and at what volume it can be heard. After a reasonable hour, put a limit on the noise level if you live in a built-up area, but until then, let the party-goers set their own volume. Bear in mind this will probably be much louder than you can bear, but try to negotiate before the party.
- **Limit numbers.** Your youngster does not have 100 friends, whatever he or she says.
- **To cut down gatecrashing,** which is a real problem in cities, advise your son or daughter to issue written invitations as near the date of the party as possible, so that only their friends know about it. Tell your youngster that it helps to have a large but amiable friend on the door, one who knows the faces of people who ought to be there, and can bar admittance to the party without too much difficulty.
- **Warn your immediate neighbours before the party.** You might want to take boxes of chocolates around to put them under a faint obligation to be good-natured about it; this is much better than taking them round as an apology afterwards.

FOOD AND DRINK

Your son or daughter may protest that they don't want food at their party. There is a stage, amongst boys particularly and in the mid-teens especially, when the charm of a party is that it's an excuse for drinking. The idea of food still smacks of the parties they had when they were children, or seems to add an air of formality, and this is something that virtually all teenagers fight shy of. Persuade them (insist if you have to) that the more guests eat, the less likely anyone is to get drunk — something to take seriously if guests will be driving home after the party. Tell them that guests like the idea of eating something, even if their young host or hostess does not, and you will find that, if you provide the right kind of food, it will vanish. Put the food out so that people can help themselves when they want to. Make it something they can eat in their fingers and keep it as simple as possible: pizza, sausages or sausage rolls, mince pies, and French bread with cheeses and cold meats.

What do you do about drinking at parties? To make them totally "dry" and stipulate only Coke is to invite the hard nuts to smuggle in vodka. The best solution is to provide low-alcohol beer, plenty of soft drinks, some wine, perhaps a punch or mulled wine which, provided that you make it up before they arrive, can be made to look much more alcoholic than it really is. Ban spirits altogether.

SLEEPING OVER

"There's a party at Kate's on Saturday and I don't want to leave before it's finished. Can I sleep over?"

An all-night party is no more likely than any other party to develop into an orgy, but many parents find this hard to believe and get very edgy when "sleeping over" is suggested. However, sleeping over means just what it says. The party-goers doss down in sleeping bags if they have them, on whatever floors, beds, or sofas are available. They pass an uncomfortable night and often help clear up in the morning.

Unless you have good reason not to, trust your child: sleeping over is a practice that makes very good sense. Public transport is not always available, and if it is, may not be particularly safe late at night. The alternatives are to give them the fare for a taxi home, turn out yourself late at night to collect them, or, least desirable of all, accept that they may be given a lift home by someone who has drunk too much.

MUSIC CAN DAMAGE YOUR EARS

Most middle-aged rock stars have some degree of measureable hearing loss. Some are seriously deaf and have to use hearing aids. This is a direct effect of their years spent surrounded by powerfully amplified music.

Occupational deafness has been recognized for many years, and nowadays people working in noisy conditions all wear some form of ear protection. Modern rock music can be almost as damaging as engine noise, and the louder it is, the more dangerous it is. But how loud is loud? Sound is measured in units called decibels (dB). A watch ticking is about 20 dB, normal conversation is about 60. Exposure to sound over 90 dB (about the noise level of a big diesel engine) carries a risk of damage to hearing; anything over 130 dB (a jet engine at 30 metres, for example) is likely to cause immediate damage. The volume of the music you play in your own room is about 80 to 90 dB, just on the margins of safety. A rock concert, however, registers about 100 dB, definitely in the high-risk area. Exposure to 120–130 dB causes immediate and sometimes permanent damage to the ears. Lower levels of noise cause damage slowly over time, what's known as a cumulative effect. Young people who have used personal stereos for several years to listen to rock music also show some hearing loss, which unfortunately may go unnoticed until the damage has been done.

Experts on hearing disorders recommend that no one should listen to noise levels above 90 dB without wearing ear defenders. An occasional visit to a rock concert is OK, but if you plan to be at the front, take some earplugs that you can use if the sound turns out to be very loud. More important, don't deafen yourself at home or in the car. Music that can be heard outside the house or car when the windows are shut is dangerously loud. And turn down your personal stereo. If other people can hear it while you're wearing the ear-pieces, it's too loud. If you don't want to be deaf by the time you're 30, keep your sound levels low.

11

SEXUALITY IN ADOLESCENCE

"

Sex is something I just don't understand,
I swear to God I don't.

"

J.D.Salinger, The Catcher in the Rye

IT CAN BE HARD TO ACKNOWLEDGE that your child is someone who thinks about sex, wants sex, maybe even has sex. More than any other aspect of growing up, your child's growing sexuality emphasizes his or her separateness from you. Your son or daughter has a private life in which you have no part, and which will take him or her into areas where you can provide little or no protection. For that reason, it's easier to believe that sexuality is an adult preserve. However, any adult who thinks back to his or her own adolescence must remember how much time was spent in sexual thoughts, fantasies, plans, and experiments. For adolescents, their emerging sexuality can be overwhelming, dominating their minds and "taking over" their bodies.

Teenagers will always be curious about sex, and they will always want to experiment. It's an area – like driving or alcohol – which is seen as both a challenge and as a mark of adulthood. The problem has always been that young people are capable of having sex, and of conceiving children, long before they are emotionally mature enough to form a close or stable sexual relationship, and usually long before they have any real wish to form sexual relationships at all.

Every parent knows the pitfalls as well as the pleasures of sex. Like it or not, we are uneasily aware of the risks of pregnancy, sexually transmitted diseases, or heartbreak which children will encounter as soon as their sex lives begin. One's natural instinct, as

Left: As a parent, you should try to ensure that your son or daughter is
emotionally prepared for a sexual life.

with any high-risk activity from smoking to learning to ride a motorcycle, is to hope they will postpone it for as long as possible.

Sex is an emotional subject, and what you say (or do not say) to your teenage children is bound to be coloured by your own experiences and attitudes. If your feelings about sex are ambivalent or your sexual experiences unhappy, it may seem very important to keep control over, and impose limits on, your offspring's sex life. As in so many other areas, though, you have to strike the right balance between keeping them safe, and letting them take responsibility for their own lives and making their own decisions.

"It's crazy, I'm living with Jake. Mother knows I'm living with Jake. And yet when I mentioned the other day that I was going to buy a double bed in the sales she said, 'What for? You're not getting married yet'."
Tessa, 19

POSSIBLE PARENTAL ATTITUDES

• **"If you do it, don't let me know you're doing it."** Simply saying "don't do it", especially in a threatening or judgemental way, will not help adolescents. It certainly won't stop them: they *will* do it at some point.

Some parents (often those who have an ambivalent attitude towards sex themselves) find it easiest to pretend nothing is happening. They act as if their child is still a child, denying or ignoring any evidence to the contrary, because this makes them as parents feel more comfortable. This attitude may do no harm as long as everything goes well, but it leaves the teenager cut off from the adult help or advice which at some stage he or she may very well need. It is an unfair attitude to take, too, until the child is secure and self-confident enough to know what he or she truly wants. The 15-year-old, for example, whose parents allow her to stay out until all hours without knowing where she is, may find herself in situations she cannot cope with and would rather have avoided. Parental ignorance in this situation is a kind of collusion which puts too heavy a responsibility on the child.

Older teenagers may hate the evident hypocrisy of this attitude and resent being forced into a false position, as may happen when they're out in the world working or at university and deeply involved (and sexually involved) with someone. What do you do when they stay overnight? You have a right to expect them to respect your rules and feelings for as long as they're living with you. Once they have more independent lives, however, it helps if you can all be honest about your teenager's growing independence.

• **"I want to know everything that's going on."** A few parents adopt a "tell-me everything" approach. They show an almost prurient fascination with their children's sex lives, probing for every detail, ostensibly to make sure they're not getting into any trouble, but also perhaps to fulfil their own adolescent sexual longings vicariously. This is an unjustifiable invasion of the youngster's privacy – and your teenager won't tell you anything he or she doesn't want you to know anyway.

- **"Don't do it because it's wrong."** This may be how you feel, but as advice it will only be effective if you and your son or daughter share the same moral code. Adolescents are busy working things out for themselves, making their own decisions about what is right and what is wrong, and their conclusions may not coincide with yours. They will probably interpret the message simply as, "Don't do it because I don't want you to do it" – which cuts no ice with many teenagers.

- **"Don't do it unless you're in love."** This can be a risky thing to tell an adolescent, who is quite likely to seize on it as a way of reconciling an irresistible sexual impulse with a self-imposed or acquired code of moral conduct. They may then persuade themselves that they're in love, and are therefore "entitled" to sex, or they may try to impose permanence on what they might otherwise have discovered to be only a transient sexual attachment.

By all means get across the message that love and lust don't always coexist (see *Dialogue: Is It Love?*, next page). Be wary, however, of encouraging a romantic attitude that justifies everything in the name of love. This may make it all the harder for them to judge a relationship realistically.

- **"Don't do it yet."** This is probably the most sound and realistic attitude you can take. It is an honest expression of your fears, and can be backed up by data. Sex too early may lead to love too early and so to marriage too early; this is widely accepted as inadvisable and unlikely to last. Slowing down teenage sexual development has advantages: in many primitive societies (and in Europe until recently) sex was postponed until young adults left home and became independent. Sex is a great consumer of time, energy, and emotion. It can swamp adolescents at a time when there are many other demands as well as opportunites before them. It can also be addictive; it is quite difficult to turn back the clock and return to a sex-free lifestyle once you've had an affair. So try, if you can, to give your children the confidence to know that they'll be losing nothing by postponing sex for a while; indeed, ultimately they may gain.

WAYS TO HELP

In the best of all possible worlds, you would do the following:

- **Accept your child's developing sexuality**. It's then much less likely to become a battleground between you. Children will quickly sense any anxiety or ambivalence in their parents' attitude to sex. If they're looking for some way to precipitate an argument, they will soon discover that flaunting their sexuality or sex life is a most effective means of provocation.

- **Let them set their own pace**. Most teenagers are quite capable of deciding for themselves when they're ready to begin a full sexual relationship. If your son or daughter asks you if you think it's all right to have sex, you can be fairly sure that he or she is feeling pushed or pressured towards a sexual relationship and is not ready. Your

DIALOGUE: IS IT LOVE?

Nicola's view: There's a girl in my class, Shireen, and her parents have arranged for her to marry someone back in Pakistan she's never met. I think that's dreadful.

Father's view: How does she feel about it?

Nicola: She doesn't seem to mind. I can't think why. She says her parents say he's really nice and she trusts them to choose someone she'll be happy with. But suppose she doesn't fall in love with him?

Father: You mean, suppose she doesn't find him attractive enough to want to go to bed with him?

Nicola: Daaaad! I'm talking about love, not just sex. Shireen says they'll probably grow to love each other. But that doesn't sound like love to me.

Father: Tell me what you mean by love. Are you talking about what makes people want to be together, maybe get married? Or what makes them stay married?

Nicola: Well, I don't know. Both, I suppose.

Father: Well, what about your cousin Ted and Anna? They certainly seemed to love each other when they got married. But are they still together?

Nicola: Dad, you know they're not. But that doesn't prove anything. Ted's impossible. Everyone knew that except Anna. She should never have got tied up with him.

Father: Well, maybe that's one advantage of an arranged marriage. The impossibles get weeded out straightaway. And don't forget, Shireen's parents want this to work. They're not going to choose someone they think Shireen won't find reasonably attractive. And they'll make sure they've got as much in common as possible. You must admit that it probably improves a marriage's chances if the two people really like each other and get on well together. And Shireen obviously feels that if her family likes this man, she probably will, too. It could be as good a basis for marriage as falling in love.

Nicola: I suppose so. But it doesn't seem very romantic. It isn't what I call love.

Father: It doesn't matter what you call it, so long as it works.

child may want you to say no on his or her behalf. Adolescents may need you to absolve them from the responsibility of saying it, confirming their own feelings of unreadiness. Your job is to set up a climate in which it's easy for them to opt out if they want to. When adolescents are ready, they won't need your permission or approval, neither are they likely to ask for it.

• **Make sure they're well informed**, and do try to talk to them about sex. If you're too embarrassed to talk to them, at least make sure there are some sound books around the house (they can read the adolescent section in this chapter). At the very least, they should know about contraception, and where to seek contraceptive advice. Your children should understand the risks of sexually transmitted disease that are increased by casual sex. They should also know more than just the basic mechanics of sex, and know something about the way men and women respond to each other emotionally as well as physically. These may be awkward conversations, but bear in mind that if you can't talk to them, they may feel too frightened or inhibited to discuss their deeper or confused feelings with you, or any real problem they may have.

• **Trust your children**. They may push you to the limits in what they and their friends say, but in what they do they are much less likely to set out to shock. If they're sensible and responsible in other areas of their life, they will usually be sensible and responsible in their sexual lives, too.

> *"My parents told me nothing about sex or birth control, so of course I got pregnant when I was 18, and they insisted I have the baby adopted. That's why it's important to me to talk to my own daughter now, even if we're both embarrassed. I never want her to feel the way I did: lost, confused, very lonely, and very sad."*
>
> Liz, 49

HOW SEXUALITY DEVELOPS

In their early teens, the closest friendships children have are usually with their own sex, even if they are at a mixed school and have the opportunity to make friends with either sex (see *Friends and Friendships*, p.97). These friendships may be so intense and exclusive that parents sometimes assume that their child may be forming a lesbian or homosexual attachment (see *Discovering Your Child Is Gay*, p.131). While it's certainly true that most teenagers at sometime or another are attracted to people of their own sex, and in boys some kind of homosexual play (usually handling each other's genitals) is very common during the early years of adolescence, none of this means much. It is a normal, usually transient stage that most children go through, but children (as well as parents) may need reassurance that it is normal. More commonly, however, adolescents usually begin their sexual lives by having friendships with members of the opposite sex.

FIRST SEXUAL FRIENDSHIP

The first boy-girl friendships, around the age of 13 or 14, are more in the nature of a game than anything else, with most of the action taking place inside the adolescent's head. They are usually brief and superficial, exploratory forays undertaken under conditions that guarantee a minimum of exposure or opportunity for a more threatening intimacy. A couple may have lunch together at school or spend time with each other at a party, but seldom will they actually "go out" together or make any serious attempt to spend time alone. On the whole, they prefer to go around in a crowd, doing things as a group; pairing-off may be done more to impress their friends or to gain status than because the couple have any real interest in or feeling for each other. They still usually feel more comfortable with the company of their own sex.

With their same-sex friends, both boys and girls spend much of their time thinking and talking about the opposite sex. They like to compare notes, discussing who has done what to whom, perhaps trying to measure the truth of what may be idle boasting. While some of this chat is harmless, an occasional reminder that the reputations of both boys and girls can be compromised by either their own poor judgement or by unprovable speculation might not go amiss. It also reinforces the idea that sex is a private matter. Unfortunately, it still seems to be the case that boys may competitively goad each other into sexual adventures, while girls discover that the unfair double standard still seems to operate during the teenage years: boys who claim to have had many sexual adventures are admired by their friends, while girls who are thought to sleep around are regarded less kindly. You may need to talk to your son, cautioning him about the risks of teenage pregnancy and the hurt this may cause a young girl, and how it might affect both their lives – especially hers.

DATING

Although boys and girls in mid-adolescence still tend to go around in groups, couples often start to split off from the group and spend time alone together: the dating ritual has begun. Girls are usually ready to begin dating at about 14 or 15, boys a year or so later. There tends to be a class difference in dating patterns, too. Girls from blue-collar families may begin wearing make-up and dating at an earlier age than their white-collar contemporaries; this pattern persists, in so far as the girls who start dating at a younger age also tend to have their first sexual experience and to marry at an earlier age.

Early dating may be seen by both peers and parents as a reassuring sign of popularity, but it is not always an advantage. Some adolescents may not be mature enough to make more than very superficial relationships, and these may come to preoccupy them so much, and take up such a disproportionate amount of their time, that they neglect or fail to develop other interests or activities. Although it is not in the nature of these first relationships to last, you should not dismiss them as unimportant. At this age, adolescents need the freedom to move in and out of relationships, learning more about

YOUR CHILD'S SEX LIFE: POINTS TO REMEMBER

Trust your child to be responsible.
Let them set their own pace.
Make sure they are well informed.
Don't be too intrusive. Sex is a private matter.

themselves and the opposite sex as they do so. But they can still be extremely intense, so don't underestimate the misery they can cause (if only temporarily) when they break up. A few children, often the ones who are finding it difficult to become emotionally detached from their parents, may develop very intense, clinging relationships from which they find it hard to extricate themselves, and which usually prove unacceptably cloying and dependent to the other person involved. When these relationships end, your child may need reassurance to restore his or her confidence.

TEENAGE SEXUAL BEHAVIOUR

There are differences in the ways that boys and girls respond to their rapidly developing sexuality. In boys the sex drive is intense, and at first, easily satisfied by masturbation – often without fantasies, and sometimes in company with other boys of the same age. Virtually all boys masturbate. Girls, at least in early adolescence, may be just as preoccupied with sex, but usually on a much more imaginative, "romantic" level: feeling is all-important, action much less so. Sexual drive seems to develop more slowly in girls, and to take longer to become genitally focused. Not surprisingly, adolescent boys have a much more active sex life than adolescent girls. Girls especially tend to develop crushes on pop stars or older adolescents, and their fantasies usually focus on these "unattainables". As with boys, however, masturbation accounts for most of the action at first. By the age of 16 about two-thirds of girls masturbate.

"Whoever called it necking was a poor judge of anatomy."
Groucho Marx

FIRST SEXUAL INTERCOURSE

On the first dates, at around the ages of 14 or 15, sex usually means petting. On average, boys tend to start having sex at an earlier age than girls, but by the age of 17 half of all boys and well over one-third of girls will have experienced sexual intercourse; by the age of 18 probably three-quarters of all boys and and about half of all girls will have had sex. All the surveys of teenage sexual behaviour seem to indicate an almost universal trend towards earlier intercourse throughout Europe and America[1]. Probably most adolescents are more sexually experienced and knowledgeable than their parents were at the same age, but only a very few teenagers are promiscuous. Most of them still want what their parents want for them: a loving relationship with one partner who matters to them. Unfortunately, many teenage sexual encounters are opportunistic. The sex is unplanned and so, all too often, is the subsequent pregnancy. This makes it all the more important for parents to make sure that their adolescents – both their sons and daughters – have a practical knowledge of contraception before they need it, not afterwards (see *Contraception*, p.135).

CASE HISTORY: THE NEED FOR PRIVACY

Jane is 17, and went away on a school holiday without her parents where she met a boy she became quite keen on. Her mother was worried about this, since she had never met him; she was also concerned about Jane's daydreaming and how it was affecting her schoolwork.

"Jane has always been so open with us before, and now I know she's having this secret correspondence with some boy. She rushes down to get the mail first, and thinks I don't know when she slips out to post letters on the sly. It's not like her to be so deceitful and secretive, but I don't feel I have the right to intrude."
Jeanette, 46

"I met someone special and I've never felt like this before. It's just so different, I don't want to tell anyone yet, least of all my mother. I think about him all the time."
Jane, 17

COMMENTS ABOUT THE NEED FOR PRIVACY
Sex is an intensely private matter. Nevertheless, it still comes as a blow to some parents if they discover that their teenager is no longer entirely open and upfront with them about his or her life. Jane is not being sly or deceitful, but she is being secretive: she has to be to protect herself. Like anyone in the throes of first love, Jane feels intensely sensitive and vulnerable, overwhelmed by feelings so powerful and private that she cannot bear them to be exposed. If she does discuss them with anyone, it's much more likely to be with a friend of her own age.
Jane's mother did not question or tease. Wisely, she realized that even if she meant to be good-natured about Jane's first important relationship, it would have been an intolerable invasion of her daughter's privacy.
Jane was allowed to set her own pace. Jane's mother didn't try to force the relationship or bring it out into the open – for example, by trying to persuade Jane to ask her boyfriend around so that she could meet him.
Jane's mother accepted that she was likely to be excluded from this area of Jane's life and that, from now on, her daughter's strongest emotions would no longer be directed exclusively towards the family.

"MINI-MARRIAGES"

By late adolescence most people are mature enough to have some sort of stable relationship just what their parents want for them, but, paradoxically, a source of yet more parental anxiety. If the relationship seems to be leading to marriage, parents are probably right to be anxious, because all the evidence is that very early marriages have a high risk of failure. But early marriage is by no means the goal of all young couples. More often, the pattern is for the relationship to run its course and then crumble, to be eventually replaced by another one.

> *"They're like an old married couple already. Spend all their time together.*
> *Never meet anyone else. They're far too young to get this serious."*
> Christopher, 54

Whether parents like it or not, that is the way things are. The advantage of these mini-marriages is that the couple is involved at all levels of the relationship; as preparation for marriage, it might even be more successful than the more superficial dating habits of their parents' generation. Against this can be set the fact that these relationships go deep, and when they do break up (which they are likely to do), the pain is intense. Serial monogamy also means serial divorce. It can also be argued that the pattern of serial monogamy, once established, may be difficult to break what the two people may actually be learning is that when the going gets tough, ending the relationship – rather than trying to understand or change the unhelpful patterns of behaviour – is one of the first options to be considered, rather than the last.

CHILDREN WHO HAVE PROBLEMS

No matter how hard you try to protect your child, you can't. Bridging the distance from the enclosed world of the family to the outside world of adult sexual relationships is always fraught, even for children who are relatively happy and well adjusted. There are, however, special problems you may have to confront.

STARTING TOO SOON

Children mature at different rates, and in itself early (or late) sexual experience is not necessarily either abnormal or deviant. Although most parents are likely to be horrified at the discovery that their 13- or 14-year-old is involved in a sexual relationship, it's important to look at it in context and not to overreact. If your child's behaviour in other ways is giving you no cause for concern, if he or she has a good relationship with you and is getting on well at school, has friends, and seems generally happy and content with life, then the sexual behaviour – although it may shock or disappoint you – should not be regarded as a major catastrophe. Boys are much more likely than girls to take a sexual opportunity if one is offered, out of either curiosity or bravado. Often adolescents do not willingly initiate a sexual relationship on their own, but may come under pressure from someone older and more sophisticated. They may not enjoy it all that much (if they did, they are very likely to repeat it), and may feel guilty, confused, or worried about pregnancy, but there is no real evidence that it will do any lasting harm. It doesn't help them if your reaction suggests that you think they have done something appalling.

Things are rather different if the sexual behaviour is part of a whole pattern of disruptive or disturbed behaviour, or if a young girl is truly promiscuous, and her relationship with her parents seems to have broken down entirely. Girls tend to "use" compulsive or irresponsible sex in the way that boys may use aggression and other forms of deviant behaviour: as a sign of real emotional disturbance. The best thing to do is to call in the cavalry and seek professional help, while making sure that the child is absolutely certain of your love and support, so that she does not have to look for these outside the family until she is ready to do so.

Very occasionally parents themselves unwittingly put pressure on a youngster to have sex before he or she is ready for it. You are probably doing your daughter no favour, for example, if you put her on the contraceptive pill as a matter of routine as soon as she reaches puberty. She may feel she is expected to have sex and is somehow failing you if she does not. Remember that she may have to cope with outside pressures from her peers in any case: if her friends know she's on the pill, they may assume she's sexually available. Certainly the pill protects her, but it also robs her of what is still one of the most acceptable excuses she has to refuse sex if she does not want it. Nor should pressure be put on your son to "be a man" and to initiate a sexual relationship just for the sake of becoming experienced. Pressure from peers is difficult enough to withstand without parental pressure.

CHILDREN WHO SEEM TO BE NON-STARTERS

Not all children conform to the picture of burgeoning sexuality which seems to be typical of adolescence. Some find it hard to cope with their sexual development, or try to deny it altogether, by giving the impression that they're totally uninterested in sex. This may be because they feel worried, guilty, or even frightened about various aspects of their sexuality – whether or not they might be homosexual, for instance – or it may reflect the attitudes of parents who are themselves so ambivalent about sex that they make it hard for the teenager to initiate any sex life at all. Eating disorders such as anorexia nervosa (see p.240), which also tend to emerge around this time, may be yet another way of denying sexuality and trying to stay (physically at least) a child.

Pressure from parents, which may be intended as well-meant encouragement, will not help. There are two things worth remembering: let your youngster set the pace,

TEENAGE PREGNANCY

Remember two things: one is that if your daughter tells you she is pregnant, it is probably one of the hardest things she has ever done, and that she is probably frightened for herself and about your reaction. The other is that there is no form of contraception that is completely reliable, and her pregnancy may have occurred despite her having taken sensible precautions.

Whatever your feelings – and you will no doubt have a very strong response to this situation – your first concern should be for your daughter. It would be extremely hurtful and damaging, for example, to say, "of course you must get rid of it"; it will be far more helpful if you first find out what she is feeling, reassuring her that you will help her to make what will be, in any case, a difficult decision. By not making any assumptions, by not forcing your own views on her (whatever they are), you are freeing her to look more objectively at the situation and make a more rational decision. Whatever her choice is, it's important that she feels she's made it freely, not under duress, and that she has your support.

Sometimes, teenage pregnancy is not just an unlucky accident, but the sign of a very troubled adolescent. The girl may want the baby as something of her own to love, and to have someone in her life to love and need her. The pregnancy may be a way of demanding more love or attention from the parents, or a deeper commitment from a boyfriend. In this situation, parents won't find it easy to help or advise their child, and it is essential that she has professional counselling to help her discuss the problems she faces and decide what she wants to do (see "I Think I Might Be Pregnant", p.137).

You may find yourself in a different, but still difficult, position if your son tells you that his girlfriend is pregnant. Again, your first reaction may be anger at his irresponsibility, but do give him credit for not walking away: many young boys in this situation simply cannot cope, and refuse even to acknowledge that the baby is theirs. He may have strong feelings about the baby but be confused about what part he wants to play, or indeed, will be allowed to play. It will help both young people if they can discuss their options together, but the bottom line is that if they disagree (for example, if she wants an abortion and he wants her to have the baby), it is her decision that should carry the day.

IF YOUR CHILD HAS BEEN SEXUALLY ABUSED

Children who have been sexually abused need three things:
- They need to be believed.
- They need the abuse to stop.
- They need an apology and reparation from the abuser: acknowledgement that what happened should never have happened, and that it was wrong.

SEXUAL ABUSE

If your child tells you he or she is being abused, believe them. It is an appallingly difficult thing for them to have to tell you, and for you to have to accept. Children who summon up the courage to tell (and it needs a lot) are too often met with a flat rejection. They are unlikely to make up such a story. What have they got to gain?

Listen to what they have to say, look at the evidence they have to offer, and start from the premise that what they are telling you is true.

If your child has been sexually abused by someone outside the family, don't take the law into your own hands, however murderous you feel. Contact the local social services or the police. If the abuse is recent (within the last 24 hours), your child may need to have a medical examination to provide evidence for the court if the abuser is to be charged.

Even more devastating is the discovery that the abuser is a parent or other family member. When this happens, it is even more difficult for the child to ask for help. Teenagers are often well aware of what the consequences of telling might be: they may hate what is happening to them and want it to stop, but still have very ambivalent feelings of both hate and love for the abusing parent. They may not want to risk losing that parent's love, or to hurt the other parent, or to cause the break-up of the family – especially if there is a risk that the abuser may go to prison. They are in an impossible situation because the consequences of telling may seem to be as terrible as the abuse itself.

There are four categories of child abuse: neglect; physical injury; sexual abuse; emotional abuse.

CARE AND PROTECTION

Ideally, the adult who has been accused of abusing a child should leave the family home, even if he or she is not immediately charged with any offence, so that the child can remain within the family with as little disruption as possible to his or her life. This option also provides everyone with a breathing space to decide what should be done, to seek help and treatment, and to start rebuilding their lives. Often the families in which abuse occurs have multiple social problems, and these must be addressed. Families can recover, but professional help is essential – especially for the abused child.

If the adult responsible refuses to leave home, or denies the charge, the youngster may feel unable to cope with the situation, and may take back what has been said. In these cases, the police, the social services department, and organizations to prevent cruelty to children have various legal powers to protect and to take into temporary care a child they believe is at risk of abuse. In an emergency, and as a last resort, these agencies may be empowered to remove the child summarily from a family home and take him or her to a children's home, a foster home, or a hospital. Parents may be refused access and may not be told where their child is.

RAPE

The incidence of rape – certainly the reporting and criminal charge of rape – is increasing. Male rape is also not unknown, and there are now counselling services for both men and women. Primarily, however, rape is a crime committed by men and boys against women and girls.

As with sexual abuse, you should believe your daughter if she tells you she has been raped. If charges are to be brought, she should not change her clothes or have a bath or shower until she has been examined by either a police doctor or your family doctor (see *If You've Been Raped*, p.143).

"When Sarah came home and told us what had happened, none of us could think straight. We just wanted to comfort her and help her get over the shock. But we telephoned our family doctor, who is an old friend, and he explained that if we wanted the rapist to be convicted and punished, then we had to persuade Sarah to see a police doctor at once and allow a full exmaination before she cleaned herself up. It wasn't pleasant, but as things turned out later, we were glad she'd agreed. Otherwise the man might not have been sent to prison."
Mary, 47

DISCOVERING YOUR CHILD IS GAY

If your son or daughter tells you that he or she is gay, your response should depend on your youngster's age and maturity. Many adolescents are dismayed to find that they have enjoyed physical contact with a friend of the same sex. That doesn't mean they are gay, and you should reassure them that such explorations are quite common.

However, this revelation from an older teenager who has clearly been thinking about this for some years is another matter. In this case, count yourselves lucky that they have been brave enough, and feel that their relationship with you is good enough, for them to risk telling you. The revelation may make you feel worried on their behalf because, whatever your own feelings, you'll know that they're bound to meet prejudice and intolerance somewhere along the line. In truth, however, you have no choice but to accept that this is the way things are. They cannot help being gay and they cannot change – even if they want to. At the best of times adolescents can lack confidence and feel unsure of themselves. Imagine how hard it must be for them to acknowledge that they are different in this fundamental way. Your loving acceptance of them as gay will be the best support you can give (see *"I Think I Might Be Gay"*, p.146).

LOVE AND SEX

Deciding that you want to have a sex life is one of the most important steps you will take. You might think it marks the beginning of your "adult" life, and in many ways you're right. You may also feel under a lot of pressure, either from friends or from images in the media, so it helps to remember that you don't have to rush into anything. You are the only person who can make decisions about your body, your feelings, and your life.

WHAT THE LAW SAYS

Because the law makes it illegal for a girl under 16 to have sexual intercourse, 16 is sometimes called "the age of consent" (see *Contraception and the Law*, below). For boys, there is no legal age of consent for heterosexual sex, but there is a law about homosexuality (see "*I Think I Might Be Gay*", p.146). Are these laws sensible? After all, sex is a "natural" activity. So why does the law put restrictions on it, and why do most parents worry so much if they think their children are starting a sex life too soon?

The answer is that there are risks involved. Most relationships between young people – even if they seem to be serious – break up quite quickly. If one person thinks having sex is quite a serious thing, and the other doesn't, someone is bound to be hurt. Sometimes young people don't want a deep involvement but want to experiment with different sexual partners, but whether you're a boy or a girl, sleeping around with no concern for someone else's feelings is never wise. You will get a reputation as someone who is selfish and uncaring, and you also increase the very real risks of a sexually transmitted disease or an unwanted pregnancy. So what are your reasons for having sex?

"IT'S GOT TO HAPPEN SOMETIME SO LET'S GET IT OVER WITH..."

What makes you decide that it's time your sex life got under way? Because you've met someone you really love and you feel you're ready? Then you're lucky! It's not like that for everyone.

For many people the "first time" happens not because they really want it or feel ready for it, but for a less positive reason. Maybe it's just because an opportunity has come along and they seize it, perhaps because they're curious, or want to make sure they can do it. Sometimes they've come under pressure from someone else and don't know how to say no. People sometimes have sex to prove they love someone, or because they think it's proof that someone else loves them, or because they think they'll lose them if they say no. Very often they have their first experience of sex at a party where they have drunk too much and cannot stay in control of the situation and themselves.

"EVERYBODY'S DOING IT"... OR ARE THEY?

You can't always believe everything you hear! No one likes to be the odd one out, and the belief that everybody else is doing it has probably propelled quite a few people into a sex life before they're really ready for it. The truth is that most people still wait to have sex until they're legally old enough.

WHY DON'T FIRST RELATIONSHIPS LAST?

Unfortunately, a good many "first times" are likely to be "last times" as well. The cards are stacked against early sexual relationships. No matter how intense they are, they seldom last. To enjoy sex, most people need a partner they feel close to, someone they know well enough to relax with and trust. They also need time, privacy, freedom from anxiety – and practice. How many people's first sexual encounters have all these ingredients? The first time is much more likely to he hurried, fumbling, and fraught with fears about pregnancy or someone (like a parent) finding them in the middle of it. So even though an experience like this may satisfy your curiosity, it may not be as great as you expected. It may leave you feeling very let-down and lonely.

Sex improves with practice. Towards the end of your teens you'll be much more able to have a relationship with someone you really like and respect and care for. These later relationships will probably last longer and may deepen to include sex you'll really enjoy. But until then, it's worth remembering that you can always say no. You don't owe it to anyone to give a reason. The fact that you just don't want to is reason enough.

MAKING SEX SAFE

Most of us are natural optimists: we tend to think we lead a charmed life. But it is very wide of the mark to believe that an unwanted pregnancy can't happen. The sad fact of the matter is that many teenage girls become pregnant every year.

It seems that even if teenagers know quite a lot about contraception, they don't often use this knowledge when they start to have sex. Most people's first sexual experience is unexpected, unplanned – and usually quite unprotected. Teenagers are more fertile than adults, so a teenage girl is much more likely than an adult to get pregnant, even if she has unprotected sex only once. She has much more to lose than an adult, too. If she does become pregnant, none of the options she has to consider – such as keeping the baby as a single parent or marrying the father, giving the baby up for adoption, or a termination of the pregnancy – is an easy one. The teenage boy who is the father has to consider these options as well.

• Start thinking about contraception before you start to have sex! This is easy to say, but not always easy to do. At the very least it means acknowledging to yourself that yes, you're ready to start a sex life or to enter a new stage of a relationship. If you're at all unsure about this – wanting it but feeling a bit guilty about it, too – then you may fool yourself into thinking that it's easier just to let things happen so that you don't feel quite so ▷

responsible. But for your own safety and peace of mind you must take steps to prevent an unwanted pregnancy. At the very least, condoms can be easily purchased, and a girl can buy them just as easily as a boy can. If you're a teenage girl, you can go to a doctor or to a family planning clinic (see *Contraception and the Law*, next page). If you're a teenage boy, you should remember that contraception is your responsibility, too. Think about how both your lives – but especially the girl's – would change if she becomes pregnant.

• **Learn to say no.** Being prepared for sex doesn't mean that you have to have sex. Contraception seems to have removed one age-old reason for saying no to someone who may be pressuring you (and sometimes girl's pressure boys!). But the truth is that no one has to explain or give anyone a reason for not having sex. The fact that you just don't want to should be reason enough. When you don't want to have sex with someone, say so, and say it as if you mean it.

• **If you're a boy**, you have to believe that when a girl says no, that's exactly what she means. It makes no difference that you feel she's encouraged you, that you thought that was where the two of you were heading. She is still entitled to change her mind or to call a halt, and however disappointed or frustrated you feel, you have to accept it. Do not pressure her, and do not even think of forcing her to have sex with you against her will. "Date rape", just like any other form of rape, is a serious offence.

• **If you're a girl**, take your share of responsibility, too. Of course you're entitled to change your mind or call a halt, even if you've been engaged in some pretty heavy petting. But it is still crazy to put yourself deliberately at risk, to make a boy think you're willing to have sex when really you don't want to at all, or to drink so much at a party that you neither know nor care what happens to you.

• **Share responsibility**. If you're in a steady relationship, you've probably talked about whether you're both ready for sex and what you're going to do about birth control. It's more difficult with someone you've met recently and don't yet feel comfortable with. You may both feel too embarrassed and anxious about the whole thing even to mention contraception to the other person.

In an ideal world every boy who thinks he's old enough to have sex should carry a packet of condoms and be prepared to use them. Unfortunately, what often happens is that a girl feels dependent on her partner's sense of responsibility. But there is every reason for a teenage girl to check that her partner has a condom; if he doesn't, she could produce one herself, and she should insist that one be used.

CONTRACEPTION

Probably the most important thing to consider before you start having sex is how to avoid an unwanted pregnancy.

CONTRACEPTION AND THE LAW

If you are a 16-year-old girl or older, you can legally receive advice from your family doctor or from a birth control clinic without your parents' knowledge or consent. Even so, you may be embarrassed about going to a clinic, and even more so about seeing your family doctor. You should then contact a birth control clinic or some other organization that specializes in giving contraceptive advice and counselling services to young unmarried people. Many are happy to counsel boys as well as girls.

For girls who are under 16, the position is more complicated. If your doctor thinks you are mature enough to know what is involved in beginning a sexual relationship, he or she can prescribe the pill or a diaphragm for you, but will also try to persuade you to allow your parents to be told. If you refuse, your doctor can still prescribe contraception if he or she believes it is in your best interests. Legally, your doctor should not break your confidence without your consent.

METHODS OF CONTRACEPTION

Although there are quite a lot of methods available, some are not ideal for young couples, either for medical reasons (the intra-uterine device, or coil, for example, isn't usually prescribed for women who haven't had children), or because they are too unreliable. Don't even think about using the rhythm method (based on the estimated time of ovulation) or relying on the boy withdrawing before he ejaculates. You may be tempted to try the relatively new contraceptive sponge because it can be bought over the counter and is simple to use; unfortunately, it has too high a failure rate to be worth risking. Realistically, you have the following choices:

• **The pill** is the most reliable method of all, but it does not suit (or is not suitable for) everyone. It is an oral (taken by mouth) contraceptive and must be prescribed by a doctor who will check that there's no medical reason why you should not take it. Also, it must be taken without fail every day, preferably at the same time each day, whether you're in a steady relationship or simply want to be prepared "just in case". If you're not in a steady relationship with a regular sex life, it seems like overkill to take the pill continuously just on the off chance that someday soon you'll meet someone you want to make love with.

• **Condoms (sheaths)** are probably the best method for anyone who does not have a steady relationship with one faithful partner. They have the huge advantage of being freely available; anyone can buy a packet without embarrassment. Once you get the hang of them, they're convenient and easy to use. They're safe and, used properly, reliable. There is now ▷

a female condom, too. Perhaps most importantly, they help to protect you against sexually transmitted diseases, including AIDS, as well as against pregnancy.

• **The cap or diaphragm** is a rubber dome mounted on a circular, springy, metal rim. Before making love it should be pushed up inside the vagina until it sits over the entrance to the womb. This acts as a barrier to sperm. Caps are quite reliable if they're used properly with a spermicide (a cream, gel, or foam that kills sperm), and have the advantage that a girl needs to use it only when she wants to make love. But even the cap's best friends can't claim that it's convenient. It's a bit fiddly to insert and unless it's the right size, it won't form an effective barrier. So a girl can't buy one "off the shelf" but must go to a doctor or to a family planning clinic for an internal examination. This helps to ensure that the cap fits properly. Caps don't have much effect in preventing sexually transmitted infections, but the spermicide used with them does offer some protection against diseases.

• **Emergency contraception** may be used if you do get carried away (it can happen) and have sex without using any contraceptive. But don't wait to see if you've been lucky. Go to your doctor or a family planning clinic and ask for "morning after" contraception. If it is available, you will probably be given two doses of a special pill, which must be taken 12 hours apart. Treatment must begin not more than 72 hours (3 days) after intercourse, and is most effective if it is given within the first 24–48 hours. The pill may make you feel sick or vomit but, provided that it's used as a once-only emergency measure, it's quite safe.

WHEN RELATIONSHIPS END

Relationships work best when the two people involved like and respect each other, and satisfy most of each other's needs most of the time. This is something to aim for, certainly if you plan to spend your life with someone, but you won't find it in every relationship.

When a relationship ends it's usually because the two people involved want different things. One partner may want more commitment, more time, or more demonstrations of affection, for example, than the other is able or prepared to give. This does not mean that it has "failed" or that either of you should feel bad about it. Your relationship has simply run its course, and given all that it has to offer. It certainly isn't a failure if it brought you at least some pleasure while it lasted, and taught you a bit more about making relationships.

The break-up of any relationship is painful; when it's your first really deep relationship, you may feel devastated. It can be difficult to believe that you'll ever feel happy or meet someone you can love as much again. Virtually everyone has felt like this at some time in their life. Fortunately, virtually everyone has been proved wrong. This is when you need friends. Most people find that it helps to talk about how you feel to someone who'll listen and help you to see it in perspective – and eventually bounce back and start all over again.

PREGNANCY

If you have a sex life, you should also be considering the possibility of an unwanted pregnancy. The first sign of pregnancy is a missed period, but when a girl starts having periods, they're likely to be irregular anyway. Unless they have settled down into a regular monthly cycle, a missed period doesn't necessarily mean pregnancy. But what if a girl has missed two periods? Other signs of pregnancy are:

- Swollen, tender, or tingling breasts
- Nausea or vomiting (at any time of day)
- Frequent need to urinate

Pregnancies happen because you haven't taken precautions, or because the method you've chosen was not properly used or didn't work.

PREGNANCY TESTING

A pregnancy test can be carried out free by your family doctor or a family planning clinic. Ring up first to check when the test can be done. Some clinics will be able to give you a test on the day your period is due, but clinics that are still using the older, less sensitive test won't test you until one or two weeks after your missed period.

Alternatively, you can use a pregnancy testing kit bought from a chemist. You can do the test on the day your period is due, at any time of day. Although the kit is fairly expensive, it is very easy to use – you simply pass urine over the special indicator – and the result is 99 per cent accurate.

"I THINK I MIGHT BE PREGNANT..."

The knowledge that you've taken a risk, that you might be pregnant, is enough to turn your whole world upside-down. Often the thought of telling your parents is the hardest thing; it may be difficult to see beyond this. In fact, the whole situation may seem so impossible to solve and so frightening that you might be tempted to put off thinking about it, or find it too hard to make a decision about what to do. But it's very important that you do go to see your doctor, or the local family planning clinic or pregnancy advisory service, as soon as you think you might be pregnant, even if you're not sure whether you want to have the baby or want to end your pregnancy by having a termination. Provided that it is carried out within the first 12 weeks of pregnancy, termination is simple and safe (safer even than childbirth itself), but after 12 weeks the risks become much greater. If you decide to have the baby, see your doctor as soon as possible so that you can have good antenatal care.

THINKING ABOUT THE FUTURE

If you are pregnant and thinking about the future, be realistic and be selfish. This is your situation and your life. No one else knows just how you feel, and no one else can make the ▷

decision for you. But it will almost certainly help to talk things over with someone who you know has your interests at heart before you make it. Your parents may be the best people to help you decide. If they can't – or won't – try to talk it over with a trusted friend.

If you can discuss your feelings with the baby's father, so much the better. If he is also very young, he may just not be able to take on any responsibility or be much help to you. But if he does want to be involved, it may help both of you. It is his child, too, and you may be surprised to discover what strong feelings he has about it.

• **If you feel you want to keep the baby**, then what about your relationship with the baby's father? Do you want it to last? If you're both young, and decide to marry because a baby's on the way, it has only a small chance of lasting a long time.

• **How would having a baby** affect any plans you've made for your own future school exams and career, for example?

• **How would you feel about bringing up a child** on your own? (Not a baby: that stage doesn't last for long.)

• **What kind of support** and financial help could you expect from your parents?

• **How would you feel** about having the baby fostered or adopted?

• **How would you feel** if you terminated your pregnancy?

You may have very complicated and conflicting feelings about any of the options open to you. It would help you enormously to go to a voluntary, professional counselling service (see *Organizations*, p.274). They won't try to make up your mind for you, but will just help you talk through the issues and see them more clearly.

If you're pregnant and have decided that you want a termination, you should act quickly. You may choose to go to your own doctor, who should be able to tell you what facilities are available, and whether he or she is willing to help (some doctors have reservations about performing a termination, but they should refer patients wanting one to a colleague who will arrange matters).

Termination of pregnancy is legal in most countries in certain clearly defined circumstances. Sometimes terminations are performed if the mother's health would be seriously harmed if the pregnancy continued, or if the baby is known to be abnormal. Another reason may be that the mother cannot face the prospect of going through with an unwanted pregnancy, and its continuation represents a greater risk to the pregnant girl or woman than does termination.

Terminations may be performed by private clinics or a termination charity; these will probably be listed in the telephone directory. Other organizations, such as the LIFE clinics in the UK, help girls who do not want an abortion, and will arrange help with the pregnancy and with adoption of the baby after it is born (see *Organizations*, p.274 for the names of these various groups). In charitable and private clinics you will be asked to pay a fee for the pregnancy to be terminated, but the charities will try to help you even if you haven't any or much money. Unfortunately, it's more difficult to have a termination performed in some areas than in others. You should find out what is available locally just in case you have to travel.

METHODS OF TERMINATION

In some countries it may be possible for a pregnancy to be terminated without an operation up until the seventh week of pregnancy (nine weeks after your last period) by using a drug called mifepristone (RU486). This method has been used for over 100,000 terminations in France (where the drug was developed) and is perfectly safe. Clearly this method will be available only if you waste no time in making the necessary arrangements. Another method of early termination is a minor operation under either a local or a general anaesthetic. If the pregnancy is advanced beyond 10–12 weeks, the simple operation is no longer possible, and a combination of drugs and surgery may be needed. You can discuss the method of termination with the advisory service, but do talk to them as soon as possible.

TELLING YOUR PARENTS

"I was only 15 when I discovered I was pregnant. I dreaded telling my parents.
It would have been easier if my boyfriend could have been with me, but he just
didn't want to know — he was the same age as me and he couldn't cope at all. I knew
how upset my mother and father would be. I thought, suppose they throw me out?
It took me days to pluck up the courage. I rehearsed over and over again exactly
what I would say, and suddenly I told my mother. 'You're not going to like this
and I'm terribly sorry, but I'm going to have a baby,' I said. At first she was
terribly upset and angry. She cried, and I cried. But even so, it was such a relief
having told her. And when she and my father got over the shock, they did everything
they could to help me. Once I'd told them, I felt I could start to think what I wanted
to do about the baby. Before I was so scared and felt so alone I couldn't think
clearly about anything."
Theresa, 16

What can you do if you know that your parents just wouldn't be able to handle the fact that you're pregnant? Obviously, if you're living at home and decide to go ahead and have the baby, they're bound to find out anyway. If you want to have the pregnancy terminated without your parents knowing, you might be able to do this legally if you're 16 or older. If you're 15 or younger, any doctor you consult will try to persuade you to involve your parents. They may even do so if you're over 16.

At any age, you will need support from friends and family, and it's usually best to tell your parents. If you can't, contact a pregnancy advisory service as soon as possible.

WHAT IS SEXUAL ABUSE?

Because your parents may not want to frighten you, or because they worry so much about you, they may not have told you about sexual abuse. They would still want to know if someone was hurting you. It sometimes happens that adults, or even older children, may want to kiss you, or touch the sexual parts of your body in a way that makes you feel uncomfortable or frightens you. It may even hurt you. For example, an older man – maybe a teacher or a friend of the family – may ask a young boy to touch his penis, or he may touch the breasts of a young girl. He may continue to do this even if the young boy or girl doesn't like it at all.

"My uncle's never actually done anything but it's the way he looks at me, and the things he says or whispers to me, because he never lets anyone else hear. It makes me feel really uncomfortable, but I don't know what to do. He'd only laugh and say he was only teasing me if I said anything."
Emma, 12

The legal definition of sexual abuse is any activity in which children (which usually means all people under 16) are used for the sexual pleasure of older people. It is not only sexual intercourse. It includes any kind of sexual touching or fondling as well, regardless of whether they do it to you, or they ask you to do it to them. If you're not sure whether someone is "teasing" (sometimes that's what they say they're doing), or if what someone is doing to you is wrong, ask yourself these questions:

- **Does it make you feel uncomfortable?**
- **Do they touch your body** in a way that you don't like?
- **Does it hurt you?**
- **Do they ask you not to tell anyone?**
- **Do they continue to do it** even if you've said you don't like it?
- **Do they threaten to punish you** or hurt you if they think you might tell someone? If you are being abused now – or if you have been abused in the past – it may help to know that you're not alone. For example, in the UK over 10,000 children a year telephone Childline (a confidential telephone helpline: see *Organizations*, p.274) to say that they are being sexually abused, or have been abused in the past. Almost as many have been physically abused, or "battered"; this means they have been severely injured as an extreme form of punishment. If this happens to you, what should you do?
- **Tell someone what is happening.** Nothing is likely to change unless you do. This is sometimes very hard. Maybe you're too frightened to tell anyone, or feel you won't be believed. You may even feel ashamed or embarrassed. Sometimes it may take months until

you decide that you have had enough, or until you feel brave enough to tell someone. It's still the best way to change a situation that is hurting you. Remember that it is not your fault. When an adult abuses a child, it is *always* the adult's fault, never the child's.

• **A parent is the best person to tell if you can**. If one of your parents is abusing you, perhaps you can tell the other parent what is happening. If you can't tell either parent, for whatever reason, tell another close relative, or a teacher at school you like and think you can trust. You can also go to the police or to the local social services department to ask for help.

• **If you can't bring yourself to talk to your parents** or anyone else you know – or if you've told someone and they don't believe you or won't help you – there is still something you can do. Look at the back of this book for the name and telephone number of organizations you can contact. Most people find it's easier to talk to someone they don't know, someone they can't see and who can't see them. Sometimes these telephone numbers are free, so there will be no record of the call on the telephone bill, even if you call from home. No one need know.

Talking to one of these support groups doesn't commit you to anything. It just gives you a chance to think more clearly about what you want. It gives you more time to feel confident about doing something to change a situation that makes you unhappy or frightened. For example, someone will be able to tell you what is likely to happen if you ask the local police or the social services department for help. If you decide this is what you want, they can contact these agencies for you. Once you have talked to them, it is usually not quite so difficult to take the next step and tell someone else.

HOW DOES TALKING HELP?

"I don't see how talking about it could help," you might think, "no one can do anything. Everything will be just the same afterwards."

But it does help to talk, even if you think that nothing can be done. It can make you feel less helpless because you're not so alone. Someone else knows what you're going through and understands how you feel. Someone else can help you see that what is happening is not your fault, and there is no need for you to feel guilty about it. They will reassure you that it is absolutely normal for you to feel angry.

WHAT WILL HAPPEN IF YOU ASK FOR HELP?

Most youngsters feel that when they've made the decision, the situation will change and that will be the end of it. They think the adults they trust will take over, and they will not have to face the person who has abused them again. But sometimes it isn't as easy as that. Even if everyone believes what you tell them, the person who has abused you –   ▷

whoever they are – cannot be punished until a court decides they are guilty. To prove guilt, the police have to check out everyone's story, and to collect evidence to support what you have told them.

You will be asked to make a statement. If you've been sexually abused within the past 24 hours, or if you have been marked or bruised by someone who has hit you, you may need to be examined by a doctor. Usually a police doctor does this, but you can ask to be examined by your own family doctor, or a doctor of your own sex.

Sometimes, even though they really believe everything you have said, the police don't bring charges against the person who has abused you because they know that there just isn't enough evidence to convict them. Sometimes they do bring charges, and you then have to appear in court to give evidence. Even then, it may happen that the person is still not convicted, because although no one thinks you're lying, it's still impossible to prove the truth. You'll probably feel very angry and bitter if this happens, and feel that it just wasn't worth telling anyone. If you feel this way, remember that the police won't forget what you've told them; by telling, you've probably prevented the abuser from doing the same thing to you again, or abusing someone else.

> *"I thought for a long time that was happening was OK*
> *because Dad said that it was a game all fathers played with their*
> *sons, a secret game that only men knew about. He said that*
> *anyway no one would believe me if I did tell."*
>
> James, 14

MY BEST FRIEND IS BEING ABUSED

Sometimes a friend may confide in you that they're being abused. Or you may suspect something is wrong, even though he or she doesn't tell you, or denies it. What can you do? Try to be sympathetic and let them know that you care about them and believe them. That's what they need. Give them an opening so that they can talk if they want to, maybe saying something like, "I thought you were very quiet/looking a bit sad today. Is anything wrong? Do you want to talk about it?"

If they do tell you they're being abused, try to persuade them to tell an adult they trust as well. Offer to go with them for moral support if you like. Knowing that a friend is in trouble like this may be a heavy responsibility. If they refuse to tell anyone else, you'll probably feel that you want to do it for them. But you should wait until they feel ready to do something themselves (unless you know for sure they're in real physical danger). Your friend needs to feel that he or she has some control over the situation, and asking for help should be a personal decision. Talking about what is happening with you is the first big step. If you help your friend to talk, you're doing all you can.

IF YOU'VE BEEN RAPED

If someone forces you to have sexual intercourse against your will, it is rape. It doesn't matter if the person is a complete stranger, or someone you know well, or perhaps even your own boyfriend. Most rape victims are female, but boys can be raped, too. Most rapists are male. Anyone of any age can be raped.

IF IT HAPPENS TO YOU

If you've been raped, your first reaction may be not to tell anybody. You may just want to get home, take a bath and change your clothes, and pretend that nothing has happened. But if you do this, it means that the person responsible may go unpunished even though he has committed a very serious crime. This may leave you feeling very bitter and angry, so think about doing these things instead:

- **Tell your parents or a relative or close friend**. They should report the rape to the police immediately. You will then have a medical examination; this may be done by a police doctor, but you can ask for your own family doctor if you wish, or for a doctor of your own sex. It's important that this is done as soon as possible, before you have had a bath and within 24 hours of the rape.
- **Keep the clothes you were wearing for the police to examine**. Together with the doctor's report, they may provide important evidence that will make it much easier for the police to prosecute the person who raped you.
- **If you notice any other symptoms** within the next day or two – a discharge, itching, soreness, or bruising, for example – go back to your doctor for treatment so that these, too, can be included in the medical report.
- **Try not to be alone over the next day or so**. You may feel very distressed, and someone who really cares about you should stay with you, look after you, and perhaps even sleep in your room for a night or two.
- **Talk to someone**. However terrible the experience, most people find they can leave it behind more easily if they can talk to someone about what has happened, and about how angry and upset they feel. Girls and women often feel guilty about being raped, even though they have done nothing wrong; they may feel dirty, as though they have been somehow "spoiled". Talking about the rape is often the best way to deal with these difficult feelings. Your doctor may arrange for you to talk to a professional counsellor, and there are now counselling services for men and boys who have been raped. You may want to be "brave", but bottling up what has happened only makes it harder to feel good about yourself. Talking about it will probably help you recover and get on with your life.

SEXUALLY TRANSMITTED DISEASES

In spite of all the publicity surrounding AIDS, sexually transmitted diseases (sometimes called STDs) are on the increase. This isn't just because people are sleeping around more, although this is part of the problem. It's also because most people are frightened and ashamed if they think they've become infected. The idea of going along to your family doctor with a problem like this may be unthinkable, and it takes a lot of courage even to go along to a special clinic where you won't know anyone. So people tend to keep quiet about it. Even if they seek treatment themselves, they may feel too embarrassed to tell anyone they've slept with and may have infected, and so the infection keeps on spreading...
To reduce the risk of catching an STD:

- **Don't have casual sex with people you don't know.** Who knows where they've been, or what they've done? You might be lucky and just catch something unpleasant but treatable. But if your sexual partner is HIV-positive, you may be risking your life.
- **Stick to one steady partner.** This is your best protection. The more partners you have, the greater your chance of being infected. If your partner makes love to other people besides you, they risk infection which they may then pass on to you.
- **Use a condom if you do make love.** This reduces the risk of infection (including AIDS) as well as of pregnancy – but it doesn't abolish it altogether.

SYMPTOMS AND TREATMENT

If you develop any of the following symptoms, see your doctor, or go to a special clinic as soon as possible (clinics are usually listed in the telephone directory under the heading Venereal Disease, or VD). Don't panic! All STDs can be treated. Nowadays people who become infected with HIV can be given treatment that greatly slows the progression of the disease, and many new drugs are under trial. Symptoms include:

- Pain/discomfort when passing urine.
- Discharge from the penis.
- Discharge from the vagina that is in any way unusual: heavier or a different colour than usual, causing soreness or itching, or smelling unpleasant.
- Pain or itching around the genital area.
- Lumps, sores, blisters, or warts on the genitals.

Do remember the following:

- **Tell your partner**, and anyone else you may have had sex with. They, too, should have a check-up in case you have passed on the infection.
- **Don't assume that, if symptoms disappear of their own accord, you are cured.** Sometimes infections do clear up without treatment, but usually there is just a symptom-free period before the disease becomes obvious again.
- **Don't have sex with anyone** until your doctor has said you're not infected.

QUESTIONS AND ANSWERS ABOUT AIDS

- **What is AIDS?** AIDS stands for Acquired Immune Deficiency Syndrome. It is caused by two types of an infectious virus (HIV-1 and HIV-2), which gradually destroy the body's ability to defend itself against some infections (like one form of pneumonia) and types of cancer (such as a form of skin cancer, Kaposi's sarcoma). The virus is passed from one person to another in semen or blood.
- **What does it mean to he HIV-positive?** If someone is HIV-positive, they have been infected with the virus that causes AIDS. Most people who are HIV-positive go on to develop AIDS, but may not do so for a long time, sometimes for up to 10 years after infection. During this time they may feel perfectly well and have no symptoms, but can still infect other people.
- **What does an AIDS test involve, and if there's no cure, is there any point in having it?** The test only involves taking a blood sample, and anyone who thinks that might have been infected should have the test done. Unfortunately the test doesn't become positive as soon as you become infected, but this will be explained to you. Obviously a negative result will be a great relief. If you are found to be HIV-positive you will be told about the disease in more detail and helped to understand what it means for you. In the past ten years the drugs available have been improved and already they greatly slow the progress of the illness. HIV infection is not yet curable but it is controllable in many cases.
- **Why should I worry? Only gay men catch AIDS.** That's what people used to think. It's true that, in developed countries, gay men and people who inject drugs and share needles are most likely to become infected. We now know that anyone – man or woman – can catch AIDS if they have sex with someone who is infected.

YOUR PARENTS AND YOUR SEX LIFE

Your sex life is your own affair, but there is just a chance your parents may think it's theirs. Certainly it's an area that many parents like to think they have some influence or control over, simply because they're only too aware of the risks involved and they want to protect you from being hurt. It's also something they may feel uncomfortable about themselves, so it's only good manners not to parade your sex life too obviously in front of them if you know they'll find it hard to cope with. For example, if you know it would upset your parents to have you sleeping under their roof with a boyfriend or girlfriend who's coming to stay, don't put them in this position: make it clear you'll have separate bedrooms and save them the embarrassment of pussyfooting around the issue not knowing quite how to ask you. It takes a very laid-back parent to cope with taking early-morning breakfast to a daughter in bed with her boyfriend.

"I THINK I MIGHT BE GAY"

The first sexual feelings you have in your teens can be very strong. But they won't necessarily be felt for anyone of the opposite sex. Almost everyone at some time or another in their teens finds themselves attracted to, or having a "crush"on, someone of their own sex. It's even more likely to happen if you go to a single-sex school and don't meet many people of the opposite sex, or are so shy and self-conscious with them that you try to avoid meeting them. Lots of boys have sex together without being gay – they may masturbate in company, masturbate each other, even have anal sex; none of this behaviour is proof that the individual is gay. It may be simply a combination of high sex drive and what's available.

You can have quite passionate feelings for a friend, but this does not mean that you're gay. Nearly always this is just a "practice" stage of sexual development. You grow out of it, but not all at once; you may find you feel attracted to your own sex when you're spending most time with them, to the opposite sex when you have a chance to meet them.

However, quite a lot of people – it may be as many as 1 in 10 (rather more men than women) – are gay. For them, homosexual feelings aren't just a stage they're going through. They go on feeling attracted mainly to people of their own sex. People who are gay usually realize this sometime during adolescence (although some remember always having strong feelings for members of their own sex, or feeling somehow "different"). It may not be until you're 19 or 20, however, that you can say with real certainty that you're not going to change and that you're gay.

Don't feel that you have to decide right now whether you're one thing or another. In any case, it's not necessarily an "either/or" choice. It's quite possible to lie somewhere along the line between people who are attracted only to the opposite sex and people who are attracted only to their own. It may be several years before you know just where you belong. Some people remain attracted to both sexes all their adult lives.

If you do realize that you're gay, it might make you feel very unhappy with yourself, especially if you've been brought up in a family where homosexuality is thought of as something dreadful, or you have come across people (and unfortunately there are many) who are prejudiced against gay people. You probably already know it isn't anything you have any choice about or any control over. Being straight or being gay is as much part of who you are as your height or the colour of your hair.

However, you do have a choice about whether to try to hide it completely or to suppress your feelings (which can cause a lot of stress and unhappiness), or whether to accept yourself for what you are, and hope that others will, too.

One decision you will have to make is whether to tell your parents. Most parents who love their children can accept the fact that they're gay. Even so, they'll almost certainly be upset at first, just because they do love you. Most of us can't help thinking that there's only one real way to be happy: our own way. If your parents have been happily married and have brought up a family – or even if they haven't – they may feel that unless you follow this common pattern, you won't be happy. They know (whatever their own feelings) that gay people are often given a hard time and treated unfairly by other people, and they won't want this to happen to you. For gay men who do not practise safe sex, there is the additional risk of contracting AIDS; this is bound to worry them, too.

No matter how difficult, there are still advantages in telling your parents and not having to keep a very important part of your life secret. You will be making an important step in being honest and accepting yourself, and you will certainly enjoy love and sex more if you make the best possible choice for yourself. If you do decide to tell them:

- Wait until you are sure of your own feelings.
- Show them that you're happy about being gay. If they're reassured about this, they will find your choice much easier to accept and be happy with.

TWO MYTHS AND WORRIES ABOUT SEXUALITY

MYTH
If you have an erection, you have to ejaculate or
it's painful/uncomfortable/dangerous.

TRUTH
Every erection subsides of its own accord in the end, whether or not a boy "comes". Boys have been known to blackmail girls ("It's all due to you, so it's only fair..."). An erection may be uncomfortable but it is not dangerous or life-threatening, and every erection subsides in the end, whether or not there has been an orgasm.

MYTH
Masturbation is harmful and/or sinful.

TRUTH
Masturbation won't harm you, and if you think it's a matter for guilt, then about 90 per cent of the population are guilty; it's something almost everybody does, even if they are reluctant to admit it.

12

LIFE IN SCHOOL

"

What should make us reflect about the educational system are the large numbers of young people who do well, or reasonably well, in life's business both prior to and after the school years, but who during those years — for a variety of reasons — are judged to be incompetent or poorly 'adjusted'.

"

Martin Herbert, Living with Teenagers

ALMOST A THIRD OF YOUR CHILD'S LIFE is spent in school. Apart from the family, school is the most important influence in your child's life, shaping friendships, successes, and failures.

Not all schools are good schools. Some have higher rates of truancy and delinquency, and more disruptive and badly behaved children than others. Not all these differences can be explained away by saying that these schools take in more difficult or deprived children. The school itself provides an environment that will influence its pupils one way or another, and there are clues that will help you predict how a particular school may influence your child's behaviour and achievement.

When you are choosing a school, what should you look for? A good "mix" of children (in both background and ability) seems to work best. The quality of the teachers and the way in which they manage their classes is vitally important, too. Specifically, these are some of the things you need to look for, and some of the questions you need to ask.

The size of a school, or even the size of classes, makes little difference to the academic achievements of a school. Buildings don't need to be new or spacious, but they should look as though somebody cares. Are classrooms and corridors decorated with pictures and posters? Are the walls kept clean of graffiti, and broken furniture or windows quickly repaired? Is the atmosphere warm and do the pupils seem cheerful?

Left: Children who are bullied need to be reassured that there is nothing wrong with them — it's the bully who is at fault — and that you can help and protect them.

SCHOOL DISCIPLINE

• **Does the school expect the children to have high standards in both work and behaviour?** Children tend to live up (or down) to what is expected of them.

• **How does the school deal with bullying?** A school should have a clear policy to prevent it and to help children who have been bullied (see p.164).

• **What is its truancy rate?** A high rate may be an indication of student dissatisfaction and poor overall academic achievement. The school may be legally obliged to tell you its truancy rate if you ask.

• **What is the attitude of the children themselves?** It's difficult for any child to work well (or indeed, to behave well) if the other children place no value on academic achievement, or if their whole ethos is anti-authoritarian. It helps if you know pupils at the school.

• **Does school discipline rely more on "carrots" than "sticks": are praise and encouragement used to reinforce good behaviour rather than punishment for bad?** It may seem easier and more effective for a school to rely heavily on punishment to maintain discipline: fear of sanctions can be a powerful inducement to good behaviour, but a school that relies on too harsh or too frequent punishment doesn't always make pupils want to work hard and behave well (which should, after all, be the primary aim of discipline). Instead, this attitude tends to produce children with a negative attitude, a determination to outwit authority or to "get their own back", and a school with an uneasy and unhappy atmosphere.

• **Do the teachers seem remote and isolated from the children?** Good teachers should be able to establish respectful relationships with the children they teach – not too friendly but not loftily indifferent or callous either. Teachers are the adult "models" your child will see day by day. If a teacher is aggressive, bad-tempered, or even violent in order to maintain control or in response to a difficult situation, you can expect the pupils to react in much the same way.

• **Does the school provide an opportunity for parents to meet staff regularly and to discuss their child's progress?** Parents should be encouraged to contact the school if they're worried about their children or they feel their child has a problem. Sometimes academic problems and discipline are interrelated.

CLASSROOM MANAGEMENT TECHNIQUES

You probably won't have an opportunity to "sit in" and observe classes to see how effectively teachers manage their classes, but talking to other children who already go to the school can give you quite a good picture of the way things actually work. These are some of the questions you might ask:

- **Do lessons begin and end on time?**
- **Are pupils praised when they do well?**
- **Are they given adequate feedback about their performance?** Are essays returned on time? It's not unknown for teachers to hang onto books, unmarked, for several weeks; this is inexcusable when the child is supposed to give work in on time and wants to know if and where he or she has gone wrong in doing it.
- **Do teachers give most of their attention** to a few individual pupils so that they lose touch with the class as a whole?
- **Is much good teaching time** spent in "secondary" activities, i.e., setting up equipment, handing out books, disciplinary measures?

NON-ACADEMIC OPPORTUNITIES

Every child needs to succeed at something. You should therefore find out if the school provides a wide range of activities and opportunities so that every child finds something they can enjoy and learn to do reasonably well.

This is especially important if your child is not particularly academic. It is all too easy for such children to feel they have failed at school because success and failure are judged so much in terms of examination results. Do check that your child will also have the chance to take part in music, sport, art, drama, or whatever else he or she is interested in. Check, too, that achievement in these areas is valued by the school (see *The Non-academic Child*, p.158).

RESPONSIBILITY

Try to find out whether the school tries to give most children a chance to take responsibility as class monitors, for example, or in helping to run school societies or organize school events. This can boost their self-esteem, and is often a very effective way of making them grow up and improve their general behaviour. Even a youngster who is very anti-authoritarian is more likely to identify with "the system" if he or she is given some responsibility within it, and yet in many schools, responsibility and status are used exclusively as a reward for "doing well", rather than as an inducement to do better.

"My mother won't believe that I can only work when I'm listening to my Walkman or with the TV on. I don't really watch it but it kind of keeps me company and helps me concentrate. I can't work when it's too quiet."

Tanya, 14

ISSUE: MIXED OR SINGLE-SEX SCHOOLS

"School should be a miniature copy of the world as we would love to have it."

The most remarkable thing about that statement is that it was made by the headmaster of a single-sex boys school!

If you think of school as preparation for living in an adult world where there are two sexes, there are powerful arguments for coeducation. Boys and girls can get to know each other in the everyday atmosphere of classroom life, with a lack of self-consciousness that just isn't possible for teenagers when they first meet on a purely social level. It's possible to learn more about each other on a very realistic level, too how the opposite sex thinks and reacts, how they respond to teasing or changes of mood. All this can be especially valuable for children from small families or those where all the children are the same sex.

Sexual behaviour The main fear parents seem to have about mixed schools is that they may lead to earlier or freer sexual behaviour. This fear probably has very little basis in reality. Girls and boys in mixed schools do inevitably learn much more about each other's sexuality. There is a good deal of sexual discussion and a free interchange of dirty jokes, but probably very little action. To a large extent, teenage boys and girls sharing a classroom have one very effective built-in safety device: the fact that they're the same age. Throughout most of the teenage years, girls are far more emotionally mature than boys of their own age, and so, although classroom romances do, of course, occur, most relationships are on a friendly rather than a sexual basis. Girls are much more likely to think their contemporaries are "too immature" to have a crush on, and usually become interested in older boys, or develop crushes on younger male members of staff. These relationships follow the same pattern as any other teenage relationships: the people involved will start to have sex when they're ready for it, and not before.

Behaviour Most teachers are overwhelmingly in favour of mixed schools. They report that such schools have a friendlier, homelier atmosphere, and that relationships between staff and pupils are better and more relaxed. There may be fewer problems of behaviour and discipline, too. Each sex, perhaps without really thinking about it, tends to behave rather better in front of the other.

Girls and academic achievement Are there academic advantages or disadvantages in coeducation? Here the pattern is not quite so clear, but it does seem that – at the moment – if there are advantages they may lie with the boys, whereas if there are disadvantages they are more likely to affect the girls.

Studies have shown that in any mixed class, teachers – both male or female – pay more attention to the boys. Even more interestingly, if teachers are instructed to give exactly equal attention to both boys and girls and their classes are then watched by an observer, the impression is that "too much" attention is being given to the girls. It's as if there's a generally accepted and scarcely conscious assumption that it's right and proper for girls to play a passive classroom role. Although things are slowly changing, a parent and daughter may well ask what effect these attitudes may have on the girl's level of achievement.

• In a mixed class, girls may not be given the attention they need unless they seek it. For many girls this may be difficult, especially as they seem to be less competitive than boys (they may have been taught to be) and don't always flourish in an atmosphere where they have to push themselves forward and demand their share of attention. If they are shy or self-conscious, they may be overlooked altogether.

• Girls are sometimes afraid of appearing too bright in case this makes them seem unfeminine. Because academic achievement may not be seen as something to make them popular, clever girls may have to learn not to defer to less able boys, and not to dampen down their own intellectual ability and interest in a subject.

> "My parents wanted me to go to a mixed school for my last two years. I wanted to go and I enjoyed it in the end but it took me almost the whole of the first term to get used to it. To begin with I found it hard to ask when I didn't understand something in class or to answer a question when the teacher asked me. All the time I was trying not to draw attention to myself or worrying about what the boys would think of me. I think I might have got better grades if I'd stayed in my old all-girls' school."
>
> Annabelle, 18

• Girls in a mixed class may sometimes be treated more gently – especially by male staff – and less may be expected of them. Boys may be given less leeway if they don't do well, and made to pull their socks up and told that they could do better. We all tend to rise – or fall – to the level expected of us, and chivalrous teachers who "go easy" on girls may not be encouraging them to do their best.

• Again, although attitudes are changing, girls still seem less likely to prepare themselves for success in the way that most boys do. Even if they have done well at school, they seem to have lower self-esteem than boys, and do not expect to be as successful in adulthood. When boys are asked to rate their chances of success in later life, they tend to take a more optimistic view of their chances (regardless of their level of academic ability) than girls do. Your daughter may need additional encouragement to overcome this "learned helplessness".

For all these reasons, you and your daughter may decide that, if she's naturally confident or pushy, she may do well, if not better, in mixed classes. However, if you have a daughter who is naturally rather shy and diffident and tends to lack self-confidence, it may be that she will feel more comfortable, and therefore will be better able to fulfil her true potential, in an all-girls' school.

HOMEWORK

It's probably true to say that parents tend to worry more about homework than their offspring do, perhaps because they see it as a predictor of future exam success (something most teenagers don't worry too much about until approximately three months before the exam). You can remind a teenager to the point of nagging that there is homework to be done. You can encourage them, offer help, show interest, but that is merely a matter of leading a horse to water. Most find their own ways of doing the bare minimum they can get away with until something (fear, awakened interest, or belated ambition) motivates them to pull more stops out. You have to remember that, while it matters to you that your children make a good impression on teachers, it often doesn't matter all that much to them; it is their peers they want to impress.

Adolescents devise many curious ways of working independently: they may believe they can "only" work last thing at night, that they can "only" work when plugged into a personal stereo, or even watching TV. You have to allow for the element of self deception because it's important that they find their own way of working. If they truly believe that watching (or listening) with half a mind enables them to concentrate better with the other half, it doesn't much matter whether it's true or not: it's become a magical ploy to help them get through something they may not particularly enjoy. It won't help them to do it well, but it may be what they need to do it at all.

At boarding school, time for homework is built into the day and there are fewer distractions, so it gets done. The student who's working at home, imposing his or her own self-discipline with an independent timetable, has a much harder time.

• **Help teenagers to plan homework** and to work out a timetable if they seem to be disorganized and never manage to finish.

• **Provide somewhere quiet for them to work** and set aside time when they're free of any family chores and commitments to do it.

• **Make sure they have a place to keep books, pens, paper, rulers** – a good environment in which to concentrate may contribute to better work.

• **Encourage them to ask the teacher for help** the following day if they don't understand an assignment. Asking for help is better than struggling and falling behind.

MOTIVATION

"Chris just isn't motivated."

This common refrain is often heard from parents and teachers who may then attempt to bribe, encourage, and nag. However, the motivation to work ultimately has to come from the adolescent; indeed, many teenagers find their own ways of doing the bare minimum they can get away with until something motivates them to do more. What are the main things to consider if you want to help?

- **Environment** is important because it's much easier to work hard in a school where the ethos is to do well, where everybody else is working diligently, and where academic achievement is admired.
- **Fear** is a powerful motivator, but unfortunately it is not a very effective one because it usually operates too late, generating only last-minute panic revision. In a teenager's timescale of life events, next year's exams are a long way away, and not nearly as important as this week's pop concert.
- **Interest and ambition** are, of course, what parents hope will motivate their children. The lucky ones have a clear aim, which gives them the energy to work towards it, but not every teenager knows what he or she wants to do, and it's not easy to work hard when you're not quite sure what you're working for. Many just don't experience the spark that awakens interest and ambition. Often they do so belatedly, after they have left school, so don't lose hope altogether.

There are a few things you can do if adolescents seem to lack motivation:

- **Don't give the impression you're washing your hands of them**. School is not their last chance or their only chance. Many non-motivated teenagers are late developers who return to further education as mature students. Many others have talents that they may not even have discovered, let alone had a chance to develop, at school. When they have something to aim for and feel commited to, you may be surprised at how hard they're prepared to work.
- **Be guided by your children's abilities**, what they think they're good at, and what teachers think they're good at. If a child loathes a subject or has absolutely no aptitude for it, don't push, however "useful" you think it would be to him or her.

DROPPING OUT

What happens when a young person below school-leaving age becomes disenchanted with school and goes absent without leave a lot of the time, hanging out with kids a year or so older who are unemployed? So long as someone is required to attend school, they need to be encouraged to get something out of it, even if they do resent the rules and restrictions. Even if the teenager is dead set against working for exams, some of the topics taught are likely to have some practical value.

Possibly changing the subjects being studied may help. Talk to the school, negotiate, but don't ignore your youngster's negative attitudes towards school because dropping out can lead to all sorts of other social problems. Many children who play truant regularly often become delinquent (see p.232). If your teenager complains about needing or wanting more money, a part-time job at the weekend may help. Sometimes a transfer to a different school may give adolescents a renewed impetus to continue their education, but there is little to be gained from forcing a young adult to stay on if he or she is determined to leave at the earliest possible opportunity.

CASE HISTORY: FED UP WITH SCHOOL

Richard was fed up with school and thought the work was boring and pointless. He had friends who had left at 16 and were earning "good money" and wanted to join them.

"All these exams and qualifications are rubbish nowadays. Everyone knows that university graduates have as much trouble getting jobs as anyone else. You can get work if you've got drive and some contacts. Qualifications don't matter."

"You don't seem to understand that I find all that school stuff irrelevant and stupid. And I'm fed up with having to ask you for money all the time."

"People who got qualified and took jobs for a lifetime with Ford or a bank still got the boot, didn't they? I want to start living now."
Richard, 16

"Why don't you stay on for your qualifications so you'll have them behind you to back you up? And in another year or two the economy may pick up."

"Those jobs your friends have got are dead ends and useless — working in a disco or selling fruit and vegetables, those aren't jobs for a lifetime."

"You may be 'living' for a few months, but you should try to think about the rest of your life."
David, 43

COMMENT ABOUT BEING FED UP WITH SCHOOL

Most schools realize that you cannot treat young adults as children, and do give them a greater degree of freedom, and often some latitude over dress. There is little point in insisting a young adult attends school if he or she doesn't want to. The likely outcome is poor attendance and a wasted year or more. Richard can try his luck in the depressed job market, and he may be lucky. People who leave school at 16 sometimes become successful entrepreneurs. And if things turn out badly, he can take up his education later, perhaps even as a mature student.

"All my boring relations are always on at me to read this and read that. They're only interested in books, and spend their weekends reading newspapers and magazines. They don't seem to understand that most people don't care about books and exams, and prefer going out to staying at home. I'm bored with school and can't wait to leave."
Cathy, 16

LOW ACHIEVERS

Few children do quite as well at school as their parents think they should. Usually this is because adolescents have a natural tendency to do as little work as they can get away with. Sometimes it's because parents are over-ambitious for their children and have unrealistic expectations of them. Occasionally it's because the child has some specific difficulty – perhaps dyslexia, for example – which limits his or her achievements.

Whenever teenagers who seem to you to be bright and alert, and reasonably intelligent when you talk to them, fail to live up to what you believe they're capable of, it's very important for you to discover why. In this situation, teachers almost always tend to blame the child ("He's just lazy", they may say, or "She's inattentive in class"), while the youngster usually blames the staff or the subject ("The teaching's lousy" or "It's all so boring"). What should you believe?

Many adolescents may be lazy, but if they're interested and motivated, they usually manage to do enough work to pull through (even if they don't achieve academic brilliance). Moreover, there are teachers who are undoubtedly poor at their job although if a teenager complains that none of the teachers is any good, it may be a case of a bad workman blaming his tools.

Some children aren't academic high-flyers.
Rather than nagging and arguing, it may be
better to accept this fact and try to maintain
a good relationship with your child.

ASSESSING YOU CHILD'S CAPABILITIES

In a few cases it's difficult for either parents or teachers to assess what a youngster is really capable of. Adolescents may sometimes give a false impression of their true abilities if their "verbal" skills – the ability to talk fluently and shape thoughts – are much greater than their comprehension. For example, a boy may be able to read a passage reasonably quickly but not fully understand what he's reading; he may be so bright and alert in class that his teachers expect the same facility in his written work. Some children do have such "specific learning deficits"; these can be bewildering and distressing for both parents and the children themselves because they feel that they should be able to do the things that their classmates are doing. They know that they're failing and cannot really understand why.

One of the signs that should make you suspect that the problem is that your youngster *cannot* do what is expected – rather than that he or she *will* not – is that behaviour deteriorates, too. Failure at school and bad behaviour are very closely linked.

If you're not sure whether you or the school are expecting too much (or indeed, too little) of your son or daughter, specialized testing by an educational psychologist might be helpful. You should have your child assessed by a psychologist attached to your local education authority. If waiting lists are long, testing can be done privately, although it is expensive. Few psychologists nowadays will give their results in terms of "IQ", or "intelligence quotient"; this is an all-round score that purports to give a general guide to a person's ability, but tends to mask the fact that performance is weaker in some areas than in others. Instead, the psychologist will use the results from a whole battery of tests to indicate the youngster's individual strengths and weaknesses, and to suggest appropriate remedial help.

*"Cathy doesn't really seem to find academic work at all interesting;
she does her homework but always gets average or poor marks. I can't
understand it; her two brothers are both doing well at university."*
Jack, 49

THE NON-ACADEMIC CHILD

Some children are intellectually gifted; some are not. You may have a child who has a pleasing personality, who seems to have no psychological problems, but who is simply slow to learn and finds books hard going. This may be difficult for you to accept if the rest of the family, including you as parents, have been high achievers.

Talk things over with the school; if their assessment confirms your own (that your child is not academically inclined), then you should accept the facts and help him or her plan a worthwhile education programme. There are plenty of occupations that do not require a university degree or a mass of exam passes. Adolescents can only choose an occupation from those they know something about. Schools often can arrange visits to local employers, and many commercial and government concerns arrange open days. Try to find out what is available and give your son or daughter the chance to attend. He or she probably won't be very interested in pamphlets and other literature, but may be stimulated by something that he or she has seen.

THE CHILD WHO WORKS TOO HARD

There are a few children who concentrate on work to the detriment of other aspects of life: friends, hobbies, out-of-school activities. Sometimes this is because they're over-conscientious, or over-anxious to please their parents. Occasionally it's because they're very gifted in a particular area and genuinely have little interest in anything else (see *Gifted Children*, p.159). Sometimes, though, it can be a sign that a child is failing to make friends and is using work as a substitute. In this case, devotion to work is not a matter for parental satisfaction but a signal that help is needed (see *Issue: No Friends*, p.104).

GIFTED CHILDREN

Kate, at three years old, had a reading and maths age of 12. She not only played the piano, but composed her own music, and could understand and discuss harmony. By anybody's standards, Kate was a gifted child. Kate's kind of intelligence, showing itself at an early age and way beyond the normal range, with an extraordinary ability in one particular field, is rare, but it's what most people mean when they talk about giftedness.

More familiar, although still exceptional, are children like Sam. At 15 Sam took ten O-levels, passed them all at A grade, and later passed three A-levels, also at A grade, before going on to university. Here he took a first, and went on to do a PhD. Sam was in his school cricket and football teams, and played cricket for his university. But perhaps the most interesting thing about Sam is that he achieved everything so effortlessly. He worked because his work interested him, but even to get his first, he didn't have to work particularly hard. "I kept thinking things would get more difficult," he told a friend, "but they didn't. Everything was easy."

Gifted children seem to fall naturally into three groups. There are those with one outstanding natural ability – perhaps they are superb swimmers or gymnasts. We can describe about the top two per cent of children in any field as being "gifted" in this way. Then there are the "all-rounders", children like Sam, for whom "everything is easy"; they're bright academically, and successful at most things they tackle. These children also tend to be taller and healthier, and to have a wide range of interests, but they do not necessarily show the unusual ability in a particular field that would make them truly remarkable. Only a very few children, perhaps about one child in 200, has Kate's kind of phenomenal ability, fascinating just because it is so far outside the normal run of most people's experience.

ADVANTAGES AND DISADVANTAGES

It may seem an obvious advantage to be gifted, but in some ways it can be a mixed blessing. Children like Sam probably do have an advantage in all sorts of ways. They are clever, but not so sensationally clever that they seem "different". They usually get along well with people, are well adjusted, and successful. Perhaps the only real disadvantage these children suffer is that things go almost too easily for them, so they may not acquire the protective "inoculation" against failure that most of us get from a very early age when we learn that occasional setbacks are an inevitable part of life, and are forced to find strategies to deal with them to restore our self-esteem when they occur. The child – or adult – who has never had to cope with failure may take it all the harder when it eventually occurs.

One-sided development Children who have a single outstanding talent are not in quite the same advantageous position. Their ability often leads them to concentrate on this one activity to the exclusion of everything else. Sports, dancing, and drama are particularly likely to lead to this kind of one-sided development because the training involved is often too intense to leave room for other interests. It may also be so time consuming that the youngster has no social life and misses out on a whole stage of adolescent development. Perhaps unexpectedly, very gifted young athletes tend to be unpopular with their schoolmates, especially if they're swimmers, gymnasts, or tennis players who are competing more for themselves than as part of a team.

Some gifted people, mathematicians especially, tend to "burn out" when they are still quite young, and may be at a social and personal disadvantage if they have not had the motivation or opportunity to develop in other directions.

Difficulties with friends Exceptional children may have problems in fitting in to a world full of unexceptional people. Very clever children often seem self-sufficient, just because they are usually involved in so many interests and activities. They may get on better with adults, and tend to seek out adult company, and yet they still need friends of their own age. The ability to get along with people is part and parcel of their development, but it is not always easy for these children to make friends.

> *Children are conventional creatures. They tend to be suspicious of anyone who is "different", or who does not fit in. Some gifted children realize this danger themselves, and tend to act down to the level of the children they're with, deliberately achieving less than they could.*

ACHIEVING THE RIGHT BALANCE

Giftedness does not necessarily run hand in hand with achievement or success. There are probably plenty of gifted children who do not develop their full potential, while others, not perhaps so naturally gifted, shine because they're highly motivated and have a great drive to succeed. Often it is parents who can make or mar a child's natural gifts by the challenge, encouragement, and opportunity they provide.

• **Don't cling tenaciously to your view of what is right for your gifted child.** Encourage him or her to discover and to develop interests independent of your advice, and to find his or her own direction.

• **Don't label your child as "gifted"**: he or she is a whole personality. Labels raise expectations. If the child's "giftedness" becomes a job description, people may expect him or her to be good at everything, and to be clever all the time; this is something that even the cleverest child may not always want to live up to.

• **Don't keep predicting a starry future.** If children are always aware of your high expectations, they may eventually opt out altogether, feeling that they have reached their limits and can no longer cope with the constant pressure to achieve.

• **Help your youngster not to feel different.** Encourage him or her to lead a normal social life and follow normal adolescent pursuits.

CLASHES WITH AUTHORITY

In his book *Living with Teenagers*, Martin Herbert[1] observed that pupils are most likely to misbehave with teachers who have offended their dignity, self-respect, and self-esteem. Pupils themselves describe a "good" teacher as one who is able to:

– Maintain control while still being friendly

– Have a laugh

– Treat students fairly and with respect

– Be understanding

– Allow students a measure of freedom

– Explain things clearly

Obviously, not every teacher is going to measure up to this standard, but then neither will every pupil react to the poor teachers they meet by being disruptive.

Personality clashes with one particular teacher can't always be avoided. In the long run it may be more useful if you try to help your child not to overreact rather than do battle on his or her behalf. If the youngster has some specific complaint, however, or feels that he or she is being very unfairly treated, do take this up with the teacher at the next parents' evening. More generalized misbehaviour with a good many teachers (such

CASE HISTORY: A GIFTED CHILD

Twelve-year-old Daniel was a very intelligent child and a brilliant mathematician. His teachers felt that Daniel was so obsessed with maths that he was neglecting everything else, and tried to persuade him to give more attention to his other subjects. But Daniel refused.

"Daniel's teachers have told us and him that he should branch out a bit, pursue other subjects, but he just won't hear of it. We're afraid he'll become too lonely, too aloof, or maybe fail to use his great abilities."

Anna, 47

"My friends don't mind I'm better at maths than anyone else – they even call me 'professor' in a friendly way. But I'm worried that if I do much better than everyone else in all the subjects, they'll say I'm stuck up and weird and I'll lose all my friends."

Daniel, 12

COMMENT ABOUT A GIFTED CHILD

Daniel has probably made an accurate assessment. In any event, he is unlikely to be persuaded to change his mind quickly. At this stage the crucial thing is for him to be happy at school and to continue to fit in and feel that he's normal, not an oddity. Broadening his educational achievements can come later; it's more important that he should have normal social relations with his school friends.

as answering back or not doing homework) is something you should discuss with the school as soon as you become aware of it. Parents are often afraid they will gain a reputation for being "difficult" if they step in to try to sort out their youngster's problems with the school, and that this will make things even worse. This can happen, but it shouldn't if you make it clear that what you're interested in is sorting out the problem, not laying blame at anyone's door.

First try to find out first exactly how your child is misbehaving, why this is happening, which teachers he or she gets on badly with, and those with whom there seem to be no problems. It does very often happen in schools that a child gets a reputation as a trouble-maker that is hard to live down (even if it is partially deserved);

GIFTED CHILDREN AT SCHOOL

Schools are geared to dealing with "average" children and do not always find it easy to cope with gifted children who may not be able to make the most of their talents without expert tuition and special provisions for learning. Schools don't always have the time or flexibility to adjust the curriculum to "stretch" these children a little more by giving them more difficult or stimulating work to do.

Unless teachers are very confident, they may find it threatening to have to deal with a very clever child. Indeed, teachers do not always even recognize that children might be gifted, perhaps not surprisingly in view of the tendency some bright children have to play themselves down when they're with other children. Sometimes a youngster is dismissed as "too clever by half", or a "show-off". In fact, a teacher's view of a child's ability may be influenced by all sorts of things, for example, whether they (and the work they turn in) are neat and orderly, whether they're "easy" (i.e., well behaved) or whether they behave badly (which sometimes happens if a child becomes bored because he or she isn't given sufficiently challenging work). Adolescent girls who are very clever and in a mixed class at school may find themselves at a particular social disadvantage, and often deliberately underplay their abilities (see *Issue: Mixed or Single-sex Schools*, p.152); your daughter may need your encouragement not to feel this way.

Sometimes a school's solution to the problem of a very clever child is to move them up a year, but this is not necessarily the best thing for every child. Those who are very self confident and grown-up for their age may take it in their stride. Others may not find it so easy: they may not be able to play on equal terms with older children and feel left out. In adolescence, this can matter especially to boys, whose self-confidence and self-image can suffer greatly if they're physically smaller and weaker than everyone else in their class. It may be better to let children stay with their own age group, or, if possible, to join an older class for just one or two subjects. You may want to find out about school activities and interests which might provide the extra challenge and opportunities they need.

in these situations, even if the youngster does make efforts in the future, they often go largely unremarked and unrewarded. It's worth taking a detailed "case history" from your son or daughter, noting the times and the reasons when he or she feels treatment has been unfair. General accusations ("He's always picking on me") are not specific enough to be helpful.

SUSPENSION FROM SCHOOL

Suspending a pupil is a school's last resort. It should never come as a bolt from the blue, but if communication between school and parents is or has been poor, it often does. In an ideal world, if your son or daughter has obviously been heading for this kind of trouble, you should have been consulted, and the school should have made very strenuous efforts to forestall such a drastic step.

Exclusion may be permanent (a very serious step for a school to take), for an indefinite period, or for a fixed period of a few days. Usually only the head teacher or head of the school can take this decision. There are probably local regulations or laws governing the procedure for informing parents; at the very least, you should be told the reasons for and duration of the exclusion order.

THE RIGHT TO APPEAL

You might wish to appeal against the school's decision to exclude your child, especially if you think the decision is unfair or if the exclusion is permanent. Such an appeal may be made to the school governors, to the local education authority, or perhaps to an independent panel.

- **Find out as much as you can** about what led up to the suspension.
- **Ask to see your youngster's school record.** You need to know whether the reasons given for exclusion are backed up by what is said in the record.
- **Talk to a sympathetic teacher** if you can.
- **Find out if the school made any efforts** to deal with trouble, especially if it had been building up. If you had no idea there was a problem, ask why you were not contacted earlier.
- **Ask why the punishment is so harsh**, especially if this is the first offence.
- **Go well prepared to meetings and hearings**, writing down the points you want to make beforehand.
- **Try to persuade your youngster** to go with you to the exclusion meeting. It will affect his or her future, and it is right that he or she should be involved.
- **Take a friend to meetings**, both to give you moral support and to help you keep a record of what has been said.
- **Try to stay calm** when you are stating your child's case. If you let yourself get too upset, it will be hard for you to make your points clearly and logically.

- **Try to stay on reasonable terms** with the staff if you want your child to stay in the same school. If communication between you breaks down entirely, it will make things difficult for both you and your child later on.
- **If the school authorities think** that they cannot fulfil the educational needs of your son or daughter, a formal assessment by an educational psychologist may be necessary.
- **Keep copies of all correspondence** you have with the school, governors, or education authorities, and notes of what happened at any meetings. You may need them at later hearings.

BULLYING

The lives of many children are made miserable by bullying, which can range from verbal and often vicious harassment to actual physical assault. Sadly, bullying often occurs at school.

Persistent bullying can have a devastating effect on a child's self-esteem. Youngsters may feel it's somehow their fault, or that there's something wrong with them; they may become more withdrawn and insecure, more cautious, and less willing to take any sort of risk. Being victimized in this way can cause days of mental anguish and leave lifelong emotional scars. It has driven some youngsters to try to murder their tormentors, and others to suicide. Your child won't always tell you that he or she is being bullied. Some of the signs that might lead you to suspect it are:

– Reluctance to go to school

– Equipment, clothing, or personal possessions that have gone missing or have been unaccountably damaged

– Bruising

– Frequent "loss" of lunch money or shortage of pocket money with vague explanations as to how it has been spent.

HOW TO HELP YOUR CHILD

When a child is being bullied at school, it's the responsibility of the school to stop it: there should be an anti-bullying policy involving both pupils and staff, and procedures should be clearly established to deal with any incidents. Unfortunately, there is no doubt that some schools refuse to acknowledge that a problem exists, while others do not take it seriously or are incapable of dealing with it adequately. In these cases, you should do the following:

- **Reassure your child** that the bullying doesn't mean there is anything wrong with him or her. It can help children to know that they're not the only victims, and that other children get bullied, too.
- **Suggest that your child tell a teacher** he or she likes and trusts about the problem, or offer to contact the school yourself.

- **Talk first to your child's teacher**, or head of year. If matters don't improve, make an appointment to see the head teacher. Be insistent, and don't allow the school to dismiss the bullying as unimportant, as a "normal" part of growing up, or something that will sort itself out.
- **Tell a parent governor about the problem** if the staff are not helpful. If you still receive no help, tell the local education authority. If this, too, produces no results, contact your local MP.
- **If the bullying persists**, keep a written record of every incident to use in future consultations with the school.

Quite often a child is adamant that he or she doesn't want you to complain to the school authorities, believing that this will only make the problem worse. In this case you need to help your child to find strategies to deal with the problem on his or her own.

- **Friends are the best protection against bullying**. Encourage your youngster to make friends, and make sure he or she knows that these friends are welcome at home.
- **Find out where the bullying takes place** (it's usually in the playground, or on the way to or from school) and help your son or daughter to work out how to avoid places and situations, or how to avoid being alone with the bullies. Finding a friend or friends to walk home with may help, for example. If bullying happens outside school, the school will not accept responsibility, even if the children involved are pupils there. In this case, contact a solicitor and ask for a letter to be sent to the bully's parents, informing them of the legal consequences if the bullying persists.
- **If bullying involves physical violence, don't encourage your child to hit back.** This may make matters worse.
- **Advise your child not to give sweets or presents in an attempt to buy off the bully**, and not to give in to demands for money (see also *School-refusers*, p.236 and *Issue: Truancy*, p.235).

SUSPENSION FROM SCHOOL

Only a headmaster or headmistress can order your suspension. Your parents must be told immediately why you are being suspended, and for how long. In the UK, if you're suspended for more than five days in one term, or at a time when you should be taking a public examination, the head must inform the governors and the local education authority.

Your parents (or you, if you are over 18) have a right to appeal against suspension or expulsion. To do this, your parents should write immediately to the chairperson of the board of governors and to the local education authority saying that they wish to challenge the decision. They should ask for information about the formal appeals procedure. Your parents also have the right to apply for a place for you at another school. If this is refused, they can still contact a local appeals committee.

STUDYING FOR EXAMS

No one much enjoys revising, and few schools give much advice about the most efficient way to do it. You might read the following suggestions to make your life easier.

- **Start in good time.** This means about six to eight weeks before the exam, or in the Easter holidays for summer exams.
- **Draw up a realistic timetable.** Don't, for example, set aside three hours each night and ten hours over the weekend if you know there's no chance at all that you'll keep up that pace. Better to start a little sooner and do a little less each day.
- **Give yourself about 40–80 minutes for each subject**, and alternate subjects you like with those you find boring or difficult. Don't attempt to revise for more than three hours at a time.
- **Plan extra time for your weaker subjects.**
- **Try to keep to the timetable as much as you can.** Just doing this gives you a sense of achievement, and makes you more motivated to carry on.
- **Set yourself definite targets for each study period.**
- **Don't feel that revising well in advance is wasted effort** because you'll forget it all again. If you've done it thoroughly once, a quick run through shortly before the exam will bring it back.
- **Build rewards and treats into your timetable.** Give yourself coffee breaks, work out which TV programmes you really can't miss, and take at least one evening off each week to go out with your friends or see a film.
- **Some people like a totally free evening the night before an exam.** Others feel the only things they'll remember are the ones they read the night before. Whatever suits you is something you'll have to discover for yourself!

How to study and review

Reading your notes over and over again, with rising feelings of panic, is not an efficient way to revise. Listed below are things you need to succeed:

Organize your thoughts. Use a fluorescent marker to highlight key points in your notes. When you've read a section through, try to summarize it without referring to your books or notes, and check that you've included all the key points. It helps to organize each topic into sections with headings, then memorize the headings to give you a summary of each topic.

Know the facts. Most of the marks in any exam are given for knowledge of the basic facts. There are no short cuts here: facts just have to be learned. It can help to write down key facts (such as physics or maths formulae, history dates, irregular French verbs) on cards that you can carry around with you and study at odd moments.

Practice. Spend at least part of your revision time working through the exam papers from previous years. Do this under exam conditions: keep to time and don't refer to books or notes.

YOUR RIGHTS AT SCHOOL

- Schools won't take responsibility for bullying that happens out of school. But suppose a teacher sees you smoking on the way home: can the school punish you?
YES School rules can extend beyond the school premises and school hours if the school so wishes.

- You are 15 years old and have a part-time job that the school say makes you too tired to work properly. Can the school force you to give it up?
YES The local education authority can make you give up a job if it thinks it is bad for your health.

- Your parents want you to go on holiday with them for two weeks during term-time. Your teacher says you should not go. Has the school the right to stop you?
NO You are entitled to two weeks' leave of absence each year, but not more than this "save in exceptional circumstances".

- Your teacher has kept the whole class in detention after school because someone scribbled graffiti on the classroom walls and would not own up. You got home late so your mother was worried (you hadn't been able to warn her because you didn't know it was going to happen). Should the teacher have kept the class back like this?
NO Teachers cannot impose detentions indiscriminately. A teacher can keep a whole class behind only as a last resort. If detention is used as a punishment, this must be made clear in the school rules, and parents must be warned in advance if their child is going to be detained for any reason.

- You want to stay on and take A levels, but the school says your GCSEs aren't good enough. Do you have to leave?
NO If you want to, you have the legal right to stay in full-time education until your 19th birthday. If your school can't or won't provide this, then the local education authority must arrange for you to transfer to another school or a further education college.

- You have a maths teacher who's always hitting you over the head with your textbook if you get something wrong or if you're fooling about. Sometimes it really hurts. Is he allowed to do this?
NO Corporal punishment (which includes any form of physical assault) is banned in all state-supported schools. However, unless it is "excessive", being hit is a civil and not a criminal offence. This means that you cannot complain to the police or bring a criminal charge, but you and your parents can seek legal advice and take out a civil action against the teacher. If you go to an independent school and your parents pay your fees, then you may have to put up with whatever physical punishment teachers care to inflict.

LOOKING AT THE OPTIONS

Some of your sixth-form friends may know exactly what they want to do and where they want to go. They're the lucky ones. For you and for others, the decision may not be as simple. Maybe you have doubts about whether you want to go into further education or training. Perhaps you feel you'd prefer to go straight into a job, or maybe even defer all decisions and take a year off before planning your next move. How do you decide what's right for you?

Further education Do you like studying for its own sake, or is there a particular academic subject you're especially interested in? If so, it will probably suit you to go to a university if you have the necessary grades, even if at the moment you don't see any practical use for it in the future. But if you feel very restless, fed up with academic work, or half-hearted or lukewarm about a particular course, it may not be a good idea to commit yourself to more full-time education. In this situation, you're more likely to drop out, and it may be harder for you if you change your mind later. Some university courses have a practical rather than a purely academic approach. Such a "vocational" course gives training for a specific career and may suit you better, especially if you have a fairly good idea about what you want to do in the future. If you discover that you're not really suited to the course you've started, don't assume that you'll have to drop out altogether. Often you can transfer to an alternative course. "Sandwich courses" offer a mixture of theory and practical training. This arrangement suits many people better than a straight academic or vocational course, and has the advantage that industrial bursaries may be available for them.

The "gap" year Taking a year off between school and college is becoming so common that most people have come to expect it almost as a right, or at least as a formal part of their education. About 25 per cent of people from independent schools and 10 per cent of people from state schools now have a "gap" year, and the numbers are increasing. A year off may be reinvigorating if you feel fed up with school and education. After the pressure of the last two or three years of school, a year away from formal education may make you feel more like going on to university or doing an academic course. It will give you time to grow up a bit so that if you do go to university, you're more mature and may be more prepared to work on your own. Finally, of course, a year off gives you a chance to travel.

Not all parents are enthusiastic about the "gap" year. They fear that it may be academically unsettling, and that you may either decide to abandon the idea of university altogether, or find it hard to study when you do get there. There is some truth to these doubts. While a year spent travelling or working abroad will make you more mature and independent, it may also make you more restless. It will break your studying routine, and it may not be so easy to get back to being a student again. It will also mean putting off your career for a year. There are financial implications, too. Are your parents able and prepared to finance it, or are you prepared to finance it yourself?

If you want a take a year off, think about the following points:

- It's essential to plan your year properly, and to use it constructively, so that you don't just drift. It can be destructive and demoralizing if time off is seen as a soft option, or an excuse to lie back and do nothing.

- Universities and admission tutors vary in their attitudes towards the gap year. They're more likely to view it positively if you plan to travel or work abroad. Universities are less likely to be enthusiastic about a year off for people who are about to embark on a long course such as medicine or veterinary science, or who want to read physics or, more especially, maths, where it's important to keep up with the work without a break.

- Think well ahead. There are various organizations that will help students find work abroad, but you may need to apply early (see *Organizations*, p.274). You will also need to earn money, unless your parents are prepared to finance you entirely.

Going straight into a job This may solve your immediate financial problems, but be sure that it's what you really want to do. You may be limiting your options for future employment by not getting any further training. If you can, choose an occupation or place of employment that will offer further training, and remember that there may be wider employment opportunities in a larger firm. Before you start looking for a job, it might help you to build up a profile of what you do and don't want from a job. The checklist below suggests some of the things you might want to include in any job specification. Although 100 per cent job satisfaction is almost impossible (and most people have to compromise and manage with much less than this), it still helps a great deal to ask yourself the following questions and to concentrate on the most important things.

- **What matters most to you?** Is it status, material success, independence, or doing a job that really interests you?

- **Do you have a particular skill** that you want to use?

- **Do you want something that will bring you into contact with other people**, or do you prefer to work alone?

- **Do you have a social conscience**, and want to be of service to others?

- **Do you want something that will be challenging**, or do you prefer an easy ride?

- **Do you want a practical job** or one that involves thinking, planning, researching?

- **Do you enjoy organizing?**

- **Are you competitive?**

Don't be disappointed if you don't end up in the right niche straightaway, but try to stay in a job for long enough (say six months) to really make up your mind about it; your first feelings may change as you settle down. You will also get some experience during this time, and it's better to look for another job while you're still employed than to be out of work. You may also be able to ask for references that will help you get your next job.

13

MONEY MATTERS

*There are several ways in which to apportion the family
income, all of them unsatisfactory*

Robert Benchley

MONEY MEANS POWER. For adolescents it spells freedom and independence, while for parents, controlling the purse strings – by stopping or cutting down on the amount of pocket money – is a well-recognized sanction. Giving pocket money "on condition" (either as payment for services or as a reward for good behaviour) is a powerful way to keep a child dependent, which may not always be helpful.

Things can be particularly difficult for many older adolescents who, even though they have achieved emotional emancipation from their parents, are still financially dependent on them. This can make for an uneasy and unequal relationship, particularly if parents, perhaps without realizing it, use their financial power as blackmail ("as long as I'm paying for you/you're living in my house, you'll do as I say/behave as I want you to").

Should pocket money be given to a child as a right, something they're entitled to? Or should children be expected to earn their pocket money, by doing their share of household chores, or carrying out extra jobs for their parents? This is a common dilemma, and a compromise might be that some pocket money – given regularly and with no strings attached – should be every child's right, and that everyone helps with routine jobs such as washing up. As part of a family, children can reasonably be expected to do their share of chores without being paid for it. It does seem reasonable, however, to offer extra payment for jobs such as decorating or cleaning the car. It also

*Left: Who pays for clothes, apart from those for school, is something that
parents and teenagers need to discuss.*

seems fair that every child should have at least some money to spend as he or she likes, even if it's on something parents don't approve of (such as trendy clothes, video games, motorcycles, or cigarettes).

The amount of pocket money you give to your child obviously depends partly on how much you can afford. Most children accept this and consider that what they get is a fair amount, or as much as their parents can afford, even if it isn't as much as they feel they need. In our survey for this book we found a wide variation in the amount of pocket money children are given. Some get none at all, or get no regular fixed amount, or get it only when they need it for some specific reason. In a very few cases parents appear to conduct a kind of means test, feeling that if a child has a part-time or Saturday job, then there is no need to give pocket money as well. Interestingly, however, few of the teenagers in our survey felt they got either much more, or much less, than their friends. Most were given pocket money weekly, although a few got a fixed amount each day. More girls than boys were given a monthly allowance, and some had a monthly or clothes allowance as well as regular weekly pocket money. At all ages we found that boys were given slightly more per week than girls, and that girls were more likely than boys to feel they didn't get enough pocket money. Perhaps parents should consider that boys and girls need to be treated equally.

ALLOWANCES

An allowance is a very important stepping-stone between the pocket money of childhood, doled out each week, and the student grant or wage that they will have to manage when they are finally on their own. When are they old enough, or mature enough, to manage this transition?

The experience of most people is that money is better doled out in small weekly amounts until about the age of 14 or 15, after which an adolescent should be able to learn to budget a larger allowance paid, say, monthly. Naturally enough, it can be a heady experience for someone used to a small, if regular, trickle of cash suddenly to acquire the real spending power of a healthy lump sum each month. To begin with, a month's allowance may be squandered in the first few days, but this is what learning to handle money is all about.

WHERE THE MONEY GOES

What should pocket money or allowances be expected to cover? This doesn't matter as long as it's worked out realistically so that your youngster has a reasonable amount to spend on what he or she is expected to buy.

At all ages, tapes or CDs, magazines, computer and video games, and sweets are the basic staples of teenage life and where much of the money seems to go. Teenagers also tend to buy minor pieces of school equipment such as pens and rubbers out of their own pocket. "Grooming" – personal toiletries and make-up – come high on the list of expenses in all age groups, too.

As their social life broadens, their expenses increase; going out with friends becomes a major drain on income for the over-15s, and both sexes spend more on clothes. In our survey several of the younger boys (for whom a girlfriend is often as much a status symbol as a relationship) mentioned that they spent money on their girlfriends, although none in the oldest age group did. Most older teenagers are expected to pay for their own films and entertainment, and to buy any Christmas or birthday presents they want to give. Leisure activities may be more expensive for this age group, too: sports equipment, membership of a sports centre, and driving lessons all call for serious money.

*As well as giving teenagers a measure of
independence, handling their own money can help them
to develop some sense of financial responsibility.*

When you're working out how much pocket money to give your children, you can use the following list (which includes most of the teenager's wants and needs) as a basis; you should be able to decide together which of these items your son or daughter should be expected to pay for.
– Clothes (apart from school clothes)
– Computer games
– Driving lessons
– Food and drink (snacks or meals out with friends, drinks at the pub)
– Going out with friends
– Entertainment (films, concerts, etc.)
– Hobbies
– Magazines
– Make-up
– Personal toiletries
– Presents
– Tapes
– Sports equipment
– Sweets/cigarettes
– Stationery (pens, rubbers, etc.)
– Savings
– Sports centre (membership, other activities)
– Leisure travel
– Videos/video games
It can help older adolescents to learn how to budget if they're given a somewhat larger allowance but are expected to cover their own daily expenses during term-time (such as

paying for travel to and from school, and school lunches). These expenses must be properly costed, and the money given in addition to their basic pocket money allowance. Many teenagers agree in principle that this is a good idea, but are realistic enough to know that there might be lean lunchtimes towards the end of the week if they're given that amount of control. A few teenagers receive a separate clothes allowance, too, although parents usually still pay for expensive items such as coats.

Managing money is a skill that can be learned.

Once you've made the decision to give them an allowance, how they spend it should be up to them. In our survey most of the children over 14 said that their parents placed no restrictions on the way they spent their money; even in the youngest age group, only nine per cent of the boys and 17 per cent of the girls said they were not allowed to spend their money as they liked. However much you dislike their taste or disapprove of their choices, remember that you and your teenagers probably have different ideas about what constitutes value for money.

ISSUE: STARTING TO SAVE

Financial expertise comes naturally to some teenagers, as to some adults. But how to help the more financially feckless, those through whose fingers money slips far too easily and long before next pay-day?

• Parents could open a high-interest bank or savings account for youngsters and encourage them to add to it; watching it grow may encourage them to save. About half of all the teenagers we questioned had either a bank or a savings account. In many cases, parents also made a contribution (see table).

• Parents shouldn't be too soft-hearted about giving advances. If people – and this includes adults! – get used to living on credit, it doesn't improve their sense of financial responsibility.

• Avoid cash cards and credit cards. This should go without saying. It's asking for trouble to give a youngster such easy access to cash until he or she has demonstrated the ability to budget and handle money.

Age	Bank account	Savings account	Parents contribute
11–14	47%	60%	42%
15–16	55%	55%	40%
17–18	65%	62%	20%

CASE HISTORY: CREDIT CARDS

When Jeremy left home to go to university, he had a small grant paid once a term, and his parents, Trevor and Sue, made this up to the standard yearly allowance with cheques at the beginning of each term. Jeremy's bank offered him a cheque guarantee card that was also a credit card. By the middle of his first year Jeremy was £300 in debt.

"I tried to keep an account of where the money was going, filling cheque stubs and so on, but sometimes if I'm in a hurry or in a shop or restaurant I don't write it down. It's amazing how you can forget buying things and paying for meals and petrol and such. Now I don't know how I'll get through the summer term."
Jeremy, 18

"In my day banks didn't allow us to get into debt. I don't see that paying off the debt is going to help him — he'll probably do the same thing next year if he knows I'm going to bail him out when he's overdrawn."
Trevor, 48

COMMENT ABOUT CREDIT CARDS

Young adults often get into a financial mess in their first efforts to manage their own money. One bad experience is usually enough to teach them the facts of financial life, but it may be best to insist before an account is opened that the bank set a tough limit on credit.

"It's my money — I earn it and how I spend it is up to me. I'm certainly not putting it in some bank for the future."
Sarah, 17

"Stephanie seemed to be a 'good manager' from about the age of six. She always seemed to have enough for whatever she wanted to do, never had to borrow to buy the family Christmas presents, and had later saved enough to pay her own fare to America for her year off. But poor old Christopher, who got just the same amount of pocket money, always needed an advance. How can we possibly teach him to manage his money better?"
Ellen, 51

PART-TIME AND SATURDAY JOBS

One of the best ways children learn about money is by earning their own. As a parent, you have to consider a few points before allowing your child to take this step.

Legally, most children in the UK who are over 13 may be allowed to take a part-time job, such as a paper round or in a shop, provided that they do not work before 7 a.m. or after 7 p.m., or for more than two hours on any school day or on a Sunday. Local authorities make their own bylaws which may impose further restrictions on children's employment, and these vary. Your child's school may also have the right to stop him or her from doing a job if schoolwork is being affected. Despite this, many children put in more hours than are legally allowed, and many employers are happy to give them the opportunity and to take unfair advantage of them as a source of cheap labour. A teenager may be willing to work for as little as half the going rate of an adult doing the same work, but you should not allow your child to be exploited in this way. If he or she can do the work, they deserve something close to the going rate for it.

It is not always exploitation, however. Many adolescents may enjoy the idea of working in a shop, and if the hours are not too long they will often gain useful experience in dealing with strangers. Over the age of 16 they should have proper terms of employment; if they work regularly, they will need to make sure that they and their employers are complying with the current regulations about national insurance. Regular earnings may also make them liable to income tax. Working in the "black economy" and taking no notice of these regulations is a risky business.

Virtually the only job open to younger adolescents is the paper round, which means that in practice few girls in this age group have a job, either because their parents are reluctant to let them take a round, or because they cannot get one. Our UK survey suggested that, on average, younger boys worked only one or two hours a week. Most of the boys of this age who didn't have jobs said it was because they didn't want one or need one. In mid-adolescence, children of both sexes who did not have a part-time or Saturday job usually said that this was because they didn't want or need one. Interestingly, by late adolescence, the number of girls who had jobs rose sharply – over twice as many girls as boys had work, and most of those girls who didn't have a job said they needed one and would have liked one. Is this because boys are more idle, or girls more motivated? Certainly far more girls than boys in this age group felt that they didn't get enough pocket money.

> *"It's not my fault there aren't any jobs for teenagers – that's the mess your generation has made of things. Why should we suffer because you lot have messed up the economy or whatever it's called?"*
> John, 16

WHAT IS A BUDGET?

Once your parents have agreed to give you more than just a bit of pocket money, you'd be wise to be systematic about your money. Having a budget simply means writing down a few things like:

– How much money you have

– Where it comes from (your parents or a job)

– Things you have to pay for (car insurance, rent, food)

– Things you have to buy (clothes, presents)

The first step is to talk to your parents and agree which things you pay for and which they do. For example, who buys the shampoo in the bathroom cupboard? Are you allowed as much as you like of the drinks (both soft drinks and alcoholic ones) in the fridge? Who pays for dry-cleaning? Who pays for holidays?

It sounds boring, but you'll probably have to try to write down what you spend each week for a month or two. If you keep careful and clear accounts, you may be able to persuade your parents that either you need a bigger allowance or that they should pay for more of the things you buy. Eventually you'll have a clear idea of how much money comes in – your allowance, cash presents at Christmas and birthdays, and money from holiday jobs (if you're lucky enough to get one) – and how much goes out. Then you can actually start budgeting. That means deciding which things you can afford and which you can't: how often you can afford to go to the hairdresser, how much you can spend over the weekend, and so on.

Try to avoid borrowing from your own friends. It's all too easy to get a reputation for always being on the scrounge. If you're hard up, don't go out for a drink and hope not to buy any – stay at home. If you need money urgently, ask your parents for it and explain why you need it.

If you want to borrow money from the bank, talk it over with your parents first. They may be willing to make a loan with no interest charges.

The most essential thing you need to know about a budget is how much money you've got coming in and where it goes. Only then will you be able to make sensible decisions. Another good reason for having your income and expenses all written down is that you may then be able to persuade your parents to increase your allowance. Show the figures to your father or mother, and ask them how they suggest you should close the gap between what you spend and the money they give you.

14

FACING UP TO ADULTHOOD

"

I have found the best way to give advice to your children is
to find out what they want and then to advise them to do it

"

Harry S. Truman

MANY BIRDS AND ANIMALS EVICT their adolescent youngsters from the family home. A few pack animals incorporate members of the new generation in the pack, but usually there is a separation after a year or two. Human families are unique in maintaining close social contacts between the generations for their whole lifetimes, but the practice of living as an extended family has become less common with recent socioeconomic changes. The result is that young people have greater geographical and social mobility. Despite this mobility, however, it still seems generally true that daughters retain close links with their mothers more often than sons retain links with either parent; once married, the son-in-law is often absorbed into the social network of his wife's family.

Most families now recognize that some degree of separation from parents – both physical and emotional – actually benefits young adults. This separation may, however, be made more difficult by the trend towards an extension of financial dependence into the late 20s or even later. If this does seem a likely prospect, it may be a good idea for parents and their adult offspring to draw up a formal financial contract.

Life is often much easier at this time for someone who knows more or less what they want to do. Uncertainty about the future can wreak havoc with temper, confidence, and self-esteem. Parents often complain that their children lack motivation, but it's

Left: Decisions about careers and plans for the future are major
preoccupations for late adolescents – and major worries, too.

difficult to become motivated without a realistic goal in mind. Once they've set their sights on something, most adolescents will almost certainly develop the commitment to work. This has always been regarded as one significant sign of maturity.

A few youngsters decide on their choice of adult occupation at an early stage. Parents sometimes say, "He always wanted to be a policeman" (or a pilot or a photographer), and quite a high proportion stay with this early choice. Many more, however, simply follow the courses their schoolteachers suggest, and may go to university with no decision beyond the subject they intend to study. It is by no means unusual for university students in their last year to have no firm career ambitions, but you should try to help your son or daughter avoid this. It would be helpful for you to encourage your children to take positive steps towards planning their future lives. You should try to discuss their plans with them, and perhaps consult those teachers whose estimation of your youngster's abilities you think are fair and reasonable.

Of the 16–18-year-olds in our survey, a great many worried about their ability to achieve their career ambitions, to get a job they liked, to live an independent life, and to support themselves. On the other hand, they seemed much less concerned than younger teenagers about having boyfriends and girlfriends or finding a marriage partner. There was very little difference in the attitudes of boys and girls: the girls showed just as much concern about their future independence as the boys did, and were less preoccupied with marriage prospects (see *What Teenagers Worry About*, below).

> *"I worry a lot that I won't be able to get a job. Lots of people*
> *don't, even people who do better at school than I do. It costs*
> *so much to buy a house and bring up a family. I can't believe*
> *I'll ever be able to earn that much."*
>
> Ross, 17

WHAT TEENAGERS WORRY ABOUT

Teenagers in our survey worried whether they could:	Boys	Girls
• Get a job	45%	41%
• Look after themselves after leaving home	38%	36%
• Earn enough to leave home	30%	50%
• Get a girlfriend/boyfriend	10%	4%
• Find someone they want to marry	25%	9%
• Find someone who wants to marry them	25%	14%

CAREER COUNSELLING

Parents can offer some advice but — as is the case with most advice for adults — the sensible course is to consult professionals. Schools and universities have careers offices (of variable quality) and these may help. Advice from academic sources may not, however, be the best source in a harsh economic climate. There is a bewildering array of career counsellors, not to mention youth employment offices, training schemes, and the like. If parents want to give practical help to adolescents who seem to have no idea what they want to do with their lives, they can assist them in finding their way through these bureaucratic mazes.

Don't try to do it all yourselves: a youngster is much more likely to have confidence in an organization he or she has found independently. Beware, too, of organizations that offer career guidance based on a couple of hours of psychological interviewing; some of these are phoney money-making rackets. A reputable organization offering a careers service should be able to suggest options that may not have occurred either to the youngster or his or her parents, and give guidance on both academic and vocational courses. Some will also advise on American degree courses and ways of spending a "gap" year (see p.168). They may also give advice on interview techniques (what an interview is and how to do well during one), and how to write a CV (see p.190).

The service should include a comprehensive aptitude test and an extensive interview to discover the kinds of work and other activities your son or daughter enjoys. It should also look at other qualities, e.g., tolerance, persuasiveness, a leadership ability, and an ability to take orders or to work on a team. This is combined with academic qualifications (or an estimate of what these are likely to be if your son or daughter has no higher qualifications yet) to produce a computer profile. This conclusion is supplemented and sometimes overridden by information gained during an in-depth interview with the candidate.

A good organization will always remember that the youngster is the client. However, they often like to see parents as well to make sure that they're happy with any options offered or decisions made. Sometimes parents are helpful because teenagers may be too disinclined to blow their own trumpets and may also undervalue their own achievements or experience. Parents can give helpful reminders about their son's or daughter's success in the school play or magazine or chess competition, which he or she might be too modest to mention.

There are youngsters whose abilities seem to point them in one obvious direction while their inclinations clearly steer them in another, such as the bright child who is a potential academic high-flyer and who is under pressure from parents, school, and friends to go to university, but who wants to abandon academic education and take a completely different direction. There are times when the function of the adviser is to point out to the parents of a bright adolescent who wants to reject a university education and become a second-hand car salesman that he or she has the persuasiveness, social skills, and business acumen to be a very successful one.

Once options have been suggested to you, take time to think about them carefully. Use your contacts to help your teenager do some independent research. Arrange for him or her to talk to friends or relatives in the field, and, if possible, to get not just advice and insights from them, but work experience in their organization (no matter how small the business may be).

> *"I've applied for so many jobs and not got them I just feel like*
> *giving up. What's the point of applying? It just makes you feel*
> *really down when you don't get it."*
> Miriam, 18

WORKING ABROAD

Many universities have a "twinning" scheme with other universities in North America and (for students who are reasonably competent in a second language) the European Community, in which students can get a grant to spend two terms studying their own subject such as engineering abroad. This way they have an opportunity to broaden their work experience as well as their knowledge of labour relations and of business practices and terminology. Now that so many firms have offices abroad, this kind of experience can be very valuable (see *Organizations*, p.274).

UNEMPLOYED ADOLESCENTS

The 16- or 17-year-old who cannot get a job on leaving school is guaranteed a training place with a training allowance or wage, but will only receive Jobseeker's Allowance in special circumstances. Unemployed youngsters are more likely to suffer depression and physical illness and to show antisocial behaviour such as alcohol and drug abuse[1].

• **Help them to maintain a normal life**. They need to feel they have some control over their lives, and are not simply drifting. Their tendency may be to do nothing, or even to stay in bed most of the day. It will help them to feel more in charge of themselves if they can get some sort of order into their day.

• **Encourage them to keep in touch with their friends**. They may be financially dependent on you, but try to make sure they don't remain emotionally dependent on you as well. Give them as much responsibility for themselves and their own lives as you reasonably can.

• **Never use their financial dependence on you as a weapon**.

• **Suggest that they spend the time learning a new skill**, preferably doing something that will make them more attractive to a prospective employer (perhaps doing a typing or word processing course, or learning a foreign language).

- **Encourage them to fill their day constructively**, and to find some sort of activity that will take the place of work. This will provide the opportunity to meet people and to make friends – especially important if many of the youngster's school friends have got jobs or gone off to college. Voluntary work is one possibility. Another is to take up a sport and practice it at regular times, even if it is only going to the local swimming baths a couple of times a week.

Sharing a Home

Often a son or daughter may be over 18 but still financially dependent on you: still living at home, either because of lack of money or lack of suitable alternative accommodation. He or she may still be in full-time education, or undergoing ill-paid training, or (perhaps most difficult of all) restlessly marking time, either because of unemployment or because he or she is unable to decide what to do. This final stage of adolescence can be one of the most difficult. Teenagers are in many respects adults – some legally so – and they certainly regard themselves as such. Once more the family has to be flexible, accommodating the needs of two sets of adults who may be leading quite different lives but are forced, maybe unwillingly, to share the same roof.

This can make for an uneasy and unequal relationship. An adolescent is both more than a lodger (with territorial "rights" over more of the house than just his or her own room) and less than a lodger (he or she may not be paying you the same rent you could get from a lodger – or indeed any rent at all – and may be subject to expectations you would never impose on a lodger).

Obviously you can lay down certain house rules, just as you would with a lodger, but these rules should be based on common courtesy and consideration, rather than limits set because you, as a parent, feel you have a right to control and set limits on your child's behaviour. This "child" is now an adult, and you cannot monitor the comings

ISSUE: DROPPING OUT OF UNIVERSITY

A few young people who are academically quite capable of doing the work suddenly decide to abandon a course or drop out of university after they have begun. Sometimes this is because they have embarked on a course that is quite unsuitable for them, perhaps a very academic course for someone who is either not capable in the particular discipline or simply not interested. A change of direction may be what is needed.

Occasionally it's because the timing is wrong. Perhaps they are not yet ready or mature enough to cope with student life. A "gap" year (see p.168) may also have the unexpected effect of making student life seem less desirable or worthwhile than life in the "real world".

Finally, depressive illness is a not uncommon reason for an able student's sudden decision to drop out, and should always be thought of as a possible cause (see *Depression*, p.238).

and goings or dictate the behaviour of another adult, even if they are living under your roof and are being subsidized by you.

HOW MUCH CONTROL SHOULD YOU HAVE?

Can you tell a 17- or 18-year-old what time he or she ought to be home? Can you demand to know where they are going or when they will be home? Remember:

- **They need to be able to come and go as they please** without having to account to you but within the limits of common courtesy. Obviously they should let you know if they won't be in for the family meal, just as you would let them know if you won't be in to cook one. Parents probably never reach an age at which they fail to worry that a child who is later than expected has had an accident. You have a right to remind your teenager that it is kind, and considerate, to let you know if they will be delayed.
- **They need privacy.** They should be able to invite their friends home and have some place of their own in which to entertain them. It's nice (and polite) if they introduce their friends to you; it's reasonable to expect this but not reasonable to demand it. They will have friends you do not know, and they may well have friends they know you would not like, and so to save friction they may prefer you not to meet them.
- **They need to feel they can get up and go to bed when they please** (as long as they don't disturb the rest of the household), and to cook themselves a snack when they feel like it (as long as they clear up the kitchen afterwards).

In short, they need to be able to live much as they would live if they were living away from their parents in a flat of their own.

LEAVING HOME

Eighty per cent of 16-year-olds live at home: 80 per cent of 24-year-olds have left, and this transition to complete independence seems to be easier for children who have a happy and secure relationship with their parents. These youngsters know that the family can, in the last resort, always be relied upon to back them up: they do not need to keep looking back over their shoulders to make sure that they haven't been abandoned. Things are much more likely to go wrong for the young adult who is anxious about or at war with his or her family.

Academic failure, an overdose, or a mental breakdown imply that the adolescent is not yet ready to go. Sometimes a young adult who is finding it hard to break away will make a desperate and self-destructive bid for freedom: pregnancy, self-starvation, running away, and drug-taking may all be attempts to gain independence.

ENCOURAGING THEM TO GO

Few young adults actually need a mother. They may, however, enjoy the services many mothers are still willing to provide. If your fledglings seem reluctant to leave the nest, it may be because you make life too comfortable for them. There are mothers who, even if they work themselves, somehow see it as their job to pick up grubby garments from their offspring's bedroom floor and return them, clean and ironed, 24 hours later. It is not their job, and it does the teenager no real favours either. A 17- or 18-year-old of either sex is, for example, perfectly capable of sorting out and doing his or her own laundry, and should be expected to do this. People of this age can make their own appointments for the dentist (and cancel them, if necessary), or buy their own stamps and toothpaste. It should be taken for granted that they're responsible for keeping their own room as they want it (which may or may not be clean and tidy) and doing a reasonable and negotiable number of other household chores. All this is good preparation for independent living.

> *Take it for granted that they will go. This*
> *isn't rejecting them or making them feel that*
> *you want them to go, but just accepting that*
> *this is the way life is, and that they should*
> *feel no hesitation about leaving you.*

Don't let your own feeling that it's nice to be needed stand in the way of your youngster's independence. Let them into the kitchen if you haven't done so before. Everyone, male or female, should know how to cook, and most adolescents enjoy it if they're given the chance. Cooking a family meal once a week or so is good experience for the teenager. Certainly by this age no parent should feel, if they are going out or away for the weekend, that they have to leave a set of pre-cooked meals in the deep freeze for the nearly-adult person they're leaving behind. By all means leave the raw ingredients – but let the person who's going to eat them turn them into a meal.

A PLACE OF THEIR OWN

In late adolescence and early adulthood, an apparent rejection of their "roots" may be part of a young adult's determined – and healthy – effort to create an identity quite separate from that of their parents. You may be horrified when you see the building your son or daughter has chosen to live as a first place of his or her own. Nowadays there is very little property to rent in most of our cities (and whose generation is to blame for that?) so young people often have to settle for run-down premises or tough housing estates. You can try to help by offering to take a look at any agreement they are asked to sign (and if you're not an expert, take it to someone who is). You may be able to offer practical help putting a good mortice lock on the entrance door, fitting window locks, and checking that there is some way out of a multioccupancy house in the event of a fire.

Even if you don't like the people they choose to share with, try not to make snap judgements based on appearance and accents. They are unreliable indicators. You may want to ask your son or daughter questions like, "How long have you known them? Do they owe you any money?" but that risks starting an argument. The important thing – if you're worried that it may be a disastrous mistake – is to make sure that your kids can come back home without losing face, so grit your teeth and offer to cook a big meal and lend the washing machine at the weekend.

If you're worried that sharing a flat with a friend of the opposite sex implies a sexual relationship, you should reflect that sexual disasters (such as unwanted pregnancy) are less likely in circumstances in which sex is neither hurried nor furtive. Whether you offer a double bed to your son or daughter and his or her partner when they visit is up to you.

CASE HISTORY: MOVING OUT

Sarah had moved out of the family home at the age of 19 and had been happily settled in her new flat for about six months. She regularly visited her parents who still missed her.

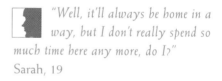 *"Sarah had come over to see us on Sunday, and after we'd had supper she said, 'Well, I think it's about time I was going home'. I felt so hurt I couldn't speak. I mean, I know she's got a flat now, but it had never occurred to me that she didn't think of this as home any more. I think her father saw how I was feeling."*
Esther, 49

"Well, it'll always be home in a way, but I don't really spend so much time here any more, do I?"
Sarah, 19

COMMENTS ABOUT MOVING OUT

Sarah was deliberately but tactfully making the point to her parents (who were disinclined to let her go) that she had made a life of her own which was not dependent on them, but it wasn't a deliberate attempt to hurt them.

Sarah's parents decided they need not feel so rejected. They recognized that "home" is really the way you feel about a place, and for most people who have had a happy childhood and feel strong ties of family affection, the childhood home will always be a special place.

Making a home of your own, and running it in your own way, is a vital part of growing up. Whether it's a luxury penthouse or an uncomfortable squat makes little difference to adolescents: the point is that, for the first time, they are not accountable to their parents for the way they live or how they spend their time. Nevertheless, parents reaching retirement are often surprised at how strongly their adult children react to the suggestion that they might sell the family home.

They are unlikely to choose the night they spend with you to have an orgy, so it won't matter in practical terms; the decision really depends on who is most likely to be embarrassed by whatever arrangements are made. But it is your house and if you are more comfortable giving them separate rooms, do so; just don't investigate where they woke up.

> *"I like a clean, modern sort of Japanese look, so I don't mind*
> *it if I sleep on a mattress on the floor and don't have a lot of*
> *furniture. My parents think it's because I have no money and keep*
> *offering me these huge, clunky pieces of furniture from the attic*
> *but I'm happy with what I've got."*
> Tina, 19

There are several things you can do to help adolescents make this important transition from living with you to living in a place of their own:
- **Don't make them feel guilty at being happy to have left home**. Of course you miss them, but that's your problem.
- **Remember when you go to see them that you're a visitor**, and that you're treading on their patch. Don't try and take over, rearrange the furniture, or exercise any proprietorial rights – even if you're contributing to the rent.
- **Don't turn up unannounced**. There may be all sorts of facets of their new life that they're not yet ready to share with you.
- **Don't criticize**, even if they're living in a squat mostly furnished with old milk crates. Find something encouraging and positive to say.
- **Offer anything you think may be useful** only if you're prepared not to be hurt or offended if they turn it down. Aunt Elsie's lace tablecloth may not fit their way of life.

CHANGING RELATIONSHIPS

During the late teens a subtle reversal of roles tends to creep into the parent-child relationship. Sometimes there is an element of rivalry between mother and daughter, or father and son, as the youngster gradually encroaches on adult territory and acquires new adult skills. Often the teenager's attitudes towards his or her parents are characterized by a fair amount of arrogance and condescension: an assumption, for example, that he or she is the first person within the family to understand the dangers of cholesterol or overpopulation, or to advocate full employment or peace in our time. It isn't that most parents mind their offspring believing that the world is their oyster; what rankles is the parallel belief that their parents' knowledge of the world and of life is inadequate, or at least outdated. What should you do?
- **Don't be condescending back** if you can help it ("I felt the same at your age, you'll soon learn that life's not that simple/grow out of it...")

• **Don't expect to be the teenager's main confidante and trouble-shooter** in the way you may have been when they were younger. They may well still want to talk to you when they're miserable or in trouble, but it's quite possible they may prefer to talk to a friend or even another adult (see the table below).

"What I found hard to take was the way Jane would stand over me while I was cooking, not exactly criticizing me, but simply acting surprised at everything I did. She'd say things like, 'You're not putting that much butter in are you?' or 'Have you ever thought about using wholemeal flour?' Finally she'd turn away, saying, 'Don't bother doing anything for me, I'll cook myself something later'."

Liz, 46

Towards the end of adolescence your relationship with your son or daughter also changes in more positive ways. As the over-sensitivity of the teen years recedes, older adolescents are able to handle you better, to turn your anger and criticism with humour, for example, or to make allowances for your own bad moods. Now nearly adults themselves, they start to see their parents as people and are more able to understand and accept them as they are, warts and all. For the first time, these young adults can be supportive of their parents regardless of their own needs, having learned that they can put others first and be more sensitive to someone else.

WHO DO TEENAGERS TALK TO?

Asked who they would want to talk to if they had a problem, older adolescents in our survey replied as follows:

	Boys	Girls
Parents	65%	54%
Friends	55%	77%
A teacher	–	14%
Another adult	25%	41%
School counsellor	10%	18%

COMMENT
Adolescents who are 16 to 18 years old are much more likely than younger children to choose a friend to confide in rather than their parents.

TALKING TO YOUNG ADULTS

You may feel you have a lot of wisdom to impart to your children. They are unlikely to agree. They may value practical advice if they ask for it (how to change the antifreeze in the car, book a package holiday, or get a survey done on a flat). They are not very likely to be interested in your opinions on sex, politics, literature, films, or religion. In any case, they'll have heard them all before.

If your children have friends around for a meal or staying for the weekend, take care that you don't dominate the mealtime conversations – and especially take care if you've opened a few bottles to show that you are a generous host. Don't become the stereotype parent figure: the talkative, middle-aged bore. Whatever your blood alcohol level, remember that one of the faults of growing older is that we all become a little repetitive, telling the same stories, making the same jokes, and, in the process, embarrassing our children. Make the effort to listen to your children and their friends. They're much more likely than friends of your own generation to come up with new ideas and to be in touch with new developments in the arts and literature. Accepting that your children are people with something to say, and acknowledging that often they have something to teach you, can mark the start of a new relationship between parents and child, when you finally come together on more equal terms as adults.

"I think the moment I consciously realized my children had grown up was when my mother and I were nursing my brother in his terminal illness. It was hard for the children, too – the first time they had to come face to face with dying. But they were incredibly supporting, so thoughtful and loving and concerned. It helped us more than they could have possibly realized."

Isobel, 43

LEAVING HOME WITHOUT GUILT

Don't feel that you're under an obligation to stay at home because one of your parents needs you, perhaps because their own relationship is not good and you're afraid that once you've gone, it may crumble altogether. Even if it does, that is not your business or responsibility. Most parents are realistic enough to know that you need your independence. You may also have disagreements about whether you're mature enough, or about where you'll be living and with whom, but they probably accept that the day you move out is inevitable. They may be sad because they'll miss you – that doesn't mean they want you to stay (see p.79).

WRITING A CV

In times of high unemployment you may apply for many jobs and be turned down many times without even getting an interview. This doesn't mean that you're not good enough, just that there are too many applicants for the same job. So how can you increase your chances?

If you can set out a clear, well-organized account of yourself (called a CV, which stands for **curriculum vitae**), you'll stand a better chance of impressing a prospective employer and getting an interview. It's worth spending some time preparing this (see example below). Include all your interests and achievements, not just exam successes. Your aim is to make yourself sound an interesting person, as well as an intelligent one.

When you're satisfied with it, ask someone to check for spelling mistakes and grammatical errors. Finally, write or type the whole thing out neatly, and make several photocopies. Each time you apply for a job, you need only write a short covering letter and enclose a copy of your CV. It's a good idea to ring up the organization beforehand and find out the name of the personnel manager, or the person who heads the department you want to apply to, so that you can address them by name.

Sample letter

5 Brookfield Close
Southampton
October 22, 1993

Ms Louise James
Personnel Director
Brown's Bank
24 High Street
Southampton

Dear Ms James,

I would like to apply for the job of counter clerk in Brown's Bank which was advertised in today's Southampton Gazette. I am enclosing a copy of my CV. I like maths and am quite good at handling money, so I think a career in banking is something I would enjoy.

Yours sincerely,

John Doe

Sample CV

Name:	John Doe
Age:	18
Date of birth	June 9, 1974

Education:	1988–1992	City Road Comprehensive
	1981–1985	Welbeck Road Junior School
	1979–1981	St Paul's Infant's School

Qualifications:	GCSEs:	English, maths, social biology, history
	A levels:	Psychology and computer studies

Work experience: I did a paper round for two years until I was 15. For the last two years I have had a Saturday job in a department store. This has involved both working at the cash till and in the stock room. I enjoyed this and got on well with the rest of the staff.

Other achievements: School prefect.
Duke of Edinburgh Award.
Secretary of Chess Club.
Member of school football team.

Spare-time interests and activities: I enjoy canoeing (especially white-water canoeing) and playing chess. I am a member of a local drama club, but enjoy the stage management and lighting side more than the acting. For the last two years I have done voluntary service for the school. A friend and I visit an old lady and do her garden and other odd jobs for her.

Career plans: I get on well with most people and would like to have a job that brings me into contact with the general public.

PART FOUR

THE ADOLESCENT
IN TROUBLE

15

THE FAMILY IN CRISIS

In my time my parents didn't hesitate to speak of death and dying. What they seldom mentioned was sex. We've got it the other way round.

Saul Bellow, Something to Remember Me By

WHEN THERE IS A CRISIS IN THE FAMILY, parents are often tempted to protect their children: sometimes they won't tell children what is really happening, and often they won't let them see what they, the adults, are really feeling.

Within a family, however, there is seldom only one person's problem. What you may think is your own personal despair may be having an overwhelming effect on your children, too, even if you don't talk about it, or try to pretend it's not serious. It's easy to overlook the effect on children, and fail to give them the comfort they need as well as the reassurance that things will get better. The problem is compounded by the fact that children do not always show their anxiety or grief. In fact, they may act in ways that seem quite inappropriate, showing indifference or lack of concern.

Most families – and most adolescents – do weather such crises. But problems such as deteriorating behaviour or schoolwork are often signs that the situation is more than the youngster can cope with. We are used to adolescents occasionally being moody and miserable – in fact, it's almost what we expect – but very often we underestimate the depth of pain they suffer, and overlook the fact that, occasionally, normal misery can become clinical depression, just as it can in adults (see *Depression*, p.238). Whatever the crisis – unemployment, divorce, or bereavement – it is almost bound to have a knock-on effect on your child and should not be overlooked. You may have to make a special effort to talk to your adolescent during difficult times.

Left: Even if it's difficult to talk, you may find ways of comforting each other.

FAMILY BREAKUP

How do teenagers cope when they're faced with the breakup of the family home through death, separation, or divorce? It's widely believed that parents have a more important part to play during childhood than during adolescence, but research shows that the consequences of parental loss may be just as traumatic for an adolescent. Even one who is truly a young adult in college with a life of his or her own may be deeply

> *"I keep telling my children that I left their mother because we were making each other unhappy. I didn't want to leave them, and I tell them that whenever they stay with me."*
> George, 47

affected by divorce. Some studies have suggested that these young adults are more likely to blame one parent rather than blame themselves (as younger children sometimes do). They are likely to deny the divorce, or to show their anger by taking an aggressively moralistic attitude towards it, and the experience may later colour their own feelings about romantic love and marriage. Whatever their ages, they're likely to feel that the parent who leaves is rejecting not just the other parent but them.

CASE HISTORY: UNEMPLOYMENT

Peter found it very difficult to accept the fact that the father whom he had always regarded as invulnerable had lost his job and was out of work. At the same time he had to try to resolve the paradox that a "good" God created a world that contains much unhappiness.

"I can't understand why my dad was made redundant. He was a good worker, and it's a big firm making good cars. So why did they pick on him?"
Peter, 15

"Peter doesn't seem to be willing to accept that the recession is no one's fault, that these things just happen, and that a lot of good men have lost jobs."
Fred, 42

COMMENT ABOUT UNEMPLOYMENT

Peter's mother intervened. It wasn't until his mother said to him, "Don't give your father such a hard time, Peter, he's feeling bad enough about things as it is," that Peter was able to show his father any sympathy, or talk about his own anger at the way he felt his father had been treated. Eventually he realized that his family was caught up in a national economic recession and that there was no reason to think that any of it was his father's fault. Things became easier when Fred found a new job for a small engineering company set up by some of his workmates, but the future remains uncertain.

For the parents the split is probably the culmination of a long, drawn-out period of conflict. They may not realize that for their children the blow may be sudden and quite unexpected. Young people are self-absorbed, tend to accept their own family situation as normal, and may take very little notice of what goes on between their parents. If those parents, moreover, have tried hard to keep their differences and difficulties under wraps, even older teenagers may be shocked at the disintegration of what they thought was a normal marriage. "All I want is for us to be a happy family again," one 12-year-old said sadly after his parents had separated, unaware that, to anyone else's eyes, his family had not seemed a happy one for a very long time.

HELPING THEM THROUGH

The breakup of a family will always cause distress, but how much children suffer in the long term from divorce or separation seems to depend much more on the quality of family life before the breakup, and on what happens to them afterwards, than on the separation itself. Some children do suffer long-term psychological problems; the most vulnerable, however, are those who have suffered chronic family discord over a long period, or who have never found themselves in a stable, happy home again afterwards. All children need extra loving care and help from both parents.

Children of 12 or older may be mature enough to be involved in any decisions made about their own future. What they want may not be practical (almost certainly what children want most is for the family to stay together), but at least their wishes should be considered and taken into account as far as possible. Often, however, both parents are so bound up in their own misery, or are unwilling to involve their children in their problems, that they don't actually talk to them much at all, let alone think to consult them about what they want. Children may thus be left completely in the dark. They may believe that it's somehow their fault that their parents have broken up. They may ask no questions, partly so as not to upset their parents further, partly in the hope that the problem may somehow disappear. If you are separating or divorcing, it is therefore up to you to explain to your children what is happening and how the future is likely to work out. Whatever your own feelings, children need to feel good about both parents.

*When a parent leaves home, he or she is
usually leaving a marriage. They may not
think of it as leaving a family, but the
children involved do.*

Almost always the children's loyalties will be divided, and they won't want to hurt anyone's feelings. Even if they feel strongly about where they want to live, for example, they may find it hard to tell you – so you may have to ask and be willing to listen to their real feelings, reassuring them when you can.

WHAT YOUR CHILDREN WILL ASK ABOUT DIVORCE

- **Which parent are they going to live with** – and do they have a choice?
- **Will they be able to see the other parent?** If so, will they be able to visit whenever they like or only at set prearranged times?
- **What about brothers and sisters?** Will they stay together or will they be separated?
- **Was it their fault you split up?**
- **Does the parent who's leaving home** not love them any more?
- **If there is another man/woman involved,** will they have to meet them?
- **Will they have to move house,** or change schools?
- **Will there be enough money** to look after everyone?

Younger adolescents, with their tendency to see issues as black and white, may find it hard to see this as a situation that has two sides. They may feel that one parent is hard done by, and that they have to "side" with them, which makes it all the more important for the "wronged" parent not to make capital out of this and turn children against the other partner. Older teenagers, on the other hand, are usually very reluctant to take sides, and are more likely to want to opt out altogether and leave the parents to sort things out for themselves.

WHEN A PARENT DIES

A parent lost through death is lost forever – although, surprisingly, sometimes this is something a teenager may be able to come to terms with more easily, and which may have fewer long-lasting effects, than the loss of a parent or family breakup through divorce. There are several ways to make this difficult and sad time bearable:

- **Don't try to hide the facts from them.** When someone close to them is dying, it is, of course, difficult not to try to protect any children involved, but it's usually wiser to tell them – partly to prepare them for what is inevitable, but also because teenagers are not stupid. They are likely to pick up the adults' own anxieties, or the feeling that the subject is taboo so that they cannot talk about it. Sometimes they may accept the reassurances they're given at face value, in which case they'll behave as if nothing unusual is happening. You may then think, unfairly, that they're behaving inappropriately or without feeling.
- **Help them to talk about their feelings.** One way to do this is to show and to talk about your own; they will then find it easier to share their grief with you.
- **Don't shut them out from what is happening.** Let them spend time with the sick or dying person; let them go to the funeral. None of this is easy for them to cope with, but they may surprise you by the strength and support they show.

STEP-PARENTING

Children do not want a "new" parent. They just want the old one back. Remarriage may seem like salvation to the adults involved; to the children it can be just as traumatic an event as the breakup of their natural family. It can be especially devastating if it happens too quickly, while the child is still mourning the loss of the old family.

Parents often feel that if they marry someone who wasn't involved in the separation or divorce, their children will accept them more easily. This isn't always the case. Very often children maintain the fantasy that somehow their parents will get together and things will be as they once were; after a remarriage the "vacant place" is filled and the fantasy destroyed once and for all.

"I know it's stupid when I'm practically grown-up now – and Dad left
when I was 12 – but it makes me feel funny, him having another family
that isn't us. It isn't that I don't like Jackie, we get on quite well. But I don't
like the idea of the baby at all. I feel it's taken my place."
Louise, 20

When parents remarry, children have to adapt to two households with different house rules and different expectations. They may not be quite sure where they belong, and divided loyalties will almost always make it hard to form a close relationship with a step-parent. Even if they find that they do grow to like, or even love, a step-parent, it may seem an act of disloyalty to the real parent to show it. The problems are worst when the step-parent brings children from a previous marriage into the household. Young boys often form good relationships with their stepfathers, but there is some evidence that the relationship tends to be more difficult if the boy is nine years or older at the time of the remarriage.

"When my mother left my dad and me, I sort of coped, but I
really hate the idea that she's going to get married again.
I guess I always thought she'd come back some time. At least
I hoped she would. I think my dad felt the same way.
Now I know there's no chance."
Tom, 15

For some teenagers the relationship is never easy. The more rejected they feel, the more miserable, aggressive, and disruptive they are likely to become. Indeed, it may seem as though they're trying to disrupt the marriage altogether. What should you do?

• **If you plan to marry again**, give your children fair warning. Don't just spring it on them. Try to explain your own feelings honestly, and listen to theirs.

• **Don't try to be a replacement for the real parent**. Your relationship with your stepchildren will probably work best (at least to begin with) if you simply try to be a good friend to them.

• **Make sure that the children have as much contact** with their natural parent as possible. They will accept a step-parent more readily if they don't feel they have to "give up" their real parent.

• **When two families merge**, give the children the chance to get to know each other before expecting them to live together under one roof.

• **Give help and advice when asked**. Otherwise keep a low profile to begin with.

The younger the child, the easier it may be to
develop a good relationship with a step-parent.

• **Realize that, as far as the children are concerned**, their lives have been completely disrupted. Where there are going to be obvious problems (a child who may have to be turned out of or share his or her room, for example), talk these over with the people involved so that at least they know you're aware of the problem and are trying to solve it.

• **When two sets of children are coming together**, work out with them what the ground rules are going to be. Be totally pragmatic about this, accept that there are going to be difficulties, that the two families will be used to doing different things in different ways, and that what you have to do for the moment is to find practical ways to help you all to live together without too much friction.

• **Make sure you give time to each other in the marriage**. The children won't like this, but it is actually in their best interests for the marriage to succeed.

ADOPTION

Families with adopted children are no more or less likely to run into problems during the child's adolescence than any other families. If your child is adopted, however, then it's natural – when times are troubled and you're engaged in an unprofitable "where did we go wrong" exercise – for you to believe the adoption lies at the root of the problem. This is very seldom true. Almost always when problems do arise in adoptive families, the cause is conflict between the personalities involved, just as in any other family; but when there is conflict, the adoption may act as a further complication. Teenagers who are getting on very badly with their adoptive parents, for example, may start to fantasize about their real parents or decide they want to seek them out.

Every country has its own laws about allowing adopted children access to information which would enable them to trace their biological or "birth" parents. A few adopted children do decide they would like to do this, and although usually they do so through curiosity or a need to know about their past – rather than unhappiness with their adoptive family – it is always desirable for them to have counselling before they embark on such a search (see *Organizations*, p.274).

> *"My parents have always seemed very reluctant to talk about my*
> *adoption, or to tell me anything about my natural parents. They*
> *hate to be reminded of it. I think they would find it unbearable if*
> *they knew I wanted to search for my natural parents. So I've*
> *decided not to say anything to them. If I find my real parents I*
> *may tell Mum and Dad or I may not. I really don't know."*
> Andrew, 20

RUNNING AWAY FROM HOME

Children who run away are voting with their feet.

Children who leave home are registering a complaint or trying to persuade their parents to listen to them. Sometimes this drastic step is the only way children can see of escaping a situation that has become intolerable. For example, a 1992 report by the National Children's Home in the UK found that about 45,000 young people run away each year; most are between 14 and 16 – and there are more or less equal numbers of boys and girls – and about 70 per cent are running away from home, and 30 per cent from care institutions. The report also found that most of those who run away from home do so only once, do not go far or stay away long, and come home of their own accord. Our own survey findings were very much in line with this report, although we did find that more girls than boys seemed to think about running away.

WHY CHILDREN RUN AWAY

Running away may be the first indication you have that something is wrong, but often you'll have some idea of what might have made your child leave home – if you're honest enough to recognize it. Listed below are three of the main causes of running away: if you spot the danger signals in time, you may be able to stop your son or daughter resorting to such a drastic solution to their problems.

• **Have there been frequent family rows, usually about your youngster's behaviour?** These rows may have been over quite trivial issues, but sometimes children run away because it seems the only way they can make their feelings known. They run away because their parents don't really listen to them or understand the way they feel, and they think their views are not being heeded, or their opinions respected. Some of the most common reasons teenagers have for running away are arguments about girlfriends or boyfriends, about clothes, or about staying out late.

You should sit down and talk. Keep as open a mind as possible; listen to what they say, and do your best to reach a compromise (see *The Tools of the Trade*, p.47).

IF YOUR CHILD RUNS AWAY

- **He or she is unlikely to stay away for long**. Most are home within 48 hours; only about two per cent of runaways stay away for longer than 14 days.
- **Few runaways go far from home**. In fact, 98 per cent stay in their own area, mostly with friends or relatives. Very, very few aim for the big cities.
- **Most runaways return home of their own accord**.

What you should do:
- **Check with friends**. Often their best friend's home is the place they'll choose to go.
- **Check with relatives**, especially any the child is close to.
- **If you cannot contact your son or daughter**, tell the local police.
- **When your youngster does return home**, your first reaction is likely to be tears of relief; your second may well be anger. Do make sure, however, that your son or daughter knows that, if you're upset or angry, it's because you love them and were so worried about their safety.
- **Make them feel it was worth coming home**. Tell them you want to understand why they felt they had to go. Listen to them when they explain, and then – together – see what can be done to change things.
- **Don't be afraid to seek outside help**. Young people may talk more easily to someone who is not directly involved, especially if reassured that they can talk in confidence. Professional counselling might help them.

- **Could they have worries they are afraid to tell you about?** When a child has a problem that he or she thinks you wouldn't understand, or that might make you either hurt or angry, running away may seem to be the simplest way out. Quite often it is because there has been trouble at school: children who have been suspended, or who know there is a letter on its way home, are often too scared to face the music, so they just don't go home. Bullying or worries about work or exams are other common causes. Sometimes a teenager has worries about sexual orientation or about pregnancy. Occasionally, they have had a brush with the law, or got themselves into debt, or are anxious about a drug or alcohol problem.

Children who are unhappy or anxious nearly always show some change in behaviour. If your child seems more withdrawn or irritable, or simply behaves worse than usual, ask them if anything is wrong. If they deny that they have a problem, reassure them that if they're ever in trouble you'll always be on their side and want to help them. Make sure they understand that no problem is too serious for them to share with you. If it seems impossible to talk to them directly because you meet a blank wall when you try, or because tempers flare up on both sides, its worth suggesting that they might find it easier to talk to a sympathetic third party. Could a family friend or relative whom they like and trust talk to them? Professional counselling can be helpful if your child agrees, and if they're reassured that what is discussed will be confidential.

• **Is there a situation at home which is impossible for your child to cope with?** Sometimes running away is a desperate cry for help, or an escape from a situation that is intolerable and that seems to have no solution. The breakup of the parents' marriage, a complete inability to get along with a parent or (more often) a step-parent, emotional or physical or sexual abuse: all are situations that the teenager cannot expect the family on its own to resolve. Although these problems are the most serious, they are also the most difficult for parents to acknowledge. A mother, for example, may turn a blind eye to abuse of a child by her partner, or refuse to listen if the child tries to tell her, either because she feels powerless to stop it, or because she feels that recognizing it would threaten her own relationship with the abusing partner.

Make time to listen to your child. Never brush aside their worries when they try to talk to you. If you are really worried about them – perhaps because you think they seem very withdrawn or unhappy, or you suspect that they're drinking too much or taking drugs – tell them you're worried, and ask them about their feelings.

RUNNING AWAY

If you have a problem, running away won't solve it. The problem will still be there when you go back. Running away, unless you have money and somewhere safe and comfortable to run to, can be unpleasant and even dangerous. Whatever the problem is, it helps to tell someone about it. Your parents are the best people to talk to because they are the people most likely to be able to change things.

If things have reached such a state that you're thinking about running away, then you have to make your parents realize how you feel. If you're hurt or angry or resentful, don't try to bottle it up, but tell them your real feelings. This doesn't mean attacking them for what they've said or done. That seldom works. The chances are that they think they behave quite reasonably. You have to explain how their behaviour makes you feel because, very often, they just don't realize this. Even if you've done something you think is bound to hurt or anger them (like getting in trouble at school), they'll have to know sooner or later, and often they are more understanding than you might expect. Almost certainly they would rather try to help you solve the problem than have you run away.

If for some reason you can't talk to your parents, tell someone else about the problem. A grandparent or other relative you're close to is often the most helpful person because they may be able to explain things to your parents. Simply talking to a friend, or ringing up a free telephone helpline can make you feel a lot better (see *Organizations*, p.274). They may not he able to solve the problem, but they can help you sort out your feelings and decide what you can do to change the situation that is making you unhappy.

COPING WITH STEP-PARENTS

If your parents have divorced or if one has died, you've probably become used to living with only one parent, sharing responsibilities, and being treated as an adult. If there's a new parent in the household, it may be upsetting. Even if you know him or her well, there's a big difference between someone coming as a visitor and someone moving in for good.

Ideally your step-parent and your own mother or father should realize that this is going to be a difficult time for all of you, but they may seem to you to be insensitive or tactless. They may be more concerned with their relationship than with anything else. The truth is that your father or mother and your step-parent are just as likely as you are to be worried about how things will work out. They may also not like admitting that they don't know how to behave or don't always know best.

Building a new family unit is going to be difficult for all of you. It will also take time. Almost certainly you will all make mistakes and there will be times when you feel very miserable and left out, especially if you're the only child. You can't be expected to "love" a stranger just because your mother or father has found a new partner. You may find it difficult even to get along with them. But it's just as likely that you will get on with them very well. This is not being disloyal to your own father or mother and you don't have to feel guilty. You should try to think of a step-parent as an extra. Certainly they are not a substitute. Even if you rarely see your own mother or father, or they have gone away or perhaps died, they are still your mother or father. Adults have ex-wives and ex-husbands; children do not have ex-parents.

If you're upset by a new step-parent trying to take over the running of the family, then say so. You will probably find it easier to talk to your own mother or father first, or possibly to a grandparent. Tell someone else anyway, and get your feelings out into the open.

You may find it hard to spend some time each month with each of your separated parents and their new partners. It may be difficult for you to feel that either household is your proper home, especially if there are other children. Again, try to talk to someone about your feelings. If your own parents are not sympathetic, you may find there is another family friend or relation to whom you can turn. Don't try to manage it all on your own. Everyone needs someone to share their troubles with.

FINDING YOUR REAL PARENTS

Not everyone who's been adopted wants to find out about their biological or "birth" parents, or to make contact with them. Still, many do – especially during adolescence, when you begin thinking much more about who you are.

Wanting to find out about your birth parents doesn't usually mean that you don't love your adoptive parents or that you want to replace them. You should remember, however, that although your adoptive parents may understand your need to find out who you are, they may still feel nervous about the search. They may feel afraid of losing you, or sad because they've done their best for you and now feel this was not enough. These feelings are understandable – just as understandable as yours are in wanting to search for your birth parents.

In most countries there is a legal age at which you have a right to see your birth certificate, and to search for your birth parents if you want to. But many experts believe that, even at 18, most people are still too vulnerable and unsettled to be able to cope with the difficulties and emotions such a search can involve. It's probably best to wait a few years if you feel you can. Your search may have a happy outcome: it may satisfy your curiosity, fill in the missing piece of the jigsaw puzzle that is "you", and it may even provide you with a new and fulfilling relationship. But before starting to search, you have to accept that you may be disappointed. You may not like the parent you find. If you've thought about them a lot, you may have built up a picture of them that turns out to be quite unlike the real thing. They may not welcome you or want to be found. You have to be ready to deal with these possibilities.

If you do decide to go ahead, it's a good idea to join an organization that will give advice and practical help (see *Organizations*, p.274). You can usually obtain details of your birth records without much difficulty. The information you'll be given will include your mother's name, address, and occupation at the time you were born, and possibly your father's name and occupation, too. This may be all you feel you want. To trace your parents so many years later will probably involve a good deal of time and detective work; it can prove expensive, too.

> *"I always knew I was adopted, but it didn't matter to me because I*
> *never felt I was loved any less than my sister. But when I was about*
> *15 I realized how different I was to the rest of the family, and I*
> *started to think about my real parents: what they were like, whether I*
> *looked like them, whether they ever thought about me, what they felt*
> *about having me adopted. I just wanted to know. But my adoptive*
> *parent seemed really hurt and upset. My dad said, 'Don't you think*
> *of us as your real parents?' I had to reassure them that they'd been*
> *marvellous. I just wanted to find out more about myself."*
>
> Tim, 18

16

RISKS AND
RECKLESSNESS

> *Accidents will occur in the best-regulated families.*

Charles Dickens, David Copperfield

EENAGERS ARE NATURAL RISKTAKERS. They need to experiment, they need to test limits – their own and other people's. It's all part of learning to manage their own lives and make their own decisions. But to begin with, because their experience is limited, their judgement is sometimes faulty. No wonder parents worry, and sometimes feel bound to step in when they fear that their youngster's health or safety is at risk.

Most parents worry about their children's health and physical safety. They fear that they will experiment with – and possibly get hooked on – drugs. Once the teenager is old enough to drive, they worry about road accidents. They worry about behaviour that might lead them into conflicts with teachers or police, about sexual experimentation, about rape or pregnancy. Most of all, parents worry about their children's happiness. How can you minimize risks?

- **Make sure you're well informed yourself.**
- **Make sure they are well informed.** Give them all the information you can about contraception, about the dangers of drinking and driving, and about drugs.
- **Set an example you want them to follow.**
- **Set limits, and make clear what they are.**
- **If you're anxious on their behalf, say so.** If you believe they're set on a course of action that involves real risks (starting a sexual relationship or riding a motorbike, for

Left: Motorbikes can become an obsession for many adolescents, who don't realize the dangers of riding them. Insist that correct safety procedures are followed.

example), don't forbid the action, but do discuss the risks. Plan together what can be done to make it safer.

• **Don't even try to protect them from everything**. For one thing, it isn't possible. For another, it isn't desirable. You have to learn to trust their judgement and accept that sometimes they'll make mistakes. Constant interference, however well meant, will simply mean that they'll make sure that you don't know much of what is really going on in their lives, and may not know when they do need help.

DEALING WITH WHEELS

Young men are reckless drivers. One recent UK report revealed that one in three male drivers is involved in an accident within two years of passing his driving test (for women the figure is about one in five).[1] Boys aged 17–19 are the most likely to have an accident. Motorbikes have an even worse accident record than cars.[2] What can you do to protect your teenage son or daughter?

DIALOGUE: THE MOTORBIKE – VERSION ONE

Teenager's view: I'm getting a motorbike on my birthday weekend. There's a special winter offer and there's a real bargain.

Parent's view: Don't be stupid. You know I'm not going to let you have one.
(Too abrupt, you've left yourself no way out.)

Teenager: I knew you'd say that. It's not fair. All my mates have motorbikes. You're really out of touch.

Parent: Only your stupid friends have them, the ones who want to die young. You can wait until you're old enough to drive the car.
(Don't mix good arguments with insults about friends.)

Teenager: I need some wheels now, I can't go on using rotten buses and my bike, and I can't wait another year to learn to drive.

Parent: I told you you're not having one and that's the end of it. And when are you going to clean those boots that have been lying in the hall for the last week?
(Don't drag in trivial side-issues that simply aggravate the argument.)

Teenager: Oh, shut up. I'll get a second-hand one. You can't stop me.

Parent: Oh yes I can.
(But can you? You should have thought it out before you started arguing.)

- **Improve their driving skills.** Basic driving lessons around town that are enough to get them through a driving test are certainly not enough to make them safe on motorways, for example. It is not usually possible to take an advanced driving test without some years' driving experience, but some driving schools do provide further instruction (an extra course of two or three 3-hour sessions), which involves driving at the respective maximum speed limit on country roads and on motorways.
- **Make sure that the car (or motorbike) they drive is mechanically and structurally sound.** It would make more sense if youngsters could drive the modern car, with its multiple safety features, and their careful parents the clapped-out old banger.
- **Where motorbikes are concerned, frighten them with statistics.**
- **Do everything you can to make sure they don't drive after drinking.** Many road accidents are drink related. This issue is one of the very few on which parents need to be authoritarian. If your youngster is the only one in his or her group with a licence, it may mean you have to collect them and bring them home more often than you would like, but it's worth doing.

DIALOGUE: THE MOTORBIKE – VERSION TWO

Teenager's view: I'm getting a motorbike on my birthday weekend. The payments are less than I earn from my part-time job.

Parent's view: Hold on a minute. You know we've always said we didn't like motorbikes. But we'd half-expected you might want one when you're 16 and we've thought a bit about it.
(Play for time, show you're prepared to be reasonable.)

Teenager: Don't start that old stuff about waiting until I'm old enough to drive the car. I can't go on waiting forever to get some wheels.

Parent: No, but you should understand that we worry about you having an accident. Lots of young people do, especially while they're learning.
(Don't be dragged into the wrong argument. Safety is the only real important point. Stick to it.)

Teenager: I won't have an accident. I'm not stupid, you know, I'll be careful.

Parent: You'll be less likely to have an accident if you make some sensible plans. January is the worst time to start to learn to ride a motorbike. We'll be happy to pay for you to go on a training course if you'll agree to wait until Easter. We know it's disappointing, but you know it makes sense.
(Probably the best outcome you could expect – and the one both parents should agree beforehand as the most likely compromise.)

ADOLESCENT DEATHS

The worst nightmares for parents are about the death or serious illness of their child. People tend, however, to exaggerate some risks and ignore others, worrying about rare events (such as teenage girls being murdered) while taking no steps to reduce the important risks, particularly those of road accidents. Each year 2,500 teenagers in England and Wales die: twice as many boys die as girls, mostly because more are killed on the road. Some other non-violent causes of death (such as muscular dystrophy) are also virtually confined to boys. The main causes of death for 1993 are shown below.

Causes of death annually between the ages of 10 and 19 in England and Wales, 1993

Cause	Boys	Girls
Infectious diseases (such as meningitis)	17	16
Cancer, including leukaemia	154	106
Nerve and muscle diseases (such as epilepsy and muscular dystrophy)	133	69
Heart and lung diseases	56	40
Abortions and complication of pregnancy	–	5
Road accidents on bicycles	15	6
All accidents	466	167
Drowning	44	8
Suicide	80	19
Murder	21	15

These deaths can be substantially reduced, however. Children and young adults who cycle should attend a training course. They should have bikes that have good lights and sound brakes; they should also wear reflective strips or jackets and safety helmets.

If and when teenagers get a motorcycle or moped, the same principles apply. Most accidents occur in the first six months of riding (indeed, if your teenage son has survived his first six months uninjured, you can relax a little). Again, training schemes and good protective clothing are important. Finally, the whole family – this includes you – must follow the principle of not drinking and driving.

The ideal car for a teenage driver is slow but safe. Many old bangers disintegrate in accidents. Make sure your children are taught to drive properly and that they don't drink and drive, nor travel as passengers in cars driven by friends who have been drinking.

All children should be able to swim. They should also know that drinking is just as dangerous if they intend to be around boats and water as it is with road vehicles.

THE TEENAGER AND THE POLICE

It's not only delinquent teenagers who can fall foul of the law. It's perfectly possible for even a thoroughly law-abiding teenager to find him- or herself involved in a confrontation with the police. In the UK, for example, random stopping and searching without "reasonable grounds" for suspicion is unlawful, but the reality is that it happens, and it happens quite often; the term "reasonable grounds", moreover, is so open to a particular officer's interpretation as to be meaningless. Owning a motorbike, looking shifty, being cheeky, mooching about with no apparent aim – all perfectly normal teenage activities – can be used as grounds for interrogation. Teenagers who drive home from a football match or after an evening out should be aware that they are quite likely to be stopped by police, so for their own protection – and to forestall trouble – make sure that they always carry their driving licence and, if possible, a copy of the insurance certificate with them.

Police can give youngsters a hard time even if they don't arrest them. Because adolescents have such a strong sense of fairness and unfairness, right and wrong, it's all too easy for them to make things worse for themselves in these situations. Their sense of outrage is more likely to dominate the occasion than their sense of diplomacy, and they may then insist upon their "rights", despite having only a vague idea about what these are. The best advice you can give them is that, when dealing with the police, it's usually wiser to be polite and co-operative rather than confrontational.

Most parents, not just teenagers, have little idea of
their legal rights, or of what they should or should
not do if they are stopped by the police. The best
policy is stay calm.

TEENAGERS' RIGHTS

The police should have reasonable grounds for stopping adolescents, and they must tell the suspect what these are. When searching, the police must say what, if anything, they are looking for. The teenager or his or her family has the right to:

- **See a copy of the search form**, on which the officers will have made notes.
- **Register an informal complaint** (if found to be justified, this can lead to an apology from the officers concerned).
- **Register a formal complaint**; this may initiate the long and complex process of a formal investigation.

Very expensive lawyers often earn their fees
by advising their clients to keep their mouths
shut tight.

DRUGS

Teenagers like to experiment, and there may seem to them to be very little difference between their own experiments with drugs, and the tranquillizers, sleeping pills, cigarettes, and alcohol that are socially acceptable for adults. Most teenagers realize that many of these "acceptable" drugs are also addictive and potentially dangerous. This does not make drug-taking by adolescents any less hazardous, but it does make it clear that a double standard operates in many parents' minds about drugs. You may need to put your own house in order before you can expect your children to listen to your advice about drugs with any degree of attention or respect. Teenagers are likely to spot and resent any adult inconsistencies and invalid arguments about drug-taking.

WHO TAKES DRUGS?

Most teenagers do not take drugs, and of those who do, most use only "soft" drugs, take them only experimentally and occasionally, and eventually give them up altogether. Probably by far the most common practice is for drugs to be taken at parties for the same reason that adults smoke and drink: because they enjoy it and because it makes them feel relaxed or uninhibited. Some take them out of bravado or because it's the socially acceptable thing to do.

DRUG USE IN 1992: TEENAGERS AGED 15 TO 16*

Drug	Current user	Previous user
• Cannabis	6%	9%
• Glue-sniffing	3%	9%
• Cocaine	0.3%	0.9%
• Heroin	0.4%	0.9%
• LSD	0.8%	2.1%
• "Downers"	0.35%	0.8%
• "Speed"	0.6%	3%
• "Magic mushrooms"	1.4%	7.5%
• Other drugs	0.9%	3.6%

*2,300 Welsh teenagers (from *British Journal of Addiction*, 1992: 87; 227–33)

A few teenagers may take drugs in order to explore new sensations and to gain new experiences, or simply to test their own limits. A survey of dancers in a Glasgow nightclub found that more than 90 per cent had at some time tried cannabis, amphetamines, and ecstasy, and 21 per cent had tried heroin. The proportion who had tried smoking was 99 per cent, and 94 per cent had tried alcohol.

WHO BECOMES DRUG-DEPENDENT?

Only a very few of those adolescents who start to use drugs for fun go on to become dependent on them as a means of personal escape, or progress from "soft" drugs, such as cannabis, to the more potentially dangerous "hard" drugs, such as heroin. Most of those in this very small group are teenagers who have other problems that make them especially vulnerable to the risks of drug-taking. They may be emotionally disturbed, lonely, or immature youngsters who find it hard to deal with the challenges and occasional disappointments that all adolescents have to face. Adolescents who do become drug- or alcohol-dependent tend to be those who take these substances often and who use them to escape from or to solve personal problems. Boys are more likely than girls to experiment with alcohol and illicit drugs and are also more likely to become dependent on them. What can you do to minimize the risks?

• **Face the facts**. Your children are going to come across drugs, be offered them, and have to make up their own minds about experimenting with them. You can't protect them, but you can prepare them.

• **Discuss the issue with them**. Make sure they know as much as possible about all the drugs they're likely to be offered, and that they understand the risks involved.

• **Be honest**. Some drugs are more dangerous than others. They won't take anything you say seriously if you insist, for example, that smoking pot carries much the same risks as injecting heroin.

• **Do what you can to make sure** that your teenager has no reason to want to use drugs as an escape route. Help him or her sort out problems as they arise, and to develop the self-confidence and social skills to resist pressure from friends.

• **Don't overreact** if you discover that your teenager has been smoking cannabis or occasionally taking amphetamines with friends. In all probability, the worst this means is that he or she finds it hard to resist peer-group pressure, or is looking for excitement. It does not mean that your son or daughter has started on the slippery slope to drug dependence, or will progress to more dangerous drugs, such as heroin or barbiturates.

• **Know what's going on around you**. Whether drugs are widely used, and which drugs are taken, will depend partly on cost and partly on what happens to be available, or fashionable, in a particular area. You will have a better idea of the exact risks to your youngsters if you know what the drug culture is in your particular

THE ADOLESCENT IN TROUBLE

neighbourhood – and especially if your adolescents confide in you and tell you how many of their friends take drugs (either occasionally or regularly).

• **Emphasize that what really concerns you are the risks** – physical, mental, and legal – that are involved. Teenagers will respond better to this approach than if you treat it as a moral issue or react as though your teenager has embarked on a reprehensible life of crime if he or she has smoked a joint at a party.

• **Take action** if you discover that a youngster is using any drug every day, even if it's one that you would regard as relatively harmless (such as cannabis or alcohol), or that he or she does this alone. Once a drug becomes a central part of everyday life, a substitute for normal social activities rather than an adjunct to them, the youngster needs help.

TOBACCO

The most widely used, easily available, and potentially dangerous drug on the market – and the one that carries more health risks than any other drug – is tobacco. People who have not smoked by the age of 20 are unlikely to start, while 85 per cent of those who smoke while teenagers become permanently hooked. Whether or not adolescents start to smoke depends largely on whether those around them – friends and family – smoke. What should you do?

• **Give up smoking yourself.** Your children will then be less likely to start, and will find it easier to resist peer-group pressure.

• **Advise your children very strongly not to smoke**, but don't forbid it completely. Such a rule is largely unforceable, and is thus unrealistic.

• **Forbid them to smoke at home.** This is reasonable, and will at any rate reduce their cigarette consumption. At the very least, if you are not a non-smoker yourself, you can create firm no-smoking zones in your house.

• **Offer a bribe**, if necessary, to help them resist temptation. Bear in mind, however, that the inducement will need to be fairly substantial to be effective.

• **Don't give up hope that they will stop.** Your adolescent may smoke until he or she is more mature and is clear-thinking and determined enough to give it up.

CANNABIS
(marijuana, dope, ganja, grass, blow, joint, weed, hash)

Cannabis is obtained from the cannabis plant. In America it's usually used as a herbal preparation (marijuana), while in Europe the more concentrated, resinous form (hashish) is more regularly used. Taken occasionally, cannabis is a relatively harmless drug and does not inevitably lead youngsters on the slippery slope to more dangerous ones.

Cannabis is the most widely used of the illegal drugs. An American survey in 1979 found that 68 per cent of young adults had at some time used cannabis, and 35 per cent were still doing so.

WHAT DOES DEPENDENCE MEAN?

The terms **addiction** and **drug addict** are no longer used by doctors working with drugs because these words are considered pejorative: calling someone a drug addict is seen to be insulting. So the current term is **dependence**, which means simply that the person finds it difficult not to take a particular substance.

Physical dependence means that the body becomes so used to the drug that, if it is withdrawn, there may be quite severe physical symptoms (such as violent tremors, vomiting, and profuse sweating) until the body has adjusted to being without the drug once more.

Psychological dependence means that the drug produces such pleasurable and satisfying sensations that the user feels driven to take it repeatedly to recapture these pleasant feelings and to avoid discomfort.

Many drugs (cocaine and the amphetamines, for example) do not cause physical symptoms when they are withdrawn. They can, however, produce just as intense a craving for the drug as those that are sometimes thought of as more addictive – the opiates and barbiturates, for example. **Tolerance** means that increasingly higher doses of the drug need to be taken to get the same effect.

SIGNS OF DRUG ABUSE

Unless your youngster actually wants you to discover that he or she is involved with drugs, the actual evidence – such as charred tinfoil, solvent containers, or pill bottles – will be hidden. Often a change in behaviour is your only clue that something is wrong, but it's easy to misinterpret adolescent behaviour: all teenagers have occasional mood swings and act oddly or unpredictably. However suspicious you are, don't panic and make accusations. Get your own feelings into perspective before mentioning your fears.

Some of the more usual signs of drug abuse are:
- Altered sleeping patterns
- General lethargy, drowsiness, or sleepiness
- Sudden mood changes
- Change in appetite
- Unusual irritability or aggressiveness
- Loss of interest in schoolwork, friends, or out-of-school activities
- Lying and secretiveness
- Chronic shortage of cash
- Unexplained disappearance of money or belongings

Most are only occasional "weekend" or party users of the drug. It is usually mixed with ordinary tobacco and smoked as a cigarette ("joints" or "reefers"). If you find cigarette papers and tins of tobacco in the possession of a youngster who is not a regular smoker (or who has previously smoked only commercial brands), this may be the reason why. The drug can also be incorporated in a cake mix, cooked, and then eaten; this is a more risky practice as it is difficult to be sure how much of the drug is being taken.

"I don't know why my parents worry about my smoking hash.
Saturdays I may sit around with my friends, smoke a few joints, and
watch a video. But I'd never take heroin or anything. I'm not stupid."
Matt, 17

Cannabis makes the user feel relaxed. It heightens perceptions, making the user feel "high" or "spaced out". Users may feel desperately hungry because it causes a drop in blood sugar. It also occasionally impairs memory and concentration. In higher quantities, it can cause raised blood pressure, rapid heartbeat and tremor, panic attacks, and, rarely, feelings of unreality or hallucinations. Although it is generally a safe drug, large quantities, or even small quantities in people who are not used to the drug, can, in rare cases, cause nausea, vomiting, and collapse.

Regular heavy smokers of cannabis tend to become psychologically dependent on the drug. They also may develop tolerance to it, so that more is needed to produce the same effect. People who have smoked a good deal of pot for a long time tend to lose their intellectual powers (memory and concentration are both affected), or may become apathetic and ineffective; they may "drop out" altogether, but this may say as much about the type of person who becomes psychologically dependent on the drug as about the effects of cannabis itself. Cannabis does not cause physical dependence, but the physical effects of long-term use (if any) are still uncertain. It has been suggested that it causes male infertility.

ALCOHOL

Alcohol is freely available, socially acceptable, and reasonably cheap. Teenagers are especially likely to drink too much if one or other parent has a drink problem themselves. Driving while over the limit is one of the commonest causes of road accidents, and people in their late teens are among those most likely to die or to be severely injured as the result. Unlike cigarette smoking, where the only sensible policy is not to start smoking at all, most people do manage to control, and not be controlled by, their drinking habits. Within a family where occasional social drinking is accepted as a pleasant, normal part of life, most teenagers learn how to drink sensibly and safely.

Young people (along with the rest of the population) are drinking more than ever before. About 60 per cent of under-age children (between 13 and 17 years old) have probably bought alcohol; about one-third of children of this age drink something at least once a week. Some teenagers drink during lunchtimes at school, and convictions from drunkenness among people under 18 are steadily rising. What should you do?

• **Forget about prohibition**. It doesn't work. It simply conjures up all the teenager's instinctive feelings of rebellion. Young people are much more likely to drink too much if their parents are rigidly opposed to their drinking anything at all.

• **Don't turn a blind eye**. Just as bad as complete prohibition is to give no guidance at all – to seem not to care. Teenagers seem to be less likely to drink too much themselves if they see that their parents drink in moderation and that they are not dependent on alcohol for their enjoyment of life or their ability to cope.

• **Teach your children to recognize when they have had enough** – and then to say no.

• **Help them learn social skills** that make it easier to resist the social pressure to drink. This can be hard for an adult, let alone a teenager, so teach them strategies for keeping their alcohol intake unobtrusively low: keeping their glass full so that it's not constantly refilled and pleading thirst every second drink and asking for water or a soft drink.

• **Get them to develop a "blotting-paper" habit**, such as eating or drinking a glass of milk before going out or to a party. Food delays the rate at which alcohol is absorbed from the stomach; the same amount of alcohol taken on an empty stomach may cause a blood alcohol peak almost twice as high as if a meal has been eaten before drinking.

• **Make sure they realize they should never drink and drive**. Also impress upon them that they should never let themselves be driven by anyone who's been drinking.

AMPHETAMINES
(pep pills, speed, sulphate, uppers, blues, black bombers, purple hearts)

Amphetamines are stimulants, reasonably cheap, and easily available. They may be taken occasionally to keep the user awake and lively, maybe because he or she is working for an exam (more often during an all-night party). Amphetamine use is more widespread among late adolescents than school-age children. They are usually taken as pills, but may be ground up and licked, sniffed, or occasionally injected. The various preparations have widely differing strengths.

Amphetamines speed up physical and mental processes, causing insomnia and making the person seem full of energy and excited. Pupils become dilated, heartbeat becomes rapid, and there may be trembling. Users often talk non-stop and move about continually (even when sitting down), are restless, and often grind their teeth or lick their lips. After using amphetamines, a youngster may feel tired and depressed. If amphetamines have been taken continually for several days and then none are taken, the "high" becomes a "low": the user "crashes", depression may be severe, and may also be marked by suicidal feelings. Sometimes acute mental disturbance with hallucinations and delusions may develop, usually (although not always) in people who have taken high doses for a long time.

SEDATIVES AND TRANQUILLIZERS

Barbiturates (*barbs, downers*) cause drowsiness and reduce anxiety. They are usually taken to counteract the effect of amphetamines and, like these, are more likely to be used and abused by older adolescents. About three per cent of 18–25-year-olds take barbiturates. These drugs are nearly always taken by mouth, but they can also be injected (in which case there is a risk of abscesses forming at the site of the injection caused by the chalk powder used to make the tablet; if needles are shared, there is also the danger of infection with the AIDS virus). "Downers" make the user seem lethargic, drunk, and confused, with slurred speech and poor co-ordination and balance. Like alcohol, they sometimes cause aggressiveness, and a few teenagers may take them deliberately for this

Barbiturates are highly addictive, causing both mental and physical dependence. Anyone who does become dependent must be eased off the drugs under medical supervision, because too rapid a withdrawl can cause fits. Barbiturates are particularly dangerous because an overdose, especially if combined with alcohol, can be fatal.

Tranquillizers (*tranks*) such as the benzodiazepine drugs (Valium, for example) are widely prescribed, and are thus relatively easy for youngsters to obtain. Their effects are similar to but less marked than barbiturates. Long-term users become dependent, and withdrawal can be unpleasant. They are not, however, as dangerous as barbiturates because an overdose is unlikely to cause death unless another sedative drug, such as alcohol, is taken at the same time. Because this may happen at a party, you and your youngster should know about the emergency procedure for responding to an overdose, known as the recovery position (see *Issue: Overdose*, p.222).

COCAINE

(coke, snow, crack, blow)

Cocaine is a stimulant with effects similar to those of amphetamines. Its use is becoming much more widespread and fashionable, but it is still more expensive and harder to obtain than either cannabis or amphetamines. Because it is expensive, dealers may adulterate it with other substances and this, if it is injected, can make it especially dangerous. Because of the expense and lack of availability, only a small proportion of late adolescents (the 17- and 18-year-olds) try it. In the USA, about four per cent of 12–17-year-olds have been found to use cocaine, whereas about a fifth of 18–25-year olds have tried it. Cocaine is usually a powder that is sniffed or, much less frequently, injected. It may also be heated (usually in aluminium foil shaped into a container) and its vapours inhaled ("chasing the dragon"); this "freebase" cocaine gives a particularly rapid and powerful "high" and is very addictive. "Crack" is an extremely addictive form of freebase cocaine: the cocaine is separated from its salt by the addition (usually) of sodium hydroxide (washing soda). Small lumps or pebbles of this substance, known as crack, are very potent; when these are heated and smoked, they produce a very intense high very rapidly (within one minute).

Cocaine rapidly induces feelings of euphoria and well-being and, for many people, heightened sexual feelings. The effects are short-lived, so the user is often tempted to take another dose. Because the effects of cocaine are so pleasurable, the drug is very addictive and the user soon becomes psychologically dependent on it. However, cocaine does not cause physical dependence; when it is withdrawn, there are no unpleasant physical symptoms. Heavy users may become very restless and anxious, and occasionally develop paranoid symptoms. People who regularly sniff cocaine may also develop ulceration of the nasal membranes.

SOLVENT INHALATION

"Glue-sniffing" is usually a group activity among younger adolescents. Although glue (in the form of contact adhesives) is the most popular substance, many other household products containing volatile substances are also used. These include aerosols such as deodorants and hair lacquers, dry-cleaning fluids, lighter fuels, paint-thinners, correction fluids, petrol, and nail-varnish remover. Because these are so easily available, youngsters do not need to become involved with the drug scene to obtain them. There is some evidence that glue-sniffers tend to move on to alcohol when they can afford it, rather than experiment with other drugs. Glue-sniffing seems to be regarded as a cheap way of getting drunk. About 3.5–10 per cent of adolescents have experimented with solvents at some time, and probably 0.5–1 per cent of secondary schoolchildren are current users. Boy-users outnumber girls.

Usually the substance is sniffed directly from the container, or from a plastic bag or crisp packet into which the substance has been poured, or from a handkerchief soaked with the substance and held over the nose and mouth. Some children risk suffocation by putting their heads into a polythene bag while they are sniffing to heighten the effect. Lighter fuel is sometimes sprayed directly into the mouth, which is particularly dangerous. These substances act very much like alcohol: they first produce a state of excitement, followed by feelings of depression. Youngsters usually recover quite rapidly from small doses, and it's quite possible for them to inhale solvents after school yet appear sober by the time they get home. By topping up the dose with repeated sniffing, though, a youngster can remain high for up to 12 hours.

Larger doses can make youngsters confused, restless, and uncoordinated. There may be dizziness, slurring of speech, and blurred vision. Some suffer hallucinations and delusions, which may make them behave aggressively or put them at risk. Vomiting, coughing, and sneezing can occur at any stage. Children who are sniffing may develop a rash or boils around the nose and mouth, red eyes, or a red ring around the nose. There may be traces of glue on their skin or clothes, and the characteristic smell of the solvent.

Long-term use of some solvents, especially petrol and dry-cleaning fluids, can cause brain, liver, or kidney damage. In the UK, for example, about 60 children die each year from solvent abuse; most are boys. Some of these deaths are caused by suffocation or by the inhalation of vomit while the child is unconscious, while others are due to the direct effect of solvent inhalation on the respiratory and cardiac systems. All these risks, of course, are that much greater if the youngster is alone than if he or she "sniffs" in a group with friends.

PSYCHOTROPIC (HALLUCINOGENIC) DRUGS

Hallucinogenic drugs are taken by mouth. LSD (*acid, tabs, microdots, windows*) is the most widely used of these drugs, and is reasonably easy to obtain and not very expensive. It does not cause dependence, although tolerance develops rapidly. "Magic mushrooms" (psilocybin mushrooms), a species of small wild mushroom with a brief season, have mild hallucinogenic properties and are usually dried and eaten. Few teenagers (perhaps 3–8 per cent) will either use or even come across these; availability varies from region to region. Those who do take them are usually older teenagers, or young adults, who are curious about the "mind-bending" properties of the drugs, but use them only occasionally.

The user's sense of reality and time are altered and their perceptions heightened. However, the effects are unpredictable: they can include powerful and sometimes frightening hallucinations. A bad "trip" may cause long-term psychological upset, and "flashbacks" – temporary re-experiences of the hallucinatory quality of the "trip" – may occur (even when someone is not on the drug).

DESIGNER DRUGS

Many of the drugs sold illegally to teenagers have been stolen or obtained in some other way from pharmacies or from illegally obtained medical prescriptions. Others, however, have no connection at all with medical sources but have been made in back-street laboratories: these may be especially dangerous because, having been developed illegally, these substances go through none of the rigorous testing that is normally applied to any new drug.

Some of the designer drugs made in these laboratories are modifications of medical drugs; changes made to the chemical make-up of an existing, approved drug may mean that its use is not technically illegal. These drugs are thus often commonly sold by people who claim that they may be taken for an evening's fun without any risk. Millions of people have taken drugs occasionally in the last 10–20 years, and the vast majority came to no harm. So what are the risks?

Some of the designer drugs are injected, a procedure that is seriously dangerous. If the dose has been miscalculated or the drug is stronger than expected, a user can lose consciousness in seconds. Injection always carries a risk of infection from the drug itself, which may contain impurities, and from the syringe or the needle, which, if shared or previously used, may transmit the virus that causes AIDS. Taking designer drugs by mouth is also risky because these drugs have been made and sold illegally and a user has no idea about what substances they contain. Their effects are therefore completely unpredictable.

ECSTASY

Ecstasy is the street name of a drug that is similar to another amphetamine that has been a listed drug of abuse in Britain since 1977. Its full name is methylene-dioxymethamphetamine (MDMA). Like other amphetamines, MDMA was first used to control or reduce appetite, and was an aid to weight loss, but concern about its possible harmful side-effects and its misuse as a mood-lifter stopped doctors from prescribing it.

Ecstasy is now widely sold illegally in clubs and discos, and many people use it regularly without seeming to come to any harm. Taken by mouth, Ecstasy makes people feel lively, alert, sociable, and happy. It had been described as not as dangerous as other illegal drugs, but in 1992 doctors in the UK began to report cases of teenagers becoming seriously ill and even dying within a few hours from the drug's effects on the brain, the liver, the heart, and the temperature control system. The frightening aspects of these reports is that some young people have died after reacting badly to their first one or two tablets of the drug, while others have taken it without ill-effects several times and then reacted badly on a later occasion. Frequent use of the drug may damage the liver. Dehydration also increases the risks, and people who do take Ecstasy should drink enough water, though not excessive amounts, to stop them feeling thirsty. Since 1990, in the UK as many as 50 people are thought to have died as a direct result of taking the drug, and others have been killed in road accidents while under its influence. Clearly this drug is dangerous, especially because its effects are so unpredictable.

"ANGEL DUST"

This is an anaesthetic drug (phencyclidine, PCP) that was widely used for a time by drug-users in America, although its popularity has declined. It is a potent and potentially dangerous drug, whose effects are closely linked to the dose taken. "Snorted" (inhaled) in small doses, it gives a "buzz" and a feeling of mild euphoria. Slightly larger doses produce hallucinogenic effects and a lack of coordination (a feeling sometimes described as "walking on marshmallows"), while in larger doses it acts as a "downer" similar to barbiturates. The drug usually produces adverse effects, and regular use can lead to "burning out", an inability to think clearly, and memory loss.

HEROIN AND THE OPIATES
(H, smack, scag, horse, blow)

The opiates, which include morphine, heroin, and codeine, are drugs derived from the opium poppy. The most commonly misused is heroin, a talc-like powder that can be brown, white, grey, or pink. It is usually sold as "wraps" or "bags", small amounts folded in paper or put in a small bag.

The discovery that their youngster is taking heroin is every parent's worst nightmare. Parents of a drug-dependent adolescent are usually desperate to talk about their problem but sometimes feel such a sense of shame and failure that the last thing they

ISSUE: OVERDOSE

If you discover someone who is unconscious and you suspect a drug overdose, immediately check that the victim is breathing. This simple procedure may save a life.

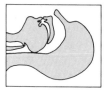 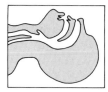

• **Kneel at the victim's side.**

• **Hold the chin**, gently pulling it up to tilt the head back. This opens the airway *(see boxes left)*.

• **Put the person in the recovery position.** Turn the head towards you.

• **Make sure** the legs are straight. Bring the arm across the chest. Place the palm on the floor.

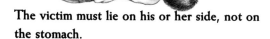

• **Place the victim's arm** nearest to you under the buttock *(right)*.

• **Turn the victim on to the side** by pulling the upper leg towards you to rest against your knees.

• **Readjust the arm** nearest to you. The palm should be flat on the floor, just in front of the victim's head.

The victim must lie on his or her side, not on the stomach.

• **Readjust the head** by lifting and tilting it back *(see box left)* to keep the airway open.

• **Make sure** both the hip and the knee are at right angles to the body.

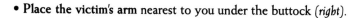

• **Get someone to call for help.** NEVER LEAVE AN UNCONSCIOUS PERSON ALONE.

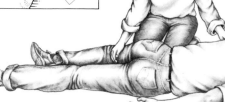

want to do is to admit to friends, who have not been through the experience themselves, that their child is drug-dependent. Most parents find that they are helped most effectively by joining a support group and meeting people who have faced the same problem (see *Organizations*, p.274) Although heroin is now more widely available and cheaper than it has ever been, probably only about one per cent of youngsters ever try heroin, and only a few of these will become regular users.

"I'd stolen this Barclaycard; I was about to be evicted from my flat and had no place to live, I had no money to eat, and my bank had bounced all my cheques. Then I managed to get a good bit of smack (heroin). No sooner had I injected it than all my problems disappeared and life was blissful and calm. I had this warm, safe feeling. Nothing else mattered any more."
Tina, 19

Heroin is an illegal, powerful drug, causing both physical and psychological dependence. It can be taken by mouth, sniffed, smoked ("chasing the dragon"), or dissolved in water to be injected beneath the skin, into a muscle or directly into a vein ("mainlining"). However, most youngsters are aware of the dangers of injection. Usually the drug is smoked or sniffed; taken this way, its effect is less powerful and the dangers of infection and overdose are reduced. It also means that you can seldom tell if your youngster is taking heroin simply by looking for needle marks on his or her body or for bloodstains on clothes.

The first experience of heroin usually only causes nausea and vomiting. The "rush" (the brief but intense feeling of euphoria and pleasure that is the effect most users crave) isn't usually experienced until the drug has been taken a few times. The rush is then followed by a feeling of calm and peace. A youngster taking heroin will seem to be withdrawn and solitary: he or she will be lethargic and difficult to get through to, and may lose interest in schoolwork and seem to have little motivation – except for obtaining future supplies of the drug.

The mortality rate in Britain for heroin users is still about two to three per cent each year – despite the fact that, in the UK, they may legally register with doctors to receive controlled doses of heroin – but there is evidence that over a third of heroin users do give it up. Many others manage to lead quite normal lives despite their dependence. Much has been learned about heroin dependence from the experience of the American soldiers in Vietnam, an estimated 70 per cent of whom became regular users of heroin during their service there. Doctors who treated these returning soldiers found that most managed to give it up – three years after returning only four per cent still used it daily – and that some who had been withdrawn from the drug were subsequently able to take it occasionally without becoming dependent again.

HELPING DRUG USERS

Drug dependence isn't an illness and it can't be cured by doctors. It is a form of deviant behaviour, something someone does because he or she likes it. Only the drug-user can decide to give it up.

There is no one way of dealing with it. Parents used to be advised to refuse to give their youngster money to buy drugs, or to throw them out so that the drug-user sank lower and lower, got more and more desperate, and was eventually forced to seek help. But most parents find it heart-breaking to take this hard line; an additional drawback is that, if and when a young user does give up a drug, you may have cut yourself off from him or her and be unable to provide additional help. Many parents prefer to give their drug-dependent adolescent money, so that at least he or she won't be forced to steal, and to keep the lines of communication open, even though the user may seem so separate and withdrawn that this is often difficult.

Giving up drugs is like giving up smoking: until the drug-user recognizes that he or she has a problem and actually wants to give up, not much can be done to help. Once the desire to give up is there, almost any method works.

WHERE TO SEEK HELP

It is not always easy for a youngster to get professional help, even if he or she has decided to seek it. You may be able to find hospital drug clinics, although most have long waiting lists; some offer out-patient treatment only. After withdrawal, people with serious drug problems sometimes spend a long time at a residential rehabilitation house, away from the influences and environment associated with their drug-taking.

Once drug-users have made this commitment, you can help them through withdrawal, and try to resolve the problems that made them turn to drugs in the first place.
• **Take someone who is injecting heroin to a doctor straightaway.** Regard this as a medical emergency. Withdrawal from heroin must be done slowly and in hospital to prevent unpleasant and painful withdrawal symptoms. Sometimes another drug – for example, methadone – is given to prevent withdrawal symptoms.
• **Persuade them to see a therapist** who can help them resolve the problems that may have led to the drug dependence or substance abuse.
• **Help them make changes in their lives in order to remain drug-free.** It's not enough simply to give up drugs: it's essential for drug-users to get away from their previous environment and set of friends.
• **Help them to find and keep a job.** This avoids the problem of having too much time on their hands and a feeling of purposelessness.
• **Don't despair if they go back on drugs again.** This is a very common pattern; although the chances are that it will happen more than once, the drug-free intervals will probably get longer and longer.

CASE HISTORY: ECSTASY

Michael and his friend John planned to go and see a local band. They knew that drugs would be available, and Michael had decided to experiment with Ecstasy. John, however, had a driving test the next day and decided not to take anything that evening. At the club, Michael bought a tablet of Ecstasy. After 20 minutes he felt nothing, decided he had been sold a dud tablet, and bought another. Another 20 minutes passed and he still felt nothing, so he persuaded a friend to lend him money for a third tablet.

"About an hour after Michael had taken the first tablet, he got really high, dancing and whirling all round the place. Later he seemed really out of control. He was sweating a lot and I tried to make him drink something, but there was no way I could get him off the floor."
John, 17

"About 11:30 that night John rang us up distraught to say that Michael had been taken off in an ambulance. He had collapsed a couple of hours after he'd taken the first tablet. In hospital he was put on a drip straightaway and he was OK. But it was a close thing."
Maurice, 47

COMMENTS ON ECSTASY

Ecstasy, like all illegal drugs, is potentially dangerous. If you do take it, stick to three golden rules:
Never take more than one tablet; it can take at least an hour to act.
Drink plenty of liquids – but not alcohol – if you are dancing after you take it.
Never mix Ecstasy with any other drug.

ISSUE: DRUGS AND THE LAW

Illegal drugs (in the UK, those covered by the Misuse of Drugs Act) include cannabis, heroin and other opiates, barbiturates, amphetamines, cocaine, and LSD. Some "magic mushrooms" are not covered by the law if they are picked fresh and eaten straightaway, but if they are dried, cooked, or processed in any way, they are counted as an illegal drug. It is an offence to possess, give away, or sell an illegal drug. It is also an offence to allow anyone on your premises to do so. It is illegal to permit anyone to smoke cannabis or opiates in your house.

If parents find illegal drugs on their premises and wish to prevent their son or daughter from using them, they are legally entitled to destroy the drugs; they need not involve the police. In any other circumstances, parents are legally obliged to hand illegal drugs to the police straightaway.

Parents do not have to tell the police if they believe their children are taking or supplying illegal drugs.

DEALING WITH DRUGS

Unless you have no friends, stay home every evening, or take yourself off to a desert island, you're going to meet people who take drugs or who want you to take them, or who try to sell them to you. You'll find it easier to deal with if you know something about drugs, so try to find out all you can about them before you're offered any (see *Drugs*, p.212).

All drugs except alcohol and tobacco are illegal. Some are dangerous. Drug dealers are not concerned about anyone's safety, and when you buy street drugs you have no way of knowing how pure they are or what dose you'll be taking. You have to make up your own mind if the risks are worth running. If you decide you want to experiment, that's up to you. But plenty of people first take drugs not because they want to, but because someone else has persuaded them.

No one can force you to take drugs if you don't want to, but they can lean on you quite hard. Not for nothing are people who sell drugs called "pushers". Remember – that these people are doing you no favours; for them you're just a source of easy money. Crack is much more addictive and dangerous than cocaine, for example, and so dealers would far rather sell you crack: it's much more profitable. Drugs are their business, and often they're using you to finance their own drug habit.

If someone you don't know tries to sell you drugs, there's only one way to deal with it. Say "No thanks" very firmly and walk away. If you hang around, or sound uncertain or curious they'll mark you down as a "possible". And because they've had more experience of selling drugs than you have had of refusing them, the chances are they'll win.

More difficult to cope with is the friend who's taking a drug and wants you to try it, too. It's worth asking yourself why they're so keen for you to join them. Would they put all that effort into persuading you to try a new chocolate bar, for example? It could be that they feel a bit uneasy about taking the drug. If they can say to themselves that "everybody" is doing it, then it's much easier for them to believe that it's all right for them.

It's not easy just to say no to friends and walk away – because you care about what your friends think, and you don't want to lose them. The more sure of yourself you sound, the less pressure on you there will be. If you're a very strong-minded and confident person, you might get away with saying, "I think you're stupid, and you're certainly not going to get me to take it". Otherwise, it's probably easier to saying things like:

- "I don't really want to, so why bother?"

- "There are lots of things I'd rather spend my money on."

- "I don't like the idea of being out of control."

- "I don't feel in the mood."

- "You go ahead, but I've decided I'm not going to."

You may think that everyone else does seem to be taking soft drugs at the weekends and you don't want to be left out. People may not be telling you the truth. It's a bit like sex, with everyone claiming to be more experienced than they really are. But if you do decide to try a drug such as cannabis, then you should wait for an occasion when you know and trust the people around you. Never forget that drugs are illegal. Don't walk around the streets carrying drugs with you.

You may also think that it's exciting to do something dangerous like experimenting with hard drugs, but you should ask yourself about the very serious health risks you would be exposing yourself to. To begin with, you risk becoming drug-dependent. Remember, too, that it's one thing to take a drug by putting it in your mouth or smoking it, but it's a very different matter if you're thinking about injecting it. It you inject a drug, you risk infecting yourself with the virus that causes AIDS, for which there is no cure yet. Ask yourself if the "thrill" of doing something dangerous or feeling high is worth risking that.

TALKING TO THE POLICE

Sooner or later every teenager is going to come into contact with the police. You may be stopped in the street and asked questions; you may be involved in a road accident; or the police may be called to a party or pub where there has been some noise and violence. Don't try to be smart, showing off to your friends. The police have got all the advantages and they're going to come off winners if it comes to a confrontation. So even if you feel you're in the right and that they're being unreasonable, try to keep calm and keep the temperature down.

Be polite. Answer all the straightforward questions, such as your name and address and where you're going. You may be asked to turn out your pockets and show what you've got in any bag you're carrying. You don't have any choice, so do it without arguing.

If the police seem to think you may have committed an offence – speeding, driving carelessly, being concerned in violence outside a drinking club or pub or after a sporting event – it may be best to say very little. You don't have to make a statement at all. At the very least, you can say that you don't want to make a statement until you have had a chance to talk to your parents or to a solicitor. All police stations have a "duty solicitor" available to give advice to people brought in by the police.

17

BEHAVIOURAL AND EMOTIONAL PROBLEMS

"

Nobody who has been in the interior of a family can say what the difficulties of any individual of that family may be.

"

Jane Austen, Emma

NEARLY ALL ADOLESCENT DIFFICULTIES arise from the normal process of growing up. All teenagers have ups and downs of mood, go through periods of boredom or apathy, show extremes of energy or enthusiasm, or become temporarily withdrawn and uncommunicative. All these can be signs of emotional disorders, but they are much more likely not to be. Even though these moods are maddening to live with, they seldom mean there's any real cause for alarm.

However, it can be dangerous to assume that an adolescent will grow out of everything, particularly a serious mood disturbance. Sometimes a problem reaches such proportions, or parents and teenagers reach such an impasse that outside professional help is needed. Although severe mental disorders are very rare among children of this age, antisocial behaviour and mild emotional disorders are probably about as common in adolescence as they are among adults.

It can often be difficult even for professionals to distinguish the symptoms of a genuine emotional disorder from "normal" adolescent behaviour, or to draw a line between true psychiatric disorders and the inevitable problems that are part and parcel of growing up and of family life. Covered in this chapter is behaviour that goes beyond being merely irritating (but normal), behaviour that indicates some real disturbance or unhappiness that may threaten the youngsters health and well-being.

Left: Some children may find it hard to recover from a setback or failure, and go through a "low" patch or even a period of depression.

DECIDING WHAT'S "NORMAL"

In trying to cope with odd or awful adolescent behaviour, apply the same principles as for childhood behaviour:

- **If the youngster behaves in a way that worries you**, ask yourself why.
- **Look at a particular type of behaviour in context** to see its real implications before deciding whether it is abnormal, rather than simply maddening or objectionable.

Tom's parents, for example, were devastated when they discovered that he had stolen a magazine from a shop on the way home from school. Neither did it comfort them much when Tom told them that "everyone" did it, that almost all the boys from his class occasionally stole small items from shops when they had the chance, that it was just a game with an extra element of excitement. Eventually, however, the realization that this kind of petty shoplifting was so common among his friends helped his parents to put things into perspective: they realized that their son was probably not a crook, but simply an adolescent conforming to the "normal", although reprehensible, behaviour of his peers. This didn't mean that they had to condone it, simply that it was behaviour that could be dealt with by firm talking at home, rather than needing professional help.

*Unhappy adolescents take it out on the easiest
targets — usually parents and teachers. When they
make life intolerable for you, it's probably because
they're finding it pretty unbearable themselves.*

WHEN TO WORRY

You should always look for, and try to understand, the cause of behaviour, not just the behaviour itself. You should be concerned, too, about any behaviour that seems to be restricting your son's or daughter's own life. The youngster who is truly disturbed is certainly not easy to live with, but the behaviour calls for action not just because it is difficult and perhaps damaging, but also because it suggests that the youngster is deeply unhappy. For example, the time to worry about cannabis is when you discover that your youngster is regularly smoking it on his or her own because he or she wants to opt out of the real world. Smoking with friends — and telling you about it — is less worrying, because the underlying causes are social (and have more to do with a need to be accepted by a group) rather than emotional.

BAD BEHAVIOUR

Most bad behaviour is a sign that the youngster is finding life difficult to cope with. It may be because he or she is uncertain or unhappy about the future, or is lonely and unable to make friends easily.

But what is it that makes some children more vulnerable than others and leads to the kind of disturbed behaviour – fighting, stealing, drunkenness, refusal to go to school or to talk to parents – that may be impossible for parents and teenagers to resolve themselves without professional intervention and help? There are several factors that may contribute to difficult behaviour:

- **The teenager's own personality** is one of the most important factors affecting both the way in which he or she handles problems, and the way other people (parents, teachers, and friends) respond to him or her (for example, youngsters who have always been "prickly" or difficult tend to attract criticism).
- **Family situations and attitudes are important, too.** Some families are able to cope with and contain or deal with problems that arise. Others may seek psychiatric help, not because the youngster's problem is particularly severe, but because the parents are at a loss to know how to handle it, or because the relationship between parents and child has deteriorated to such an extent that resolution seems impossible.
- **Low self-esteem often lies at the root of problem behaviour.** Continual failure is damaging to anyone's self-esteem, and this is why children who fail at school often

CASE HISTORY: POT-SMOKING

Jane's parents regarded all drug-taking as delinquent behaviour. They knew that Jane smoked cigarettes occasionally, but were horrified when they found out that she and most of her friends smoked pot at parties, too.

"I can't tell you how bad I felt when I found that Jane smoked pot. I felt I'd really failed as a mother, that it must be something her father and I had done wrong that had made Jane take drugs. I wanted to take her straight off to our family doctor and ask him to refer us to a drug clinic."
Mary, 41

"It was hard to explain to my parents that it wasn't like what they thought. My friends are just ordinary kids. None of us takes drugs, but everybody smokes pot sometimes. It's just a social thing like having a cigarette or a drink. It doesn't mean we're all going to be shooting up hard drugs."
Jane, 17

COMMENTS ABOUT POT-SMOKING

Jane's parents told her that the fact that "everybody" smoked pot didn't, in their view, make it either right or harmless.

Jane's father could see that Jane didn't need to be treated for drug dependence, but did need some straight talking about not always going along with the crowd, and reminding that smoking anything is, in the long term, bad for health reasons.

behave badly, too. This is not to say that clever children behave well and that less able ones behave badly. "Failure" here doesn't simply mean the inability to pass exams, but means instead the failure to live up to other people's expectations, some of which may be inappropriate. Some children seem to fail consistently at school because they have given the mistaken impression of being more academically able than they really are (see *Assessing Your Child's Capabilities*, p.157). Others may fail in an attempt to call attention to more serious emotional problems, such as family breakup.

SEEKING HELP

Knowing what type of behaviour needs professional attention – such as anorexia, compulsive stealing, drinking – may be difficult. If in doubt, you should either discuss it with your family doctor or a professional psychologist.

If you decide that your child needs more help than you can provide, what do you do? Occasionally an adolescent will seek help for him- or herself. In this case, a youngster is already halfway to success, because he or she has obviously recognized a problem and is willing to work at it. But how do you persuade a reluctant adolescent to see a family doctor or even a psychologist or psychiatrist? Almost always the best approach is to make it clear that you see the problem as a family one, for which you all need help.

• **Tell the youngster** that although you desperately want to help, you don't seem able to find the right thing to say.

• **Make it clear that you feel responsible, too**, and that although you may seem to be getting on badly and are unable to talk to each other, you are as much to blame as the teenager. Reassure him or her that the problem is not anyone's "fault", but a situation you have all got yourselves into and cannot resolve by yourselves.

• **Arrange an appointment with your doctor** once both of you are convinced that outside help is necessary. Even if reluctant, your son or daughter will probably go along with this.

• **Don't enter into any hypothetical arguments** about what will happen next, or worry if your youngster agrees to go but not to cooperate. Take things one step at a time and deal with whatever is in front of you at the moment.

DELINQUENCY

Many, perhaps most, teenagers break the law at some time or another. The legal definition of a juvenile delinquent in the UK, for example, is someone between the age of 10 (the age of "criminal responsibility") and 17, who has been found guilty of a criminal offence by a juvenile court. However, in practical terms, only the youngster who has had repeated convictions will be considered truly delinquent.

Usually the law-breaking behaviour of adolescents is confined to such petty offences (riding on buses for free, trying to get into a football stadium without paying, or into an adult film while under age) that they can scarcely be considered "crimes". Only a few ever appear in court, and most appear only once.

Most youngsters "outgrow" their delinquency, and only about 25 per cent of delinquent children go on to become persistent law-breakers after adolescence. Nevertheless, about half of all crimes are committed by people between the age of 10 and 21, most of them boys. Over 90 per cent of these crimes include breaking into premises, theft, driving off cars without the owner's consent, and vandalism.

We tend to think of delinquency in terms of breaking the law, but this is not necessarily so. Any behaviour that is a deliberate and subversive deviation from the norm can be thought of as delinquent. In girls, for example, law-breaking is very uncommon; delinquent behaviour is much more likely to take the form of sexual promiscuity or of early pregnancy.

The more a child is regarded as difficult, the
more this becomes a self-fulfilling prophecy.

WHAT MAKES A DELINQUENT

Many children who become delinquents were regarded as "difficult" almost from birth. Antisocial – that is, noisy and aggressive – children who are disobedient and fight a lot run a relatively high risk of becoming delinquent teenagers. It may be that they were born with difficult temperaments that created or contributed to their difficulties in relating to other people.

Much of the evidence suggests that delinquents are not happy youngsters. Many have deprived or unstable backgrounds; many, but by no means all, have parents who tend to be uninterested, unloving, intolerant, and inappropriately or harshly punitive. Delinquents tend to be more impulsive, defiant, and resentful of authority than other youngsters, but few have any real psychiatric problems. Often the adolescent feels he

Adolescents under 17 are rarely violent, but
those who are 17 to 20 years old have the
highest conviction rates for crimes of violence.

or she has been wronged, and, in these situations, see their behaviour as morally justified, as "getting their own back". They tend to dislike their classmates, and are often disliked or not accepted by them. Often they have failed at school and so may have low self-esteem and self-confidence; this creates a vicious circle because, disliking or having failed in school, these teenagers tend to be truant. When they leave school they may then find it difficult to get or keep a job and thus have ample opportunity for getting into trouble. The more serious kinds of delinquent behaviour thus often begin around school-leaving age.

DELINQUENTS AND THE LAW

In the UK and many other countries, changes in the law during the 1960s and 1970s were intended to ensure that prosecution for criminal acts should be avoided altogether in the case of "juveniles" (defined as children under 14 years of age), and wherever possible, in the case of "young persons" (defined as children between 14 and 17). Because several studies had shown that locking youngsters up in institutions did not help to reform them (and may even have made it more likely that they would commit criminal offences again), the police and other authorities were expected to cooperate in finding ways to help both the child and the family without court action.

However, things have not worked out in quite this way. In Britain, legal statutes have never been fully implemented; in many cases, the police have discretion about prosecution, and sometimes resort to it where an alternative might be preferable. Even if the offence is trivial and the offender comes from a "good" home where parents are prepared to cooperate and take responsibility for their child, the police often feel that justice must be seen to be done and are reluctant to let an offender off the hook.

ALTERNATIVES TO PROSECUTION

Once a youngster's behaviour has reached the attention of the police, what alternatives to prosecution are there?

• **The official "caution"**, a ticking-off from a senior uniformed police officer. One objection to this is that before the youngster can be "let off" in this way, he or she has to admit guilt. If a youngster denies the offence, he or she may well be taken to court. Another objection, of course, is that if the youngster is not taken to court, any victim loses the chance of a court order for compensation.

• **Informal supervision by the police or the social services.** Again, a youngster may be put under pressure to admit guilt and agree to supervision so that he or she can be kept out of court.

• **No action or intervention.** Many surveys have suggested that, from the point of view of the teenager's future behaviour, this works best of all.

• **Counselling and psychotherapy.** These may work for a few emotionally disturbed children, but as a general rule, they have not been found to be particularly helpful.

• **Practical forms of "treatment" such as help in finding a job.** These seem to work quite well. Youngsters may benefit from a proper assessment so that they and those teaching them have a realistic idea of their capabilities; they can then be encouraged to achieve realistic educational goals.

• **Social skills training** that will give youngsters more confidence, more self-esteem, and a better chance of getting and keeping a job.

• **Firm and consistent handling,** whether they are living at home or an institution or an approved school. This approach contributes to a sense that they are expected to live up to someone's high (but realistic) expectations of them.

ISSUE: TRUANCY

Some youngsters play truant on just one occasion, perhaps because they want to avoid some sort of trouble at school or are worried about an exam. Occasionally, a few classes may be skipped as a lark. For a few youngsters, however, truanting becomes a way of life so that they're out of school more often than they're in it.

- **Who plays truant?** Boys truant more frequently than girls. Often, they'll pretend to go to school but never actually arrive. Truanting is most frequent around the age of 13 and reaches another peak around school-leaving age.

School drop-outs share many of the same characteristics as delinquents, although not all truants are delinquent. Many are simply youngsters who can think of better ways of spending their time than going to school. Sometimes they're merely bored by their classes, but more frequently they actively dislike school. Often they have good reason to: most truants are of below-average ability, and often they have had frequent changes of school so that their schoolwork is usually poor (and made worse by constant truanting). As a result, they tend to be frequently criticized, or be regarded as stupid, and their self-esteem tends (understandably) to be low. Academic failure can lead to social failure, too, because often these youngsters are kept back a year and find themselves with younger children who don't easily accept them. Their friends tend to be other youngsters who have dropped out. Truancy may be just one of the adolescent's behavioural problems.

- **What should be done?** Parents are legally responsible for their children's attendance at school until the age of 16. When a school discovers that a youngster is persistently truanting, the school governing body should inform the local education department. Local authorities vary enormously in their attitude to truanting, but in most cases the educational welfare officer will visit the child's home to discover why he or she is truanting, and try to resolve the problem without resort to statutory powers.

Persistent truanting usually needs professional intervention. Helping the family may work best, because quite often these children are unhappy at home. Parents who are unsure how to deal with bad behaviour are sometimes too harsh or punitive or (just as bad) tend to overlook it. It's important that parents show concern; otherwise youngsters may get the impression that their parents don't care – either about the truancy or about them.

A change of attitude on the part of the school may be needed, too:

- **Has the school actually got something to offer children who truant?** Is the curriculum right for them? Do they feel they're getting anything out of going to school? If not, who can really blame them if they truant?

- **Teachers should treat the teenagers courteously** and make it easy for them to rejoin the class. Finally, a school's truancy records (which parents are entitled to see) can tell quite a lot about the school, as well as about its pupils. As a parent, you have every right to be angry if you discover your child has been truanting before the school finds out.

EMOTIONAL PROBLEMS AND ANXIETY STATES

In adolescence, anxiety most often takes the form of intense fears called phobias. For example, a social phobia or intense shyness, or school refusal (which may reflect anxiety about school itself or anxiety about leaving the family).

SOCIAL PHOBIAS

Mild social fear (such as shyness or anxiety about dating) is quite common in adolescents, as it is in the general population. However, a few youngsters develop social anxieties in adolescence that are so intense that they cannot make friends, even with people of the same age. They may develop an uncontrollable fear of doing some specific but quite normal activity, such as eating, drinking, or writing in public, to the extent that it becomes a very serious handicap. Children who have these phobias may tend to try dealing with them by simply avoiding the feared situation, but this does not constitute or lead to a cure. A much better way to deal with phobias, and one that usually works very well (provided that the person concerned really does want to be rid of the phobia), is a "behavioural" approach, in which the person, encouraged and supported by his or her family, is actually helped to do whatever it is he or she fears.

If your child tries to avoid all social contacts so that he or she cannot make friends and has a very restricted life, then you should seek professional help.

SCHOOL-REFUSERS

Children who refuse to go to school present a quite different problem from those who play truant (see previous page), and need to be treated in a quite different way. Truants usually avoid school because they can think of better ways to spend their time. They may dislike school, or be bored by it, but they do not have an active fear of it. School-refusers, by contrast, are filled with real terror and distress at the prospect of going to school; it isn't just that they won't go, but that some aspect of school life makes them so intolerably anxious that they cannot go. Although this problem most often occurs at around the age of 14, it is nonetheless rare and accounts for only about five per cent of all children with psychiatric disorders. However, there are probably many other children who have some mild form of the problem, but who are helped by their parents or family doctor before their anxiety reaches unmanageable proportions.

In a few children, school refusal can be a sign
that they are suffering from depression.

Usually the problem develops quite gradually. At first, the youngster may simply be reluctant to go to school and presents all sorts of excuses about why he or she should not go. Sometimes the child may not actually refuse to go to school, but develops vague physical symptoms (headaches, stomach-aches, or nausea, for example) each morning. Eventually, anxiety builds up to a point where he or she absolutely refuses to leave home at all, and becomes panic-stricken if pressured.

Often an initial reluctance to go to school becomes outright refusal after the change to senior school. Sometimes refusal starts after a temporary absence from school due to illness or holiday that has made a youngster fall behind in a subject he or she finds quite hard at the best of times, or after some crisis or upset in his or her life. At the same time,

CASE HISTORY: SOCIAL PHOBIA

Seventeen-year-old Rachel had always been quite shy, and all through her teens the thought of eating in front of other people made her feel anxious and panicky. She always took a packed lunch to school and would go off somewhere by herself to eat it. Even at home she would sometimes ask to eat in her room rather than with the family. One day after school she was persuaded to go out with some friends where a boy she liked bought her a hamburger. Rachel made a desperate attempt to eat it, but was immediately sick. This reinforced all her fears about eating in public and made her problem very much worse.

"We hadn't realized how anxious Rachel felt about eating until we took her to a restaurant on her birthday. She seemed to be looking forward to it and ordered her meal quite happily. But when it came, she was quite unable to eat it. Rachel didn't seem to be worrying about her weight; in fact, she worried that she wasn't getting enough to eat."
Lisa, 39, and Michael, 39

"I just knew that if I took a single mouthful I would be sick, right there in front of everyone – and I was."
Rachel, 17

COMMENTS ABOUT SOCIAL PHOBIAS

With her parents' encouragement and support, Rachel tried hard to overcome her problem. She managed first to eat just a few mouthfuls with friends at home, then at a small, quiet restaurant with the family. Now, two years later, things have improved, but the problem still recurs when she is socially very anxious. Someone who really wants to be rid of a phobia and live normally can sometimes be helped if they can be supported by their family while actually trying to do whatever it is they fear.

Don't struggle too long on your own and allow a phobia to become a focus for family conflicts. Instead, seek professional help: psychologists have developed several ways to assist people in overcoming phobias such as Rachel's, or fears about, for example, dogs, spiders, or flying.

the youngster may become more generally withdrawn, unsociable, and reluctant to leave home.

In most cases, it is anxiety rather than depression (see below) that accounts for school refusal. Sometimes the anxiety, which amounts to a phobia, is specifically about school itself. In some cases (often in children who have a particularly close and dependent relationship with their mothers), the anxiety may be primarily about leaving the family. Sometimes children are worried by a family problem, and feel that they are somehow "safeguarding" the family by staying at home, that something fearful may happen if they leave to go to school. Most children who refuse are of at least average ability, so difficulty with school work is seldom the root cause of the problem. Boys and girls are equally affected. Cultural background, and attitudes to education in general, may be another important consideration; in Britain, for example, school-refusers are less often from Asian families.

If you're faced with an adolescent who will not go to school, it's important to seek help from your family doctor. While it is obviously important to discover why the youngster refuses to go to school, the first step is simply to get him or her back. The longer a child stays away, the more likely it is that he or she will fall behind with schoolwork and lose touch with friends, and this will make school an even less attractive prospect. It is best for parents, doctor, and school to cooperate – especially because it may be hard for you to be firm with a child who is distressed and anxious – so that the youngster can be reintroduced gradually to school (perhaps for only part of the day at first or to attend only a favourite lesson). Ideally, you should take the youngster to school and spend some time there; if a schoolfriend can be drafted in to go along, too, this can often make the child less anxious. Alternatively, your family doctor may arrange for someone outside the family to take the child to school at first. If your doctor cannot help you persuade your son or daughter to go back, a referral to a psychiatrist is the next step. Usually the youngster will be treated as an out-patient, but in some very severe cases of school refusal, admission to an adolescent unit as an in-patient may be necessary.

Your child will settle back in school eventually, but be prepared for times in the future when he or she may be especially vulnerable and likely to manipulate you into letting him or her stay home: Monday mornings, after half-terms, holidays, or absence through illness (see also *Issue: Dropping Out of University*, p.183).

DEPRESSION

The emotional highs and lows of adolescence are one of its hallmarks. It's quite common for teenagers to have extreme swings of mood and to suffer periods of intense gloom when life is difficult or disappointing. Our own survey found that about half of the 14-year-olds interviewed had felt like this at times, but most children are very resilient and quite quickly come to terms with whatever is bothering them. They seldom remain miserable for long and may recover before their unhappiness has even been noticed by the adults around them.

A very few children, however, do not recover easily from a setback or failure. Their misery may persist even though the youngster no longer has any particular reason for unhappiness. Sometimes the depression is so severe that it interferes with life at every level, affecting schoolwork, social life, friendships, and family relationships. The evidence is that between three and six per cent of 14- to 16-year-olds are suffering from a true depressive illness. Although younger children (below the age of nine) do sometimes suffer depression, they seem somehow to be emotionally protected: they do not feel things so deeply and therefore do not have the extreme swings of mood or reach the depths of unhappiness that many adolescents experience.

Perhaps even more interesting, depressive illness seems to affect twice as many women as men, and one suggestion for this finding is that, during adolescence, young women are first likely to show the sense of helplessness in the face of failure that is one characteristic of depression. Girls are more likely to see failure as being due to their own lack of ability; if they fail in what have always been considered "male" areas (for example, maths or science), they may interpret this to mean that no one really expected them to succeed. When boys fail, however, they're more likely to be told to pull their socks up and that they could do better if they tried. The unspoken message boys receive is that failure isn't inevitable and that they are certainly not helpless in the face of it (see also *Issue: Single-sex Schools*, p.152).

You have good reason to worry about any teenager who has been in a continual state of misery for longer than two weeks, and cannot seem to shake it off and join in normal life even temporarily. You should be quite concerned if your youngster's behaviour or personality has changed in other ways as well, especially if he or she has become very withdrawn and shows no interest in their normal activities, or displays a sudden, and perhaps uncharacteristic, outburst of aggressive behaviour, or loses interest in school, or finds it difficult to concentrate on schoolwork (but see also *Drugs*, p.212). You should be especially concerned if they talk about suicide. People – including teenagers – who are depressed often have vague physical symptoms: they may not eat or sleep properly and, if severely depressed, may even lose weight. Youngsters may have recurring headaches or stomach-aches, necessitating frequent days off school. Depression can indeed sometimes be a cause of school refusal (see p.236) and, in late adolescence, it is by far the most frequent and most significant factor in the decision to "drop out" of college or university.

Although antidepressant medicines can sometimes help adolescents who are seriously depressed, they are seldom used as a "first-line" method of treatment. Most doctors prefer to try some kind of psychological treatment (counselling or psychotherapy) first; this may help a youngster to cope more effectively with any future stress.

ISSUE: ANOREXIA NERVOSA

Anorexia nervosa (AN) is an illness in which the sufferer (90 per cent of whom are girls) believes she is fatter than she really is, whereas everyone else sees her as painfully thin. The girl with AN eats less and less in a hopeless attempt to get rid of fat that is simply not there.

There are many theories as to why young girls should develop this distorted view of their own bodies, but the experts still have not agreed on the underlying causes. It is known, however, that AN is found only in cultures in which thinness is socially desirable. It has become much more common because our society has become dominated by images of models, actresses, and entertainers (some of whom have themselves been victims of AN, and some of whom have died from it). AN is especially prevalent in young women working in occupations where women must be thin to be successful.

Anorexia is the medical term for loss of appetite, but someone with AN has not, in fact, lost their appetite: they are often hungry, but refuse to eat. Typically, the disease begins in the mid-teens when a girl decides that she's overweight (one-third of girls who develop AN have been overweight when younger). The dieting and weight-losing pattern becomes relentless, however, and continues even after the girl has become very thin. Parents and friends urge the girl to eat more, and this leads to conflicts at mealtimes. Before long the girl with AN learns to conceal how thin she is by wearing loose, shapeless clothes; she claims to eat alone and, if forced to sit down with the family at mealtimes, will insist on making her own food, devising a salad of raw vegetables that is virtually calorie-free. She may get hold of appetite suppressants to help overcome her natural hunger and may compulsively exercise to burn up the calories she does eat. She may learn how to make herself vomit to get rid of food (a disorder called bulimia: see below), and this repeated vomiting may damage the teeth, which become eroded by the stomach acid.

Symptoms and signs Eventually, malnutrition may make an anorexic depressed, irritable, and unable to concentrate. Her skin becomes dry, and a growth of downy hair may appear on her face, arms, and legs. From a normal weight (at about the age of 15 or 16) of 50 or 60 kg, her weight may fall to 40 kg or less. Usually, once she has lost about 12 kg, the girl's periods will stop. Some girls lose their periods quite early in the illness before they have lost an appreciable amount of weight, so there may be other factors besides weight loss which lead to the cessation of menstruation. If the disorder begins before puberty, the girl will fail to enter the normal "growth spurt" of adolescence: her breasts will not develop, her pubic hair will not grow, and her periods will not begin. However, once the anorexic is treated and an appropriate weight has been reached, normal development will begin.

Bulimia is a variant of anorexia nervosa, in which someone (again, usually a girl) is of normal weight but has "binges", during which vast amounts of food (such as two huge bowls of ice cream or a dozen chocolate bars) are eaten in one sitting. The sufferer then makes herself vomit or takes powerful laxatives to get rid of the food. ▷

Parents should suspect AN if a daughter has continued to follow a diet to lose weight after she has become thin, if she conceals her appearance in shapeless clothes, and if she avoids eating with the family. Often someone with AN will say she does not want or need treatment, and it may be difficult to overcome this refusal.

Treatment One line of persuasion is to arrange a meeting with a specialist in eating disorders (usually attached to a hospital unit) to help resolve family arguments. Consult your family doctor, who may be able to arrange a specialist consultation. For both anorexia nervosa and bulimia, help is needed. Argument and persuasion within the family is not enough; the underlying condition is a form of mental illness that requires specialist care. The sooner treatment is started, the better the chances of success.

Unfortunately, there is no quick, easy, effective treatment. Most specialist units try to involve the whole family in the treatment programme, which may require a period of in-patient hospital treatment. The aim of treatment is to set goals for regaining weight while providing psychotherapy to overcome the refusal to eat.

Anorexia usually lasts two to three years, but about half of all those who develop the disease eventually recover completely, and about one-quarter improve considerably. In the rest, however, anorexia outlasts adolescence and remains a continual threat to health, as well as social and sexual life. In about five per cent of girls who develop anorexia, the disorder proves fatal, occasionally as a result of infection (to which these undernourished youngsters are especially vulnerable), dehydration caused by the excessive use of laxatives, or suicide.

CASE HISTORY: DEPRESSION

Maggie had always been a lively and reasonably hard-working schoolgirl, but she inexplicably changed quite dramatically when she was 15. Her work deteriorated, she was apathetic in class, and showed no enthusiasm for activities that she had previously enjoyed. Maggie's parents were first critical, and then concerned, of what they took to be laziness.

"I couldn't talk to my parents because they were part of what was worrying me. They seemed to be quarrelling a lot and I was afraid they were going to split up. I just had no energy to do schoolwork. Then one day my chemistry teacher talked to me after school. She said that often if you're depressed or worried about something, it's hard to concentrate on anything else. It helped to talk to someone, and the next week I made an appointment to talk to my doctor."
Maggie, 16

COMMENT ABOUT DEPRESSION
Sometimes an outsider, who is emotionally distanced from the family and its problems, can have more success in persuading someone who is depressed to talk (see *Seeking Help*, p.232).

SUICIDE AND SELF-INJURY

Children under 12 almost never try to kill themselves, and it is rare for children under the age of 14 to do so. Those few children who do make a serious or successful suicide bid are likely to be rather older. The rate increases as adulthood approaches, and suicide accounts for nearly eight per cent of all deaths in the 15–19-year-old age group.

Suicide is four times more common in boys than in girls and has doubled in frequency in the past 20 years. One reason for the greater numbers of deaths in boys is that methods chosen are different. Girls tend to take drug overdoses, while boys are more likely to choose violent methods, such as shooting or hanging. There is also some evidence that boys who attempt suicide are more likely to have severe psychiatric problems than girls who do so, and are perhaps more determined to commit suicide. Because many of these boys and girls have severe psychiatric disturbances, they are often socially isolated, are unable to talk easily with their parents, and have no particularly close friend or confidant. They may not attend school in the days before their suicide, which many youngsters have secretly planned so that they are not prevented from carrying out their intention. Very often, it is some disciplinary crisis that precipitates the attempt: the youngster may be afraid that some misdemeanour is about to come to light, such as that parents are to be told about truanting or perhaps trouble with the police.

The realization that their child has been in such depths of misery that he or she has tried to commit suicide is appalling for a parent. Fortunately, most suicide attempts fail, but it is important to realize that if your youngster has tried once, he or she may remain vulnerable. Some form of therapy – which may involve the whole family as well as the child – is essential and should be started as soon as possible.

About half of all children who do commit suicide
had talked about, threatened, or attempted suicide
within 24 hours of their deaths.

RISK FACTORS

If your child attempts suicide, you may, with hindsight, be able to remember changes in his or her behaviour during the days and weeks preceding such a desperate cry for help, and so will be able to recognize similar signs in the future. Encourage the youngster to talk to you, listen attentively, and sympathize – and seek professional help straightaway. Whether or not you believe that your son or daughter will carry out a suicide threat, you should always take any such threats seriously – especially if your youngster has a friend who has recently committed suicide. Listed opposite are some of the risk factors that indicate that you may need to take immediate action to rescue a child from despair. If your youngster is feeling suicidal, you may notice that he or she:

SUICIDE AND THE MEDICINE CUPBOARD

The 100 or so children and teenagers who kill themselves each year in Britain do so mostly by taking overdoses of drugs, often combined with alcohol. Many more attempt suicide, usually intending to make a gesture and not meaning to do themselves any serious harm (see *Parasuicide*, next page). Sometimes a teenager who takes a handful of pills as a gesture chooses the wrong ones and dies by mistake. As few as 20 tablets of paracetamol may cause fatal liver failure several days after the suicide attempt.

Paracetamol is a good, safe drug for relieving headaches and sore throats, but if there is an emotionally disturbed teenager in the family, it may be more sensible to have aspirin or ibuprofen tablets in the family medicine cupboard.

- **Cries a great deal** and seems persistently sad
- **Doesn't see friends** and becomes increasingly isolated
- **Doesn't eat properly** or sleep well
- **Can't talk or explain** his or her feelings to you
- **Becomes self-destructive** (driving recklessly, drinking heavily, taking drugs)
- **Sometimes says things like "There's nothing to live for"** or "I wish I was dead"
- **Talks about ways and means of committing suicide** (asks how many aspirins make a lethal dose, for example)
- **Thinks that life is impossibly difficult**: a romance has broken up, for example, or there has been some trouble at school, or schoolwork has deteriorated markedly.

TELLING THE SCHOOL

Sometimes, of course, a suicide attempt is the result of some trouble at school, and may even take place on school premises. Bullying, for example, can make a child feel desperate and helpless and may prompt a suicide attempt (see p.164). In this case, obviously the school will not only know about it, but must also be involved in helping to sort out the problems and the distress that may have caused it.

Suppose, however, that the attempt was made out of school for reasons that had nothing to do with the school itself: is it then in the youngster's best interests to involve the school? This depends very much on what you know of the school and its attitudes. Sadly, schools do sometimes overreact and, in rare cases, may even refuse to have a pupil back. There is also no doubt that the attitudes of some teachers towards a youngster can be coloured by this information in a way that is not always to his or her advantage. On the other hand, the more support a troubled teenager has, the better. If the school can be relied upon to give this sympathetically, and especially if you believe that your son or daughter is still vulnerable and may react in a similar way to future episodes of stress, it may be best for them to be told.

PARASUICIDE

The term "parasuicide" is often used to describe a suicide attempt that is not really meant to succeed. Girls are more likely than boys to display parasuicidal behaviour. Such attempts are also usually made at a younger age, and more often as a result of some acute personal crisis than because of serious depressive illness.

Poor communication with parents, and disruption in a personal relationship (usually either with parents or a boyfriend or girlfriend) are the problems that seem most likely to precipitate a suicide attempt, and the youngster's predominant feelings at the time are usually those of anger, loneliness, and simply wanting "out" of a situation. The methods chosen (often a drug overdose or wrist-cutting) are potentially less lethal than in a genuine suicide attempt, but because youngsters may lack real knowedge about drugs, for example, they're risking their lives – even if they do not really wish to die. Their behaviour can be seen more as an attempt to bring about some change in their lives rather than an attempt to end them.

It is easy to dismiss this kind of half-hearted suicide attempt as just "attention seeking", but children who attempt or threaten suicide most certainly do need care and attention. Any child who attempts suicide, for whatever reason, does need psychiatric help, and so, very often, does their family. Conflicts between parents and the youngster may have led to the crisis which must be resolved. The youngster also needs help to understand his or her own feelings and to learn better ways of coping with the problems and crises of life. If your son or daughter refuses treatment, such as counselling, or maintains that he or she does not need it, the best you can do is to watch for signs of problems developing in the future and to offer help if you think it is needed.

"I felt so miserable after Jenny finished with me, and I couldn't bear the thought of telling anyone. I felt it made me look foolish. It was right before my exams, too, which didn't help. The last thing I felt able to do was work. When I took the overdose I wasn't really thinking straight. I thought, 'I wish I were dead', but I don't think I really wished that. It was kind of a way of letting people know what I was feeling without actually telling them. Mostly it was that I wanted Jenny to know how much she'd hurt me. Maybe I thought it would make her change her mind."

Neil, 17

ISSUE: SELF-MUTILATION

Teenagers – girls more often than boys – occasionally deal with problems and tensions in their lives by inflicting some deliberate injury on themselves. Usually this takes the form of cutting their skin or burning themselves with cigarettes. The injuries are usually to the wrists or arms (only very rarely do they ever mutilate their faces) and are almost always trivial in themselves, although sometimes cuts can he deep and dangerous. They are intended as a way of relieving tension, not as an attempt or even a threat of suicide.

"I feel so tense and restless beforehand that I know I'm going to have to do it. It doesn't hurt, although it may be painful later. In fact I don't feel anything much while I'm doing it, just numb and unreal. All I feel is relief, and then afterwards I feel 'real' again."
Jane, 15

Adolescents who mutilate themselves like this usually seem to have some difficulty in interpersonal relationships: episodes often occur when the teenager feels he or she has been abandoned in some way. Most have severe family problems and many have other emotional problems. Sexual problems, such as promiscuity or confusion about sexual identity, and eating disorders seem to be particularly common. Many of these "cutters" are girls who have special fears about menstruation, and cutting does seem to be more common at the time of menstruation (although not before it, which suggests that it is not merely a symptom of pre-menstrual tension). Psychiatric treatment for teenagers who do this is advisable.

OBSESSIONAL SELF-CONSCIOUSNESS

Very occasionally some teenagers may become obsessed by a conviction that they are ugly or have some gross physical defect, even though to anyone else's eyes their appearance is perfectly normal. No matter how much they are reassured, it makes no difference: the conviction that they are deformed dominates their lives completely, so that they may refuse even to go out or to meet people. If matters reach this pitch, you should seek psychiatric help for them, because sometimes this kind of delusion about a perfectly normal appearance (called dysmorphophobia) can be a symptom of an underlying psychiatric illness.

A few very sensitive or shy adolescents may develop this kind of delusional belief in their own ugliness as a method of self-defence: their "deformity" gives them an excuse to avoid experiences that make them very anxious, so that they do not have to meet people or try to form relationships they're afraid they might fail at. Try not to reinforce this belief or collude with adolescents in any way (it's probably best to refuse to be drawn into a discussion about the supposed abnormality). At the same time, do whatever you can to increase the teenager's self-confidence and self-esteem (see *Boosting Morale*, p.83).

PSYCHIATRIC DISORDERS

The previous pages have discussed emotional and behavioural problems that may or may not need professional attention. The more serious psychiatric disorders, however, need urgent medical intervention.

SCHIZOPHRENIA

Schizophrenia is a psychiatric disorder that usually appears for the first time in late adolescence or early adulthood. It affects girls and boys equally, although boys tend to develop the disorder at an earlier age than girls.

In the general population, about one person in 100 is affected by this disorder. It is more common in inner-city populations and in certain geographic areas (for example, western Ireland), but the reasons for this variation are not known. Those people who have close relatives who are schizophrenic are most at risk: one in ten of those children who have a parent with the disease will eventually develop it, for example, while for those with no family history of the disease the chances of developing it are much less.

Some children who develop the disorder show certain personality traits: they tend to be "loners", shy, withdrawn, over-sensitive, and suspicious. Schizophrenia develops in about ten per cent of children who show this kind of personality.

Causes Schizophrenia is believed to be due partly to an abnormality of brain chemistry which can be inherited. However, this inherited tendency is by no means the only factor; brain damage and other causes may be involved.

Symptoms The typical symptoms of schizophrenia are bizarre and disturbed ways of thinking known as delusions. A youngster may be convinced that he or she is being directed by some outside influence, that thoughts are being put into his or her mind, or that personal thoughts and feelings are being controlled by outside agencies or broadcast to others. Adolescent schizophrenics may hear voices (auditory hallucinations) talking to or about him or her. Thoughts may become jumbled, so that you won't be able to understand what your youngster is trying to tell you. He or she may seem unable to feel or express the right emotion at the right time, laughing or crying quite inappropriately or without reason.

Often, however, the disorder does not begin with these recognizable "psychotic" symptoms (that is, when a person makes obviously incorrect or incoherent inferences or improper evaluations about external reality, and continues to make these errors in the face of contrary evidence). An adolescent may have other symptoms that are not quite so distinctive. It may start, for example, with behaviour that can look very much like a severe depression. The youngster may become progressively more isolated and unsociable, gradually withdrawing from family and friends. He or she may seem to lose all energy and ambition (often sleeping a lot, but not always at the same times as the rest of the family) or simply wanting to lie in bed all day. Occasionally the child may be found "posturing" – standing like a statue in odd poses. Often the adolescent may have no interest in being clean or tidy. Some young schizophrenics show to an exaggerated degree the feelings of self-consciousness that most adolescents have, believing, for example, that they have some quite disfiguring physical defect that everyone notices and talks about. A few young schizophrenics may show an intense interest in mysticism, and sometimes – especially in very emotionally immature children – there may be incoherent speech and odd, uncontrolled, or occasionally aggressively violent behaviour.

The illness may recur, usually at unhappy or stressful times in the person's life, but there is a good chance (especially if the illness started suddenly and the youngster seemed quite normal before) of a complete recovery, or at any rate of considerable improvement, if treatment begins immediately.

Treatment If your doctor suspects that your child may be schizophrenic, he or she will probably arrange for admission to hospital, so that the diagnosis can be confirmed and treatment given. Some units prefer to admit the youngster in the most acute stage of the illness to an adult ward, even though space may be available in an adolescent unit. The reason for this is that adults are often more able to accept into their group someone who is very mentally disturbed; other adolescents, disturbed themselves, may be anxious and therefore less tolerant. Some hospital units, however, treat psychotic adolescents alongside teenagers with other psychiatric disorders on an adolescent ward.

Treatment will involve the use of drugs (major tranquillizers or antipsychotic drugs such as chlorpromazine or haloperidol), which can very effectively relieve the symptoms of schizophrenia. However, these drugs are powerful, and may have side effects (usually on the muscles), which may themselves have to be treated with additional medication. The acute symptoms of schizophrenia disappear quite quickly, usually in a matter of weeks, and, as the symptoms disappear, medication will be reduced and may eventually be discontinued altogether. Other symptoms, however – apathy and lack of energy, for example – may continue for much longer. Sometimes long-term medication is needed to help prevent future schizophrenic episodes. Usually this is given by "depot" (slow-release) injection every 2–4 weeks, and occasionally it may be given in the form of daily tablets.

The parents of any chronically handicapped youngster have to cope with their own often bitter and confused feelings, as well as with their child. As well as treatment with drugs for the adolescent schizophrenic, the family as a whole will be offered help in dealing with these feelings, and with the stresses and tensions that may have precipitated the youngster's illness.

Living with schizophrenia Schizophrenia is distressing and extremely difficult to live with, both for the sufferer and those who care for him or her. Although there are problems, it has been found that – just as with all adolescents – some ways of dealing with these problems work much better than others.

When your youngster's acute symptoms have subsided and he or she returns home, you can help best by doing everything you can to bring his or her life back to normal, to become firmly rooted once again in the real world. In the aftermath of any serious illness, it's natural for parents to want to give children special protection, to make it up to them in some way, but an adolescent schizophrenic should not be singled out from other family members for special treatment. You must also try not to become too involved with him or her; try not to be over-vigilant by watching every move or by being over-directive about domestic tasks. People with schizophrenia have been found to be less likely to have relapses when their families are warm towards them without being over-involved, and manage not to be too critical of or angry with them. None of this is easy. Sadly, many schizophrenics simply cannot help provoking their parents into just the kind of criticism or hostility that makes their own condition worse. What are the best ways to cope with this illness?

• **Try not to spend too much time together.** The more you can be apart, the less likely you are to get on one another's nerves and, therefore, to become critical and angry. An adolescent schizophrenic may not be able, for some months at any rate, to go back to school or college or to hold down a job, but the hospital may be able to arrange for visits to a day centre.

• **Pinpoint the things that most irritate or anger** you about his or her behaviour. Often these are not the obvious "schizophrenic" symptoms such as hallucinations (these tend to resolve quite quickly with medication): they are things like refusing to get out of bed, or to wash, or to have any thought or consideration for anyone besides themselves – behaviour which in a way seems not "abnormal" but simply perverse. You may tend to think of it as "laziness" or "slovenliness" or "selfishness" and therefore get angry, but it is a real symptom of the illness which takes much longer to resolve.

• **Make sure your child takes medication regularly,** even if he or she feels well.

• **Don't try to bring the adolescent back to reality.** You cannot argue schizophrenics out of their delusions, or persuade them that things aren't as they see them. This doesn't mean that you have to agree with them; just stay neutral and try not to let yourself get embroiled in an argument.

• **Keep life as steady and uneventful as you can.** Schizophrenics find it hard to cope with change, so if some major event is coming up, its a good idea for them to be told so that they're prepared for it.

• **Do what you can to bring the youngster's life back to normal.** Encourage him or her to see friends and to return to any hobbies and activities. The more independent an adolescent schizophrenic can be, the better.

• **Take time off.** You cannot be a 24-hour carer. Nobody can. Even if you're worried about leaving him or her alone, it's vital that you get away on your own or as a couple some of the time. It's worth making a real effort to keep in touch with friends and keeping up your own interests, especially if they get you out of the house.

- **Don't expect too much too soon.** You probably will see a very rapid improvement when treatment first begins, and the most bizarre symptoms quickly disappear. After this, however, the process of recovery can be painfully slow, and you may be disappointed if you expect your son or daughter to go on improving at the same pace. It may be easier if you can think of your goal as helping your youngster "stay well" without relapsing, rather than "getting better". That way you can rightly be encouraged if you see that he or she is holding steady and not slipping back, even if you don't notice many signs of change for the better.
- **Join a support group** for relatives of people with schizophrenia. People who have lived with schizophrenia themselves will know what you're going through, and you may find it easier to talk to them than to good friends. Joining a group is another useful strategy to get you out of the house.
- **Accept that eventually you or your doctor may feel that the time has come** for your son or daughter to live in a hostel. This is not a betrayal or failure as a parent on your part. The truth is that many people with schizophrenia do better if they are living a more independent life away from their parents (see *Organizations*, p.274).

AFFECTIVE (DEPRESSIVE) PSYCHOSIS

Very occasionally, some adolescents may develop a depression so severe that their thinking becomes seriously disturbed (psychotic). They may feel that life is not worth living or that they're worthless, and they cannot be persuaded that these beliefs are irrational. Even more rarely, depressive psychosis can take the form of a manic illness. When this happens, the youngster behaves as though he or she is on a continual high, becoming excessively talkative, excitable, and overactive, and often easily irritated and quick to anger. Some youngsters have recurrent manic attacks, and in a very few cases (often those who have a family history of this same type of depressive psychosis), manic and depressive phases alternate.

Although affective psychosis is a serious, lifelong, and even life-threatening illness, treatment with lithium can very effectively reduce the risk of further attacks. Lithium, an anti-manic drug which controls mood swings, can have serious side-effects if the dose is not carefully controlled, and if the person taking it is not in good physical health. Treatment will always be started in hospital, and the youngster will be given regular check-ups for as long as he or she has to take the drug.

AUTISM

Although autism is usually diagnosed quite early in childhood, it may pose new problems when the child reaches adolescence. Autistic children, like all adolescents, will be experiencing strong sexual feelings for the first time, but they won't have the maturity and social skills to cope with them appropriately. They are not sensitive to other people's feelings and cannot easily pick up social cues and modify their behaviour accordingly. Their naïvety and childish sexual curiosity may lead to socially embarrassing behaviour, such as masturbation in public or touching other people in a sexual manner. This does not mean that they have an abnormal sexual drive and may be promiscuous, but it does mean that they may be vulnerable if someone makes sexual advances to them.

Autistic children often become more interested in making social contact with other people in adolescence, but here again they run into problems because of their failure to be aware of other people's feelings and responses, and their tendency to make irrelevant and inappropriate remarks. Sympathetic training in social skills can often help a few of these children to appreciate the effect on other people of what they say and do, but others may require long-term care and may never be able to live independently.

HYPERACTIVITY AND AGGRESSION

Parents and teachers often complain that a child is "hyperactive". By this, they may simply mean that the child seems unable to sit quietly or to be still. They have to be constantly on the move and are fidgety and restless. This kind of overactivity is irritating; it may be a sign that the child is anxious or agitated about something, but it may also simply show that he or she has a high level of energy.

Medically, the term "hyperactivity" is used more strictly. As well as being physically over-active, such children are inattentive and excitable. They tend to be impulsive, easily distracted, and find it hard to sustain attention for long. They are often disruptive, and may also be aggressive and defiant. This "cluster" of behaviour patterns is also called the hyperkinetic syndrome.

There is no general agreement among doctors about whether the cause of hyperactivity is physical (for example, due to slight brain damage at or before birth) or psychological. One view is that some dietary constituents are responsible, and claims have been made for diets that exclude food additives and fast foods. However, all the evidence is that, while a very few children may benefit from excluding such foods from the diet, most do not. Many doctors believe that diet is very rarely a cause of hyperactivity, and that dietary treatment is inadvisable without professional guidance.

In many children, hyperactive behaviour becomes less marked during adolescence, but sometimes it tends to worsen – with important consequences. Their antisocial behaviour may get youngsters into trouble at school; many fail academically, and about one-quarter become delinquent. It is therefore important to seek professional help early, during the pre-adolescent years. Various treatments are available, and include family therapy, behaviour therapy, and drugs. Children who are hyperactive often have multiple problems, both at home and in school. They need individual assessment and, often, a combination of treatments.

WHEN YOU FEEL DEPRESSED

- **Tell someone how you're feeling**. Putting your feelings into words often makes them seem less overwhelming, and a friend can usually reassure you that they, too, sometimes feel depressed and that the mood will always pass.
- **Take some exercise**, like jogging, swimming, or even a brisk walk. You'll be surprised what a good antidepressant such physical activity can be.
- **Plan a treat for yourself**, something to look forward to, even if it's something as simple as renting a video you want to see.
- **Don't be tempted to stay home from school** or miss an outing with your friends. Keeping up a routine is important. In fact, go out of your way to find company. After all, your own isn't much fun at the moment.
- **Concentrate on how things are now** and how to make yourself happier now. Worrying about the past doesn't help, and the future may be quite different from what you may be imagining.
- **When sad thoughts come into your mind**, make a deliberate effort to push them away. This is difficult when you're depressed and everything looks bleak, but "thinking sad" just feeds your misery.
- **If there is something positive you can do** about your unhappiness – making up after a quarrel with a friend, for example – do it. Positive action always makes you feel better.
- **See your doctor or a counsellor**:
  - if you don't know why you feel depressed
  - if you're sleeping badly because you wake up with negative thoughts
  - if you're losing weight because you're not eating
  - if you've been depressed for more than two weeks
  - if you have suicidal thoughts

Help is always available; you may just have to ask for it.

18

ADOLESCENT ILLNESS AND HEALTH

"

I was going through a difficult patch: I looked awful…with a complete absence of tact, [my father] would pass remarks about my complexion, my acne, my clumsiness, which only made my misery worse…

"

Simone de Beauvoir, Memoirs of a Dutiful Daughter

BECAUSE THEIR IMMUNE SYSTEM is on top form, teenagers are a healthy lot, in contrast to their younger brothers and sisters attending primary schools, who come down with every possible cough, cold, and sore throat. Of course, serious illness does occur; teenagers may develop leukaemia or bone cancer, and teenage drivers are more likely than at any other time in their lives to be involved in an accident, especially in the first 12 months after starting to drive or ride a motorcycle. Nevertheless, only a handful of diseases are most common in the second decade, so most of this chapter is devoted to advice for maintaining a healthy diet, and to those adolescent disorders, such as glandular fever, that you are most likely to encounter.

At some point in their teens, young adults will want to go to see the family doctor unaccompanied and will expect the consultation to be confidential. In most cases, anyone over the age of 16 is thought to be legally competent to consent to medical or surgical treatment or to refuse it. Local laws may govern the age at which an adolescent can expect any medical consultation to be confidential; in the UK, for example, a 16-year-old has the legal right to insist upon confidentiality. However, the circumstances in which a doctor may respect a request for confidentiality for a patient who is under 16 are not so clear-cut. Doctors try to persuade young patients to tell their parents about any serious condition, but they will not usually override a patient's request for confidentiality. Contraception advice is available in many cities from walk-in clinics,

Left: Adolescents are closer to their peak condition than at any other time in their lives.

and many young girls may choose to go there rather than to a family doctor whom they think may not be completely trustworthy; they may also be reluctant to consult someone they see as their parents' doctor, someone whom they associate with the childhood they're leaving behind.

> *Wanting to see the doctor unaccompanied and*
> *in confidence is as much a part of growing up*
> *as having a bath with the door shut.*

If you believe that your teenager wants to see the family doctor alone and to keep quiet about his or her reasons, you should try not to interfere. Your son or daughter may quite possibly not even tell you about the visit, let alone what it was for and what was decided. Do not assume that there is some guilty secret. Quite probably he or she may simply want to get a prescription for acne or athlete's foot without the whole family knowing about it, or may want to ask advice about some topic that is making him or her unduly anxious (such as a fear of bad breath or a worry about a heart condition). Teenagers may believe (perhaps with justification) that if you knew about the consultation, it would be made into a family joke. Certainly you should neither threaten nor ask the doctor about the consultation; if you do, you ought to be told firmly that legally doctor-patient meetings are always confidential. If your doctor trangresses this, you should not be pleased: you should be outraged on behalf of your son or daughter and make a formal complaint to the doctors' professional regulatory body.

DIET AND EXERCISE

Hunger is a natural state for teenagers: they have to eat enough to supply the energy needed for a combination of rapid growth and frequent bursts of physical activity. What they eat rarely seems to matter to them: they come home, open the fridge, and eat what they find. Yet the choice of foods is important for two reasons. Optimum growth requires an optimum diet, and the eating habits established in the teens are likely to determine those of adult life.

Good exercise habits are best established in adolescence, too. Few adults take enough exercise, and few are really fit. Surveys in many countries suggest that it is during the teen years that most people (and especially most girls) lose the habit of taking exercise. This is at least partly because organized sports tend to be given up during adolescence, sometimes because the school doesn't provide the facilities or the time for them. Yet when they are asked, most adolescents say they would like to be fitter. If your son or daughter gets little or no chance for exercise at school, encourage them not to be a "couch potato", but to take up a sport that they enjoy. If it is one they can make a lifelong habit of, it will pay them real health dividends in the years to come.

NUTRITION AND GROWTH

In the UK, the United States, and most developed countries, the children of manual workers do not grow as tall as those born to middle-class professionals and managers. This class difference is apparent only when thousands of young people are measured, when it is then indisputable. The gap was 3–4 inches at the beginning of the century, but it has now been reduced to approximately one inch. For around 30 years, however, no difference in height between classes has been seen in countries with little social deprivation, such as Sweden. Moreover, health experts believe that the reason that many British children do not attain their predicted full height is that their diet throughout childhood has been nutritionally second-rate[1]. Few children nowadays go seriously hungry, but a diet that includes little meat, fresh fruit, or vegetables and relies heavily on bread and potatoes (usually fried) does not provide all the nutrients required.

The diet best suited for growing children is the same as that recommended for adults. Most of the required daily calories (50–55 per cent should come from complex carbohydrates, and these should be mostly wholegrain cereals, root and leaf vegetables, peas, beans and other pulses, and fruit. The diet should have little refined white flour or sugar. About 30–35 per cent of the calories should come from fats (or lipids); these should be derived from plant sources (such as olives and nuts as well as vegetable oils), from animals (such as meat from beef, chicken, turkey, and oily fish such as mackerel), and from dairy sources (milk, butter, and cheese). Protein from sources such as meat, fish, cheese, and eggs should comprise the rest of the diet.

Most of us still eat too much fat in fat meats, sausages, pies, cakes, and pastries, as well as in butter, milk, and cream. We eat too much salt, added to food during cooking and at the table, but also included in manufactured sauces, ketchups, relishes, and in convenience snacks such as peanuts or crisps. We eat too little vegetable fibre, and should all be eating more fruit and vegetables, preferably fresh and uncooked. A high fibre, low-salt, low-meat, low-fat diet – such as that eaten in the countries of southern Europe – seems to contribute to substantially lower rates of heart disease, raised blood pressure and stroke, and several common types of cancer.

Youngsters who learn to like such a diet in their formative years will not have to change their eating patterns in middle age when they start to worry about their health. In practical terms, this means teenagers should be encouraged to snack on fruit and vegetables (apples, oranges, even carrots, celery, and other raw vegetables) rather than on potato crisps, biscuits, or chocolate bars. They should be introduced to a mixed, well-balanced diet that includes rice dishes (most young adults like curry once they've tried it), pizzas, oriental cuisines, shellfish, and salads, rather than the boring, repetitive succession of hamburgers, steak, and fried fish and chips that so many adolescents eat. Although girls tend to feel more guilty than boys about eating what they think are "fattening" foods, they enjoy sweets and snacks as much, and usually eat just as many as boys do. With maturity, however, youngsters may learn to choose a healthy diet.

VITAMIN SUPPLEMENTS

Advertisements commonly claim that most people's diets are vitamin-deficient and that by taking multivitamin pills they can improve health. From time to time, research reports are published in an attempt to persuade the public that vitamin supplements will lead to an improvement in their children's behaviour or in their performance in IQ tests. Most mainstream medical research workers dismiss these claims as a mixture of commercial propaganda and misinformation. There is no good evidence that children whose diet is slightly deficient in vitamins perform less well at school, or that giving them vitamin pills could boost their academic performance.

The crucial advice for parents is that children and adolescents with a badly-balanced, vitamin-deficient diet need to be persuaded to eat a healthier selection of food, not to swallow vitamin pills. The teenage diet of burgers, chips, and fizzy drinks is harmful not so much from its lack of vitamins as from its excess of fats, salt, and sugar.

FOOD PREFERENCES

Virtually all growing children, boys as well as girls, go through periods when they want to eat foods that are different from the rest of the family's. This is one of the first ways a young teenager attempts to assert his or her independence from parental control, and there can be few rational grounds for refusing to allow adolescents their "favourite" food on occasion – even if no one else in the family likes pink frankfurters with tomato ketchup. Parents should also recognize that there are some foods that they themselves simply do not like, and that youngsters are no different. On the other hand, there is no reason for the whole family to follow teenage fashions, and if one member consistently wants food that is different from the rest of the family's, then he or she should be prepared to cook it.

GOOD AND BAD FOODS

Encourage teenagers to eat:	Try not to buy or offer:
• All fresh fruit	• Tinned fruit in syrup
• Dried fruits such as raisins	• Chocolate bars
• Wholemeal and pitta bread	• White bread and rolls
• Rice (especially brown)	• Cakes and biscuits
• Potatoes, baked or boiled	• Chips and crisps
• Fish, preferably poached or grilled	• Sausages and hamburgers
• Poultry	• Fat meats such as pork
• Skimmed milk and fruit juice	• Whole milk and carbonated sugar drinks
• Pizzas	• Fried fish and chips
• Pasta dishes such as lasagne	• Hot dogs

Some adolescent habits are less acceptable, however, since they may encourage the development of lifelong, unhealthy habits. Many teenagers seem to prefer a "grazing" eating pattern, in which they eat something small and inconsequential every hour or so and hardly ever sit down to a proper meal. This pattern is likely to lead to the consumption of too much nutritionally inferior snack food, and it also devalues the social importance of the whole family eating together (see *Issue: Mealtimes*, p.69). An effort should be made to have at least one or two meals each week at which the whole family sits down to eat some proper food. The exact menu can be negotiated and perhaps even prepared and cooked together.

Most families nowadays seem to eat snacks of some kind while watching television. If your family is one of these, try to encourage them to eat healthy snacks: unsalted nuts, raisins, apples, and oranges will disappear if they are in the vicinity.

DIETING

Because eating habits established during adolescence tend to become permanent, teenagers who are overweight should be encouraged to shed their excess pounds by making long-term changes to their diets. Parents should not talk about "puppy fat" in the hope that it will go away; children who are overweight at the beginning of adolescence are likely still to be overweight at the end. An overweight teenager needs a lot of help and support from the rest of the family since his or her self-esteem is likely to be low.

*Don't make jokes about fatness or the efforts
your son or daughter is making to lose weight
and stick to a sensible diet.*

The key to long-term control of a tendency to being overweight is readjustment of the hunger controls in the brain to a lower food intake. This means staying away from sugary or sweet foods, fried food, and high-energy snacks such as potato crisps. These restrictions need to be lifelong: anyone who has ever been overweight will gain weight easily again if they allow themselves to slip back into old eating habits. The family can help by adopting the same restrictions for all its members; they are no great hardship and will probably improve everyone's health.

Most teenagers, however, are not overweight. Even so, almost all adolescent girls (more than boys) are concerned about their weight, and almost all decide at some stage that they need to diet. Usually this need not be a cause for concern, since such dieting is short-lived, spasmodic, and terminated by natural, healthy hunger. In about one in every 100 teenagers, however, it becomes an obsession and develops into anorexia nervosa (see p.240). Only in these extreme circumstances do you need to worry about or take action over a young girl's preoccupation with weight and diet. If your daughter is determined to diet, there is nothing whatsoever you can do to make her eat more except to cook things you know she will find it hard to resist. Even this is likely to backfire; she may feel put under uncomfortable pressure and you may feel aggrieved if she refuses to eat what has been cooked. Either way, it may only make her more determined to exert her own independence and stick to her diet (see also *Weight*, p.265). The best thing you can do is to ensure that the menu prepared for the entire family is well balanced: low in fat, low in salt and sugar, and high in fibre.

"I take a packed lunch to school and it's a perfectly healthy one, a sandwich and some fruit. But whenever I open it, I find Mum's slipped in something really fattening, like a piece of cake or a chocolate bar. It really irritates me. I don't eat it and then she gets mad at me."

Rose, 15

CASE HISTORY: APPETITE AND GROWTH

Kathleen had always had a good appetite while at primary school and was a well-built, healthy-looking child. When she had just turned 13, she began to shoot up in height; at the same time she started to weigh herself every day. Then she began refusing to join the family for meals, claiming to be not hungry.

"Kathleen will only make a sandwich and then throw half of it away. I worry about how little she eats. I know some girls do become ill in their teens from trying to become too thin."
Mary, 38

"I'm not hungry when the rest of the family eats, I prefer to get myself something later. And I can't bear being spied on, I'm old enough to know when and what I want to eat. I just don't want to end up a six-foot beanpole."
Kathleen, 13

COMMENTS ABOUT APPETITE AND GROWTH

Kathleen and her mother agreed to visit their family doctor, who consulted Kathleen's medical records and reassured her that she would soon stop growing, and that her final height would probably be about 170 cm (5 ft 7 in).

The doctor's reassurance helped, but it was six months before Kathleen had regained normal eating habits.

Early medical consultation is essential if there is a suspicion that a teenage girl is starving herself. If the doctor persuades the parents that nothing is wrong, the teenager who is reluctant to eat may be persuaded as well.

ISSUE: VEGETARIANISM

Children of the 1990s are more ecologically aware than those of previous generations, and one of the ways in which this may show itself is a strongly held belief in vegetarianism. Sometimes, however, teenagers simply decide they don't like meat without any very clear reason for the decision (or perhaps they have a few friends who have decided to become vegetarians). Parents may see this as yet another subtle form of rejection and implied criticism – an indication that a youngster is making choices quite different from their own – or as a cause for friction because it plays havoc with the family's schedule and diet. It cannot be disputed, however, that millions of people are vegetarians and are perfectly healthy. If family members want to become vegetarians, there are no nutritional reasons for discouraging them.

Vegetarianism comes in varying degrees. Someone who decides not to eat meat but is still willing to eat fish presents no nutritional problems (and in the irritating way that teenagers have, some decide that sausages don't count as meat). If the restrictions cover fish, poultry, and meat, then some care needs to be taken to ensure an adequate intake of protein: eggs are one good source, but vegetable proteins are perfectly adequate provided that a full range is eaten. Cereal grains, pulses, and vegetables are all required to provide the full range of essential amino acids and vitamins. Too heavy a reliance on milk and cheese is likely to push the fat content of the diet up to unhealthy levels. Skimmed milk contains all the non-fat nutrients and is a good drink for anyone, vegetarian or not.

A full-blown lacto-ovo-vegetarian who will eat no foods of animal origin, including dairy produce, is at risk of developing nutritional deficiencies, especially of vitamin B_{12}. If a teenager seems determined to follow this strict rule, he or she should contact a local vegetarian society for advice, whose experts are well informed and persuasive. There are three practical approaches for the family:

• **The first is to alter the whole family's diet**, not necessarily to make it completely vegetarian, but simply to put more emphasis on vegetarian dishes, to eat fish in preference to meat if the committed vegetarian allows this, and certainly to eat meat less often (say two or three times a week instead of every day). There is no need to abandon meat completely, and it certainly won't do the teenage vegetarian any harm to cook baked beans in a baked potato on the family's meat-eating days. This is probably the best and healthiest solution for everyone, if the rest of the family is prepared to try it.

• **The second is to cook special meals for the vegetarian**. This is undoubtedly the worst solution. Few parents have the time or energy to run a regular double menu; if they try, the vegetarian member of the family will almost certainly find they have to put up with either a monotonous diet or a rapidly deteriorating relationship with the cook.

• **The third and probably best idea** is to hand over some responsibility for cooking vegetarian meals to the people who want them. If they intend to be a lifelong vegetarians, then they should in any case learn to provide themselves with an interesting and balanced vegetarian diet.

CHRONIC ILLNESS

Around one in every 20 teenagers has attacks of asthma; one in every 100 has a chronic illness such as diabetes or epilepsy. Chronic illness is a burden for anyone, but can be particularly stressful for a young person whose peers take their own health so much for granted that it is seldom a matter for conscious thought, let alone concern.

But disorders of this kind do not inevitably restrict everyday activities; for example, many famous athletes are people who take medication for asthma and for epilepsy, or who have to take daily insulin injections for diabetes.

Parents of a young person with a chronic illness have to achieve a difficult balance: they're naturally concerned that their youngster does not run unnecessary risks with his or her health, but it's important not to be too over-protective and make it more difficult for the teenager to become independent. It's also important that the illness is not used as a prop or as a way of manipulating people.

The youngster will usually find their illness less of a handicap if he or she understands it or takes an active part in its treatment. There are patient associations for all of the common diseases, and these provide leaflets, books, and videos explaining the illness and how to live with it. Ask your family doctor for the name and address of the local association and encourage your youngster to join.

GLANDULAR FEVER

Teenagers are usually healthy, but one infectious illness that may strike in the teens or early '20s is glandular fever, also called infectious mononucleosis or "mono". This is a virus infection like chicken pox and causes a raised temperature, swollen glands in the neck, under the armpits, and in the groin, and a very bad sore throat with swollen, inflamed tonsils. Other symptoms may include a headache, painful muscles, loss of appetite, and a feeling that the abdomen is swollen. Sometimes a pink rash may develop, and there may be some enlargement both of the liver (which may cause yellowing of the skin, or jaundice) and the spleen.

Because the illness is caused by a virus, antibiotics are no help. Simple pain-killers such as paracetamol will help the sore throat. All that can be done is to wait for recovery. Sometimes this takes a week or two, but quite often it drags on so that even if the temperature has returned to normal and the swollen glands have gone down, some people still have no energy and feel depressed. A very few people may have serious complications, needing hospital treatment for a ruptured spleen or for muscle weakness.

If your son or daughter develops glandular fever in the run up to important exams, it may be necessary to consider postponing them for six months or a year. School and university doctors are familiar with the debilitating effects of the virus and are usually both sympathetic and helpful.

MYALGIC ENCEPHALOMYELITIS

Doctors prefer to talk about the "chronic fatigue syndrome" rather than myalgic encephalomyelitis or ME, since so little is known for certain about this puzzling illness. The symptom and signs are sufficiently distinctive for the diagnosis to be reasonably certain in most cases, but the underlying cause remains controversial, nor is there any clear agreement or treatment.

Fatigue commonly follows certain virus infections, especially glandular fever and flu. Someone who has recovered from the acute illness and who no longer has symptoms of infection, such as a temperature, sore throat, and swollen lymph glands, may still not feel well. Both physical and mental energy may be lacking, and full recovery may be delayed for several weeks and sometimes longer.

A diagnosis of chronic fatigue syndrome will be made if this post-viral fatigue lasts longer than six months. Sometimes, however, long-standing fatigue develops gradually with no obvious link with a viral illness. Additional symptoms include aching pains in the muscles on brief exertion, headache, and problems with memory and concentration. Some people suffer from depression and loss of appetite. No laboratory tests can be done to confirm a diagnosis of CFS; but the combination of persistent lack of energy and muscle pain on exertion will usually leave little doubt about the nature of the illness. Even so, tests may be done to rule out other possibilities, such as brucellosis or tuberculosis.

A teenager who becomes ill with CFS has to face the possibility of a long illness, but the long-term outlook is good: almost all people with this disease make a full recovery, though it may take many months and sometimes years.

A working party on CFS, set up by the Royal College of Physicians of London, reported its findings in 1996. It was unable to come up with a cause for the disease, and its comments on treatment were mostly negative: it found, however, that some people got better faster when given morale-boosting psychotherapy, and others improved after taking antidepressants, which are used to treat other diseases in addition to depression.

For most people with CFS, however, the approach most likely to be effective is a combination of emotional support and gradually increased physical activity. If the muscles are not used, they will lose bulk and strength, so every effort should be made to maintain a regular routine of movement and activity. Many hospitals now have treatment programmes designed for sufferers from CFS. Information, practical advice on various methods of self-help, and a review of the treatment that have been tried are all available from the ME Association (see p.274).

Finally, the family of someone with CFS should realize that this is an unpleasant, long-drawn-out disease that may strike anyone. Telling a victim of CFS to "make more effort" or to "pull themselves together" is cruel, insensitive, and ineffective.

PROBLEMS WITH APPEARANCE

Personal appearance is very important in the teenage years, and few young people are totally satisfied with how they look; indeed, those who are the most good-looking are often most obsessed with imagined imperfections.

The teens are, however, a period of rapid growth. The proportions of the face change (as do those of the nose, for example, which often becomes relatively smaller) and so do the size and shape of the legs, the shoulders, and the breasts. There is little you can do to affect these changes, but you can take care of your skin and hair, and you can choose a healthy diet.

SKIN

Acne is the hallmark of adolescence: the term comes from the Greek for the "prime of life", and although acne may sometimes persist, most people find that the condition fades away by their early 20s. Before puberty, most children have unblemished skins, but the surge of sex hormones in adolescence has dramatic effects (see *Your Changing Body*, p.22). The most obvious is the growth of hair in the armpits and genital areas in both sexes and on the face of boys. The same hormones increase the size and number of glands in the skin (called sebaceous glands) that produce a greasy substance called sebum to lubricate the hairs.

In adolescence, then, the sebaceous glands become bigger and more active, and the sebum they produce often becomes thicker. In addition to making the face greasy, this thick sebum may become trapped within some of the glands by a plug of skin debris and hardened sebum. The plug or block is easily visible as white- or darker-coloured spots the size of a pin whiteheads and blackheads. If the blocked gland becomes infected, it will become inflamed, red, and sore. These raised red pimples may be quite small, but sometimes one becomes very inflamed and turns into a really painful boil. Someone who suffers from bad acne for several years may eventually have large numbers of scars from old inflamed spots. These spots, and the scars they may leave, are most obvious on the face, neck, and shoulders, where there are large numbers of sebaceous glands.

Several factors make acne worse; jobs that involve oil getting on the skin or that cause a lot of sweating, such as working in a hot and steamy environment, are well-known factors. Other aggravating factors include some prescribed drugs, such as steroids. The oral contraceptive pill (see p.135) may make acne worse, but sometimes makes it better. Experts disagree about whether diet makes any difference; some recommend a low-fat diet and the avoidance of chocolate and fizzy drinks, while others say that diet has no effect at all. Certainly masturbation has no effect on acne. Sunlight in moderation may help.

The first line of treatment is to soften and remove the grease, and every pharmacy has a wide choice of acne lotions, which are probably cheaper and easier to get than a similar lotion prescribed by a doctor. Often this is all that is needed. If lotions don't work, you'll   ▷

need to see your doctor because the next step is to get rid of the bacteria that make the spots inflamed. This requires treatment with a safe, simple antibiotic (usually tetracycline) for about four to six months. If symptoms persist, then young women may be recommended hormone treatment to block the effects of the androgens (the male hormones). The hormone preparation used also acts as a contraceptive.

If none of these treatments works, then the final weapon is a synthetic variant of vitamin A, isotretinoin. This reduces the size of the sebaceous glands by about 90 per cent, it makes the skin much less oily, and it damps down inflammation. Why isn't it the first-line treatment? Partly because it is very expensive and partly because it is powerful stuff. If a woman is taking isotretinoin, she must not get pregnant since it causes serious fetal deformation. Acne is now curable, and indeed surveys of schoolchildren have shown that severe acne has become very rare.

Your appearance at the age of 13 or 14 is
little guide to how you will look at 20,
let alone 25.

HAIR

Your hair, like your sex and your shape, is something that you have been born with. Adolescents usually spend a lot of time wishing their hair was straight (if it's curly or wavy) or wavy (if it's straight) and dyeing it various (sometimes unnatural) colours, but any drastic change will also alter the texture and health of the natural hair shaft.

Each hair on your body goes through a growth cycle that is independent of the others. Typically, a scalp hair grows for 1,000 days – three years – and then stops. The root of the hair, the hair follicle, rests for about 100 days and then a new hair begins to grow, pushing out the old one which becomes loose and falls out. Most people have between 100,000 and 300,000 hairs on the scalp, and between 100 and 300 of these fall out each day.

• **Hair loss** During a severe illness of any kind (and during pregnancy) many hairs grow in the same phase at the same time. When normal health returns, they all go into the eight-week resting phase, then they all start growing at once, and lots of hair falls out. This, however, indicates that growth is occurring and the appearance will soon return to normal.

Someone who is totally hairless may otherwise be in perfect health, but that is little consolation to you if your hair is falling out. Alopecia areata is the name given to a common but ill-understood condition in which patches of scalp hair fall out and there is no immediate growth of the bald patches. These patches usually have a clear edge and are often round or oval in shape. The cause of this type of hair loss is unknown, although most people who suffer from it are often under some kind of stress. In such cases, dealing with   ▷

the source of the stress usually restores normal hair growth. There is no other really effective treatment, although steroid injections into the scalp sometimes seem to make a difference. The outlook is unpredictable: sometimes the condition progresses to complete loss of hair from the scalp, eyebrows, and body (alopecia totalis), but more often the patches come and go for a few months, and then there is a gradual return to a full growth of hair.

If your hair seems to be falling out in patches, consult your doctor. There are several other possibilities; the most likely is a fungus infection of the scalp (ringworm – which has nothing to do with worms!) and will clear up quickly with treatment with an anti-fungal paste.

• **Male pattern baldness** Whether or when a man goes bald is determined by his genes, not his health. The inheritance of baldness is complicated; if a boy wants to know whether he's likely to become bald at an early age, he should look not at his father but at his mother's male relatives: his uncles and his maternal grandfather. He is likely to have inherited the same sort of hair.

Some young men begin to lose hair in their late teens, thinning at the sides of the forehead and in the middle of the scalp at the back. Nothing can be done to slow down this process. Vast sums of money are spent by young men on various treatments for premature baldness. These include several types of hair transplantation and the application to the scalp of a drug called minoxodil. These treatments are expensive, and, at best, they only postpone baldness by a few years. If there was a really good treatment, it would have been given to fiim and pop stars; in fact, the ones who have gone bald early have stayed bald, except the ones who wear wigs or who have had hair transplants. It may be some consolation to know that men only go bald if they have normal sex hormones; after removal of the testes, the hair on the head grows thick, while the hair on the face disappears.

• **Excess hair** The amount of hair on the body varies enormously among the different human races. Asiatic races have little hair, whereas among Mediterranean, Indian, and Arabic peoples dense hair on the chest and back is common in men, and women usually have substantial amounts of hair on the arms, legs, and even the face. You can expect to grow up looking like your relations of the same sex, and there is little you can do about it.

Nevertheless, many young men become distressed because they have little or no growth of facial hair, whereas young women are more often concerncd about unwanted dark hair. If you're worried about the amount of hair on your face or body – either too much or too little – look at the rest of the family. It is reasonable to consult your doctor only if you are clearly different. Vigorous growth of hair may also be a side-effect of some prescription drugs.

Medical conditions causing excess hairiness in women are rare, but they do occur. A young woman whose body hair suddenly becomes more dense or who develops other symptoms suggesting a hormonal imbalance, such as change in the voice or menstrual disturbance, should certainly see a doctor. If there is an underlying hormonal disturbance, it should be treated, and effective treatments are available.   ▷

Someone who has simply inherited a tendency to have a lot of body hair and does not like it has several options. Excess hair can be removed by depilatory creams bought from the pharmacy or by shaving, and there is no evidence to support the folklore that these treatments encourage the hair to grow quicker: they don't. Bleaching the hair makes it less obviously visible. Hair can also be permanently (but painfully) removed by electrolosis. Waxing, which is best done professionally, also seems to reduce hair growth. In any case, it may be worthwhile to postpone a decision about the method of hair removal until the adolescent hormonal upsets are over.

• **Dandruff and seborrheic dermatitis** People who have dandruff are usually easy to spot: the shoulders of their clothes are dusted with a mass of white specks that have come off their scalp, and they may also scratch their heads a lot. Dandruff is the name for the specks (which are in fact scales of dead skin) from the scalp. The underlying disorder that causes dandruff is called seborrheic dermatitis, and it leads to the skin of the scalp becoming mildly inflamed and thickened. Itching of the affected scalp leads to scratching, and the scratching scrapes off masses of yellowish-white, greasy scales that shower down on to the person's shoulders.

Often the only part of the skin affected by seborrheic dermatitis is the scalp, but it may also cause patches of inflamed, scaly, crusted skin in other hair regions such as the eyebrows, the groin, and the armpits. The creases between the nose and the corners of the mouth may be affected, as may the whole of the beard area of the face in men.

Simple dandruff will usually clear up if the hair is washed twice a week with an anti-dandruff shampoo, obtainable from a pharmacy or supermarket. These shampoos, which contain chemicals such as selenium and zinc pyrithione, are usually effective, but someone with a tendency to dandruff may continue to have symptoms for their whole lives and may need always to use a dandruff shampoo.

More extensive seborrheic dermatitis needs treatment by your doctor. Unfortunately, there is no certain cure. The inflammation usually improves quickly after treatment with a steroid cream, but it often returns when treatment is stopped. Creams based on sulphur or containing antifungal drugs are sometimes effective. The condition usually improves and often disappears in early adult life.

WEIGHT

During the adolescent growth spurt, the shape of your body changes very rapidly, and this is a time at which many teenagers become conscious of their weight. Attention in the media is directed mostly to anorexia nervosa, the slimmers' disease that affects as many as one in 100 girls (see *Issue: Anorexia Nervosa*, p.240), but being overweight is far more common as many as one in five young adults are seriously overweight, and being too fat is not only unattractive but unhealthy. If you know you are seriously overweight, it's no use hoping   ▷

that the excess fat will go away. It won't unless you decide to do something about it. Being overweight is usually due to bad eating habits; like other bad habits such as nail-biting, they can be changed, although it's not always easy. However, the longer you put off the attempt, the more difficult the change will be.

Crash diets are not much use, although rapid weight loss may improve your confidence. In the long term you have to learn to eat a healthy, balanced diet that keeps your weight in the right range. Swinging from a week of starvation to a week of overeating is no good for your health and will irritate the rest of the family.

TEETH

Having a nice smile is a confidence booster and a help in making new friends, and no one should be ashamed of their teeth. So if your teeth are uneven or discoloured, or if one is broken or missing, go to a dentist to find out what can be done. Having your teeth straightened or replaced takes time, but it really is worth having done.

HEADACHES

Most people get headaches, although a lucky handful never do. The pain of a headache does not come from the brain, it comes from the muscles and blood vessels in the scalp, and the membranes covering the brain (the meninges).

Among the many causes of headache, some are obvious, such as the headache of a hangover from drinking too much alcohol the night before. Others soon become obvious, such as the headache caused by flu and other acute infections (these usually cause a raised temperature and a sore throat). A headache that affects the forehead, mostly on one side, or the cheek bones may be due to an inflammation of the sinuses. During an attack of sinusitis, your nose feels blocked and your voice sounds different. Treatment with antibiotics and nose drops usually clears things up.

If you get a lot of headaches, do a bit of detective work to see if you can find out what brings them on. You may find that you wake up with a headache if you have slept in too long; this will usually disappear in an hour or so after you get up. You may find that working in a stuffy, airless atmosphere gives you a headache. Learn to recognize whatever situations or circumstances bring on your headache and avoid them. If you often get a headache after studying or watching TV, have your eyes tested (see *Short Sight*, p.269).

The most common type of recurrent headache is the so-called stress headache. The pain is caused by the over-tightening of the muscles in the face and the back of the neck, and this seems to be a common response to emotional stress and anxiety. Sometimes the source of the anxiety is easy to recognize, such as worry about exams or conflicts in the family, ▷

but sometimes it's not. You can relieve these headaches by taking paracetamol tablets (which are just as good as the more expensive headache tablets advertised on TV) or by learning relaxation techniques. A hot bath often helps, and so may massage.

SEEING YOUR DOCTOR

If you want to have a private consultation with your doctor, you should ask for one, making it clear that you want the consultation kept confidential. If you are over 16, you have a legal right to ask for this and your request should be respected.

If you are under 16, your doctor may be unwilling to see you on this basis and reluctant to be caught in the middle of a family conflict. In this case, your doctor should then help you find another doctor. You still have the legal right to insist that he or she says nothing about your conversation to your parents or anyone else.

MIGRAINE

Migraine is a particular kind of very severe headache. It affects about one person in 10 and often starts in the teens; in fact, most migraine sufferers have had their first attack by the age of 20. This first attack may be a frightening, very unpleasant experience, but once you know what is wrong with you, you will be able to get effective treatment.

A migraine headache has two features that make it easy to recognize. It almost always affects only one side of the head and is accompanied by a sensation of feeling sick. Vomiting often relieves the pain. In one type of migraine, called classical migraine, the attack begins with something going wrong with your sight: there may be a blind patch affecting some but not all of your vision, and this blind patch may have a jagged, sparkling edge. Both eyes may be affected. A severe attack of migraine may be so bad that all you can do is lie down in a darkened room until you feel better. This usually takes a few hours.

Usually your doctor will have no difficulty in deciding whether your headaches are due to migraine. Often you will find that some of your relatives also have attacks. Once it becomes clear that you do have migraine headaches, you can try to reduce the frequency and severity of the attacks. As with other headaches, do a bit of detective work to identify what triggers attacks. Some common triggers are too much or too little sleep, various foods and drinks (chocolate, cheese, fried foods, citrus fruits, and red wine often affect migraine sufferers), emotional stress, travel, menstruation, and the contraceptive pill.

Fortunately, there are some effective treatments, and you will need to discuss these with your family doctor. If you have only occasional and/or brief attacks, you may need no more than paracetamol tablets. More severe attacks may be relieved either by tablets or by injections or capsules beneath the skin. There are also drugs that can be taken daily to reduce the frequency of attacks. Many hospitals have special migraine clinics that you can attend if the attacks interfere significantly with your life.

GLANDULAR FEVER

Glandular fever, as the name implies, is an infectious illness causing swollen glands in the neck, a raised temperature, and a sore throat – often described as "the worst sore throat I've ever had." No one really knows why this illness (also called infectious mononucleosis) should be most common in the teens, but you are most likely to get it between the ages of 15 and 17, and it often affects people in their first year at university or college. Glandular fever is sometimes called the kissing disease, as this is one way in which the infection might be transmitted, but the link with kissing is probably simply to do with the age at which the disease occurs. Like measles and chicken pox, glandular fever is caused by a virus, or, to be precise, by either of two closely related viruses, cytomegalovirus or the Epstein-Barr virus. One attack usually gives lifelong immunity against further infections.

The illness usually starts with a high temperature and a headache, rather like flu, but within a day or so there are obviously swollen, tender lymph glands in the neck, under the armpits, and in the groin, and the throat has become very sore from swollen, inflamed tonsils. Because the illness is due to a virus, antibiotics are no help; indeed, if someone with a sore throat due to glandular fever is given the antibiotic ampicillin, the usual result is a dramatic rash over the whole body and a worsening of the symptoms. All that can be done, then, is to wait for recovery to occur from the attack on the virus by the body's natural defences. Unfortunately, this usually takes some time. The swollen glands and sore throat may last for a couple of weeks or more, although the pain and the high temperature may be relieved by regular doses of paracetamol. Once the worst is over, the person with glandular fever often feels washed out and lacking in energy. He or she may also feel depressed, sleepy, and apathetic. These symptoms of weariness may persist for another month; occasionally, they drag on for even longer. Fortunately, college doctors are usually familiar with these problems and are sympathetic. There is little that can be done to speed up recovery, although a nutritious diet with plenty of vitamins will certainly do no harm.

KEEPING SLIM

The key to keeping slim is finding a pattern of eating that you enjoy but that keeps your weight within the normal range. That means permanent changes in what and when you eat.
- **Eat regular meals** at the same time of day and try not to eat between meals.
- **Avoid foods that contain a lot of fat or sugar, or both.** This means most snack meals, chocolate bars, potato crisps, biscuits, cakes, buns, and pastries.
- **Go for snacks that are filling but low in calories:** apples and other fruit, carrots, celery, a salad sandwich.
- **Avoid sugary, carbonated drinks;** drink tea, skimmed milk, and mineral water.

SHORT SIGHT

Can you read bus numbers from a distance? Can you read sentences and sums written on the blackboard? Can you read the subtitles of foreign films at the cinema? If you can't, you may be short-sighted. Quite commonly, someone whose vision was normal during childhood becomes short-sighted in their teens.

You will be surprised at the improvement in your vision when you wear your glasses, but you may not want to wear them all the time, especially when meeting new people. Remember, however, that you should always wear them when riding a bike or driving a car.

So what are the alternatives? Contact lenses have improved enormously in the past 20 years, and it's well worth giving them a try. The only drawbacks are that lenses may be expensive, they need to be replaced regularly, and you have to buy special fluids for cleaning and storing them. The two main types are hard and soft lenses. The hard ones are made of plastic and are tough and long-lasting; gas-permeable hard lenses do not last as long but are more comfortable to wear. Both types, however, are uncomfortable to wear at first, and by no means everyone is able to get on with them. The smaller, soft lenses are much less uncomfortable in the eyes and are ideal for occasional use since they don't take much getting used to. A wide range of soft lenses are available, from the daily disposable type to those that need to be replaced only every 12–16 months. If you're thinking about getting lenses, talk to friends who have them about the pros and cons before spending a lot of money. One thing is certain: if you need glasses in your teens, you're going to need them all your life.

The third possibility for someone with short sight is an operation to change the shape of your eyes. This operation is called a radial keratotomy and was pioneered in the Soviet Union. Results have been carefully evaluated over the past 10 years and the operation is safe and effective, but it is not for everyone. Only two out of three people who have the operation are able to do without glasses completely; the rest usually need weaker glasses. Also, very few surgeons want to operate on young people whose eyes might still be changing their shape. So you should put off any thoughts about surgery until you've tried various sorts of lenses for a few years.

Surgery can correct both short and long sight, but is most successful for minor degrees of short sight. The operation uses a laser to change the shape of the cornea, shaving off a precise amount of tissue. For short sight, the cornea is made flatter; for long sight, it is made steeper.

The procedure takes only a few minutes and is painless at the time, but the eye will be painful for a few days afterwards. After the operation, vision will be much improved but may still not be perfect. In some cases the vision is blurred for several weeks after the operation, and there is a very small risk of some permanent damage to the eye. You should make sure that the clinic offering the surgery is staffed by properly trained eye surgeons: consult your family doctor or your optician for advice.

CONCLUSION

"

When I look back on those years when I was neither fish nor flesh, between the ages of 16 and 22, I remember them as an uncomfortable time, and sometimes a very unhappy one. Now...I may at last be allowed to say: Oh dear, Oh dear, how horrid it was being young, and how nice it is being old and not having to mind what people think.

"

Gwen Raverat, Period Piece

WE HOPE THAT WE HAVE GOT ACROSS three main ideas in our book. Firstly, the changes in a teenager's behaviour during adolescence are complicated, but they are mostly predictable from observation of millions of teenagers in the past. Many families have no idea what is coming, what is normal, and what is unusual. We believe that parents and their children will find it easier to deal with the physical and emotional changes of adolescence if they have been told broadly what to expect.

Secondly, parents should not expect to be able to deal with all the problems of adolescence simply by relying on intelligence, instinct, and good nature. When they started a family, most parents bought books on baby care and backed these up by consulting their own parents and friends. Parents of teenagers, too, need every bit of help they can get, and we hope that the advice given in this book will be of practical help. Some of it is based on research studies, some on the teaching given to doctors and health workers, and some has come from our own experience as parents.

Thirdly, every child and every family is different. Young children pass developmental milestones (such as the age at which they walk or learn to read) at predictable times. Most teenagers pass their milestones – menstruation, the voice breaking, dates with the opposite sex – at predictable ages, too, but these emotional and physical markers may sometimes be reached months or years earlier or later than average. The range of variation is enormous, and children who develop early or late are still entirely normal. Humans are not like peas or sardines; we accept some being taller than others, and we should be just as ready to accept variations in the pace of development.

Our children all grow up and eventually leave home, and in their late teens and twenties they eventually separate emotionally from us, their parents, and lead free, independent lives. They may stop communicating except at birthdays and holidays, they may tell us little about their plans, and they may take new jobs and partners without letting us know what is happening. We should be pleased that they have become independent, and worried if they do not – or if they cannot, because they struggle to find work and financial security in an era of economic uncertainties.

Some parents find this adult separation upsetting, but they should try not to complain or nag their children about it. After 20 or 30 years of being a full-time parent – the source of food, shelter, and income, taking decisions, and giving advice – it comes as a shock to find that the last child has left the house and that it is empty. Adult children vary enormously in the amount of contact they retain with their parents, but many do become distant – for a time. In most families, separation is a temporary, transient stage. As soon as there are grandchildren, the three-generation family is likely to come together again, although there is a trend for sons to be assimilated by their wives' families.

We believe that parents of young adults should take full advantage of the decade or so of temporary freedom when they have the house to themselves. These years are potentially a golden era, when the pressures of work should be easing, the mortgage should have been paid off, and, with luck, there are no health problems. Now is the time to travel and to take up new interests, before the arrival of the next generation.

ENDNOTES

Chapter 1 Physical Development
Page 17

1. Tanner, J.M. (1966). Galtonian eugenics and the study of growth: the relation of body size, intelligence test score, and social circumstances in children and adults. *Eugenics Review* 58: 122–35.

Chapter 7 The Quest for Freedom
Page 75

1. Elliott, Michelle, *Keeping Safe: A Practical Guide to Talking with Children*, New England Library, 1988.

Chapter 9 Friends and Friendship
Page 102

1. Eidel, Michael (1962). Cited by Treadwell, Penny, *A Parent's Guide to the Problems of Adolescence*, Penguin, 1988.

Page 104

2. Herbert, Martin, *Living With Teenagers*, Basil Blackwell, 1987.

Page 105

3. Brody, Lora, *Growing Up on the Chocolate Diet*, Henry Holt, 1985.

Chapter 11 Sexuality in Adolescence
Page 125

1. Bancroft, J., *Human Sexuality and its Problems*, Churchill Livingstone, 1989.

Chapter 12 Life in School
Page 161

1. Herbert, op. cit.

Chapter 14 Facing Up to Adulthood
Page 182

1. Donovan, A. et al. (1985). Employment status and psychological well-being. *Journal of Child Psychology and Psychiatry*, 27: 65–76.

Chapter 16 Risks and Recklessness
Page 208
1. British Medical Association, *Living with Risk*, Penguin, 1987.
2. Ibid.

Chapter 18 Adolescent Illness and Health
Page 255
1. Knight, I. and Eldridge, J., *The Heights and Weights of Adults in Great Britain*, HMSO, 1984.

ORGANIZATIONS

The telephone numbers and addresses listed below were correct at the time the book went to press.

ABUSE

Childline 0800 1111
Free child protection helpline.

National Society for the Prevention of Cruelty to Children (NSPCC)
0800 800500
Free child protection helpline.

ADOPTION

General Register Office
St Catherine's House
10 Kingsway
London WC2B 6JP
0151-471 4200
(All telephone enquiries go through Southport.)

General Register Office
New Register House
Edinburgh, Scotland EH1 3YT
0131-334 0380

The National Organization for the Counselling of Adoptees and Parents (NORCAP)
(01865) 875000

DRUGS

Families Anonymous
88 Caledonian Road
London N1
0171-278 8805
Help for families of drug-users.

Release
388 Old Street
London EC1V 9LT
Offers advice on all types of drug abuse and dependence
0171-729 9904 10 a.m. to 6 p.m.
Monday through Friday
0171-603 8654
24-hour emergency telephone service for people who have been arrested for drug offences.

SCODA (Standing Conference on Drug Abuse)
49 Copperfield Street
London E1
0171-928 9500
Produces lists of drug services available both for users and their families. Also coordinates activities of the various voluntary agencies that give advice on drugs and drug-associated problems, arrange counselling, or referral to hospital clinics or rehabilitation houses.

Narcotics Anonymous
PO Box 1980
London EC13 32RB
0171-251 4007
Self-help organization for drug-users.
0171-730 0009
24-hour helpline.

FAMILY CRISES: THERAPY AND LEGAL SERVICES

Association of Child Psychotherapists
120 West Heath Road
London NW3
0181-458 1609

Children's Legal Centre
University of Essex
Wivenhoe Park
Colchester
Essex CO4 3SQ
(01206) 873820
Concerned with law and policy affecting children and young people.

Families Need Fathers
0181-886 0970
Information line.

Family Network Helplines
0181-514 1177
Careline Counselling Services.

Institute of Family Therapy
24–32 Stephenson Way
London NW1 2HX
0171-391 9150

National Family Mediation
9 Tavistock Place
London WC1H 9SN
0171-383 5993

**National Council for
One-Parent Families**
255 Kentish Town Road
London NW5 2LX
0171-267 1361

National Stepfamily Association
Chapel House
18 Hatton Place
London EC1
0171-209 2460
(0990) 168388
Counselling service.

Parentline
(01702) 559900
National office.

Parent Network
Room 2
Winchester House
Kennington Park
11 Cranmer Street
London SW9 6EJ
0171-735 1214

BEHAVIOURAL PROBLEMS AND MENTAL ILLNESS

Alateen
61 Great Dover Street
London SE1 4YF
0171-403 0888

Eating Disorders Association
Sackville Place
44–48 Magdalen Street
Norwich NR3 1JE
(01603) 621414
Youthline: (01603) 765050

ME Association
Stanhope House
High Street
Stanford le Hope
Essex SS17 0HA
(01375) 642466

National Schizophrenia Fellowship
28 Castle Street
Kingston-upon-Thames
Surrey KT1 1SS
0181-547 3937
Helpline: 0181-974 6814

SCHOOL PROBLEMS

**Advisory Centre for Education
(ACE)**
1B Aberdeen Studios
22 Highbury Grove
London N5 2EA
0171-354 8321

British Dyslexia Association
98 London Road
Reading RG1 5AU
(01734) 668271

**Gabbitas, Truman, and Thring
Educational Trust**
6–8 Sackville Street
London W1X 2BR
0171-734 0161
Counselling and advisory service
on education and careers.

**National Association for Gifted
Children**
Elder House
Milton Keynes
MK9 1LR
(01908) 673677

SEXUALITY AND PREGNANCY

National AIDS Helpline
0800 521 361

British Pregnancy Advisory Service
7 Belgrave Road
London SW1
0171-828 2484

Brook Advisory Centres
24-hour helpline:
0171-617 8000
National Office:
165 Gray's Inn Road
London WC1
0171-713 9000

LIFE
Pregnancy Care & Counselling
70 Claremont Road
London W13
0181-566 7618
For those who wish to give their
infants up for adoption.

**London Lesbian and
Gay Switchboard**
24-hour telephone line that
provides counselling as well as
legal, housing, and medical advice.
0171-837 7324

Pregnancy Advisory Service
11–13 Charlotte Street
London W1
0171-637 8962

Rape Crisis Centres
The Centres may be able to offer
counselling or referral to any local
groups for incest survivors or
victims of sexual abuse. For
nearest centre, call Directory
Enquiries, or ring:
0171-837 1600

Terrence Higgins Trust
52–54 Gray's Inn Road
London WC1X 8JU
0171-831 0330
AIDS charity that provides
educational material as well as care.
Helpline: 0171-242 1010

WORKING ABROAD

Camp America
0171-581 7333
24-hour telephone service.

Gap Activity Project (GAP)
Gap House
44 Queen's Road
Reading, Berkshire RG1 4BB
(01734) 594914

INDEX

T

ACKNOWLEDGMENTS

Revised edition team:
Senior editor: Louise Candlish; **Senior art editor:** Tracy Hambleton-Miles; **Editor:** David Tombesi-Walton; **DTP designers:** Zirrinia Austin, Mark Bracey; **Senior managing editor:** Sean Moore; **Deputy art director:** Tina Vaughan; **Additional editorial support:** Christine Winters; Nichola Thomasson, David Williams, Jo Marceau; **Additional design support:** Heather McCarry, Richard Sinclair.

Jacket picture credits:
The publisher would like to thank the following for their kind permission to reproduce their photographs:
c=centre; t=top; b=bottom; l=left; r=right
Bubbles Photo Library: Perry Joseph back cover cl; Jennie Woodcock back cover c;
Photofusion: Giles Barnard front cover bl; Crispin Hughes front cover br; **Tony Stone Images:** Nancy Honey back cover cr.

Dorling Kindersley would like to thank the following people:
Anabel Worrell for organizing the photo shoots; Daphne Razazan and Charyn Jones for distributing the questionnaire for the survey; the Chestnut Grove School, London, and the Hurlingham and Chelsea School, London for participating in the survey; Linda Grierson and Ellen Dupont for reading parts of the manuscript; Ben Jones, Josh Jones, and Karen Grierson, our adolescent readers; Audrey Cotterell for proofreading; Kay Wright for preparing the index; P4 Graphics Limited for outputting the film; Simone End for the illustrations; and Dorling Kindersley staff members Fiona Courtenay-Thompson, Philip Gilderdale, Stephen Knowlden, and Philip Ormerod.